Deconstructing the Monolith

Markets and Governments in Economic History
A series edited by Price Fishback
Also in the series:

Deconstructing the Monolith

The Microeconomics of the National Industrial Recovery Act

JASON E. TAYLOR

The University of Chicago Press
Chicago and London

The University of Chicago Press, Chicago 60637
The University of Chicago Press, Ltd., London
© 2019 by The University of Chicago
For more information, contact the University of Chicago Press, 1427 E. 60th St., Chicago, IL 60637.
Published 2019
Printed in the United States of America

28 27 26 25 24 23 22 21 20 19   1 2 3 4 5

ISBN-13: 978-0-226-60330-8 (cloth)
ISBN-13: 978-0-226-60344-5 (e-book)
DOI: https://doi.org/10.7208/chicago/9780226603445.001.0001

Library of Congress Cataloging-in-Publication Data

Names: Taylor, Jason E., author.
Title: Deconstructing the monolith : the microeconomics of the National Industrial Recovery Act / Jason E. Taylor.
Other titles: Markets and governments in economic history.
Description: Chicago ; London : The University of Chicago Press, 2019. | Series: Markets and governments in economic history | Includes bibliographical references and index.
Identifiers: LCCN 2018030491 | ISBN 9780226603308 (cloth : alk. paper) | ISBN 9780226603445 (ebook)
Subjects: LCSH: United States. National Industrial Recovery Act of 1933. | United States—Economic conditions—1918–1945. | Industrial policy—United States. | United States—Economic policy. | New Deal, 1933–1939.
Classification: LCC HD3616.U46 T36 2018 | DDC 338.973—dc23
LC record available at https://lccn.loc.gov/2018030491

Contents

Preface

On a visit to the National Archives in College Park, Maryland, an archivist asked what I was researching. Upon hearing my answer, he replied with a discouraging tone, "The National Recovery Administration stuff has already been heavily mined. You're unlikely to find anything new." But I was not searching for a smoking gun suggesting that the National Industrial Recovery Act (NIRA) was not what it seemed. Instead I was there to get a better sense of what the program really did by examining documents detailing how the NIRA affected the day-to-day lives of workers, business owners, and consumers during its nearly two-year run. What was the view of the program — and how did it affect economic decisions — *on the ground*?

Economists generally, though not always, treat the NIRA as a macroeconomic program and attempt to assess its overall impact — that is, they take a view from high above. Did the NIRA raise inflation expectations? Did the NIRA's labor provisions exacerbate the national unemployment situation? Was the NIRA a negative supply shock or a positive demand shock? And perhaps most importantly, did the NIRA promote or impede recovery from the Great Depression? These are the questions economists most often tackle when it comes to the program that is often considered the most far-reaching and significant piece of legislation from President Franklin Roosevelt's New Deal.

When I began studying the NIRA two decades ago, these macro-oriented questions were the ones that captured my attention. But as I dove more deeply into the industry-specific codes of fair competition, I realized that these codes were like snowflakes in that no two were alike. Some codes were scores of pages long and dramatically restricted economic behavior in ways consistent with a profit-maximizing cartel by, for example, employing production quotas, pricing restrictions, information-sharing provisions, and constraints on adding new productive capacity. Other industry codes were just a couple of pages long and did very little to constrain firm behavior. *If the rules imposed by the NIRA varied so dramatically from industry to industry, should we not expect the effects of the program to likewise vary from industry to industry?* And if the effects did indeed vary dramatically by industry, is the view from above really the best way to examine and assess the effects of the NIRA?

This book challenges the view of the NIRA as a monolithic program whose impact can be measured via macroeconomic or even manufacturing-sector-level price or output data. The focus here is on the vast heterogeneity within various aspects of the NIRA. This heterogeneity certainly exists at the industry level to the extent that the program affected firm behavior. To illustrate, I find that industries with longer and more complex codes of fair competition were more affected by the NIRA than were those with short and simple codes. But the heterogeneity also exists temporally. While some industries' codes of fair competition were approved and implemented as early as July 1933, the median industry code (i.e., number 279 out of 557) was not approved until mid-February 1934. Importantly, the codes could not (officially) affect industry trade practices until they were approved by the government. The NIRA also had major compliance issues, and these likewise varied over time, place, and industry. Some industries experienced high rates of compliance with their codes throughout the entire program, but many saw compliance wane dramatically in the fall and winter of 1933/1934, so that the NIRA had little or no effect on firm behavior. In other industries, compliance with the NIRA's labor and trade practice provisions continued even beyond May 1935, when the program was ruled unconstitutional.

When one treats the NIRA as a monolithic macroeconomic program that began in June 1933 and lasted through May 1935, the heterogeneous aspects of the law—both by industry and over time—are completely ignored. Importantly, this type of treatment can provide an inaccurate view of the law's impact. By viewing the NIRA through a microeconomic lens, this book strives to provide a better understanding of how the program affected the behavior and well-being of workers and firms during the twenty-three and a half months that it existed as well as in the period that immediately followed its demise. The answer varies dramatically by industry and by time period. Accounting for this heterogeneity not only leads to a better historical understanding of the NIRA but is also important for economists who wish to employ the policy experiments enacted by the legislation to gain insight into labor, cartel, and political economic theory.

Introduction

On November 8, 1934, a hearing was held by the National Recovery Administration (NRA) in which multiple affidavits were presented against the Liberty Baking Company of Washington, DC. The main charge against the bakery's proprietor, Pete Theodor, was that he was selling loaves of bread for five cents each.[1] "If this man is allowed to continue his unfair practices, he will cause a disruption of the bread market in the city of Washington . . . his competitors are daily losing business to him and are on the verge of dropping their prices in order to meet his." So said Harry T. Kelly of the baking industry's regional code authority in Washington. At the end of the hearing, Theodor agreed to raise his price to six cents in line with the baking code.

Over the next three days, the NRA sent various undercover buyers to Liberty Baking to determine whether the firm was complying. Theodor must have been suspicious of one of these agents because he charged him the proper six cents, but the agent covertly remained on the premises and caught Theodor selling bread to another customer at the illegal price of five cents. As punishment for selling bread at a price below the one agreed upon in the industry, a November 12 telegram was sent to Liberty Baking stating that the bakery could no longer display the NRA's Blue Eagle compliance emblem — an emblem whose presence (or absence) President Franklin Roosevelt and members of his administration asked consumers to consider when deciding where to make purchases. The company was ordered to return all its Blue Eagle paraphernalia to the local postmaster. On November 19, Assistant Postmaster W. M. Mooney reported to the NRA Compliance Division that Liberty Baking continued to display the Blue Eagle. The case was then referred to the program's Litigation Division, where fines and imprisonment could be imposed if the company was found guilty in the courts. However, by the time this layer of the NRA bureaucracy began its investigation in mid-December, Theodor had sold the bakery; hence, the case was dropped.

On December 11, 1933, Bernard Levine, proprietor of Home Food Market in Port Huron, Michigan, fired Joseph DeLawrence. The next day, DeLawrence filed a complaint against Levine alleging violation of the NRA's Wholesale Food and Grocery Code.[2] According to the code, employees in cities the size of Port Huron were entitled to a minimum pay of $13 per week. Levine actually paid DeLawrence $2 more than this minimum, but the code also stipulated that managers were entitled to at least $27.50 per week. In his complaint, DeLawrence noted that he was head of the meat department and hence entitled to executive pay. Levine told NRA investigators that DeLawrence never had any managerial duties and was simply a regular employee. Furthermore, Levine noted that when he approached DeLawrence about this accusation, DeLawrence said that if Levine would just give him his old job back, he would drop the complaint. Levine told the NRA that he was unwilling to succumb to this blackmail and said that he would not rehire DeLawrence because he would be a detriment to Levine's business—which was why DeLawrence had been fired in the first place. Another of Levine's employees, Irving Freeman, filed an affidavit to the NRA in support of Levine's contention that DeLawrence did not perform any managerial duties and was simply employed as a butcher and clerk at the meat counter. After several months of uncertainty, on July 13, 1934, the NRA ended the case in Levine's favor.

In Blanks, Louisiana, the proprietor of the A. N. Smith Lumber Company freely admitted that he was in violation of the NRA lumber code's minimum wage provisions. W. L. Evans of the NRA lumber code authority visited the company on May 11, 1934, and said that Smith was very "determined in his attitude toward code compliance and assures me that nothing except a court order will change him."[3] In a letter dated May 26, 1934, Smith defended his wage payments by saying that his employees freely agreed to work at the level of compensation he paid. NRA deputy administrator J. C. Wickliffe noted this was not a reasonable defense. A hearing was held in New Orleans on June 7, and the NRA ruled Smith Lumber in violation of the lumber code, and hence the company was ordered to cease displaying the Blue Eagle—an emblem that Smith had never displayed in any case given his antipathy toward the program. The file was forwarded to the Litigation Division for prosecution. On April 20, 1935, however, the NRA's lawyers decided not to pursue the case further.

These three cases provide a window into a bold experiment—the National Industrial Recovery Act (NIRA)—that eliminated normal antitrust at the height of the Great Depression. The program attempted to reorganize labor and product markets around codes that were written by industries themselves (though subject to government approval) and hence had the potential to lead to collusive outcomes throughout the manufacturing sector. Getting the competing interests within each industry to agree on the rules embedded in each industry code was difficult. Getting firm owners to then abide by the codes presented further challenges. Still, the NIRA was met, at least initially, with great enthusiasm by businesses and consumers. As a result, compliance with the codes was surprisingly high. But as the cases above suggest, the NRA codes were not always able to accomplish what their framers had hoped. Over time, defections from the codes became increasingly rampant. An examination of the NIRA can lend insight not only into the historical issue of whether the program helped or hindered recovery from the Great Depression but also into contemporary issues such as how the administrative state operates inside the federal system as well as into labor or cartel theory. Existing research about the NIRA has often painted the program in overly broad (macroeconomic) brushstrokes. The goal of this book is to break the program down into its components—in terms of both what it did and when it did it—and thus better understand the impact the program had on firms and consumers during the 1930s.

The NIRA Monolith?

The NIRA is generally viewed as a monolithic negative supply shock that lasted for nearly two years between 1933 and 1935. Macroeconomists, in particular, have pointed toward the NIRA's promotion of collusion and its imposition of minimum hourly wage rates as clear obstacles to recovery from the Great Depression. After all, cartels reduce output, and, coupled with exogenous wage increases, this was likely to have exacerbated the unemployment situation. Although there is some validity to the view of the NIRA as an obstacle to recovery, this assessment of the NIRA monolith is also a gross oversimplification.

The NIRA was a multifaceted program that affected different industries very differently. Importantly, it also had very diverse temporal effects across the 710 days of its existence. Without understanding this heterogeneity, scholars cannot fully assess the NIRA's role in the Great Depression. Rather than painting the legislation as a one-size-fits-all shackle, I disaggregate the NIRA into its components—collusion, wage increases, work sharing, and recognition of collective bargaining—to better evaluate the impact of each. And because the NIRA's economic impact varied over time, the legislation is also separated into four key periods: the code formulation period, the President's

Reemployment Agreement, the effective cartel era, and the postcompliance crisis era. Additionally, this book documents the wide industry-level variation of the NIRA's impact. In some industries, the program looked very much like the caricature that many economists now paint, with harmful collusive outcomes being achieved and workers being priced out of the market by dramatic wage spikes. But in many other industries, the NIRA codes brought little or no collusion and only minimal changes to wages and hours.

The NIRA can provide important insights into economic theory, and the legislation has been employed to this end by many scholars. However, these insights can only be properly gleaned if researchers carefully isolate the impact of each facet of the NIRA. Additionally, scholars must understand which specific windows of time to examine within the NIRA period to correctly garner such insights. To illustrate this point, consider two industries, yarn production and cement, both of which were covered by an NIRA "code of fair competition."

The yarn industry employed forty-one thousand people in the summer of 1933—more than it had employed at the start of the Depression in 1929, which was certainly not the norm. The average workweek in the industry was forty-five hours, and the average hourly wage rate was around 36 cents.[4] The yarn code was passed on August 26, 1933, ten weeks after the NIRA was implemented. This code was a scant two pages long, and it specified a forty-hour maximum workweek and a 32.5-cent minimum wage for the industry. The code—as was the case of every approved NIRA code—also forbade the employment of children under age sixteen and required firms in the yarn production industry to recognize the rights of employees to bargain collectively. Aside from these provisions, the code did nothing else to regulate the activity of yarn producers.

The cement industry employed around twelve thousand workers, which was a sharp decline from the thirty-four thousand workers in the industry in 1928. Furthermore, the industry's production had fallen by 54 percent since 1928. Unlike the yarn industry, the cement industry had a trade association in place, the Cement Institute (created in 1929), which helped formulate the industry's code of fair competition and represented the industry in the hearings in which the code was evaluated. The cement code was passed on November 27, 1933—more than five months after the NIRA took effect. This code was twenty-four pages long and, in stark contrast to the yarn code, contained a plethora of detailed wage and trade practice provisions. An employee's workweek could not average more than thirty-six hours over a half-year period, and could never exceed forty-two hours in any one week. Minimum hourly wage rates varied throughout twelve specific geographic districts, with a high of 40 cents and a low of 30 cents. The code also set up a seven-member code authority to help ensure its smooth execution, and all firms in the industry had to regularly submit data on wages, hours, and production to this body. The code included a detailed plan for "the equitable allocation of available business" among firms. The code required firms to submit to the code authority, in advance of any action, plans for increases in their productive capacity, and these increases could be disallowed if it was determined that this would increase "the problem of over-production and over-capacity" in the area. The code forbade firms from selling below cost, and it required firms to file with the code authority any price changes five days in advance—and the code authority would make this information available so that other firms could choose to match the price cut (thus limiting the rationale for the price cut in the first place). The code even forbade, among several other specific attempts at non-price competition, the providing of banquets or lavish entertainment for purchasers of cement.

In light of the contents of these two codes, one of these industries looks a lot like a cartel and the other does not. Indeed, Chicu, Vickers, and Ziebarth (2013) "cement the case" that collusion occurred under the NIRA by examining establishment-level data from the cement industry in the 1930s. But which type of code was more common—the type that resembled the yarn industry or the type that resembled the cement industry? Although these two industries offer extremely different examples of codes with respect to their content, they are not strong outliers; many codes were similar in complexity (or lack thereof). This book demonstrates that industries with longer, more complex codes were more likely than industries with simple codes to have achieved collusive outcomes.

But even in the case of the cement industry, it is important to note that the cartel-oriented code was not put into place until the end of November 1933—if one employs monthly data in a test for cartelization, the date of each industry code's implementation should also be considered. Some industries were not covered by codes until 1934, or even early 1935—just a few months before the NIRA was ruled unconstitutional. The bowling and billiard equipment industry was the subject of the 557th, and final, code passed on March 30, 1935. Since the NIRA was ruled unconstitutional on May 27, 1935, this code was in effect for only about eight weeks. The 277th and 278th code—that is, the median ones in terms of timing of code passage—were approved on February 10, 1934. Thus, to paint the NIRA as a two-year cartel program is to use an overly broad brushstroke. Furthermore, to employ the NIRA to gain insight into cartel theory, this heterogeneity of the timing of code passage must be accounted for. The use of macroeconomic, rather than industry-level, data could be particularly problematic given the heterogeneous effects of the NIRA on different industries.

Another important factor to consider with respect to potential collusive effects under the NIRA is that a widespread "compliance crisis" hit the program in the spring of 1934. Cartel theory suggests that collusion is difficult to maintain absent an effective enforcement mechanism. After all, cartels are a classic example of a prisoner's dilemma scenario; even though collusion is collectively optimal, each individual firm's best strategy is to defect. The NIRA set up what appeared, on its face, to be a formidable enforcement mechanism. The law specified that violations of the codes could be punished with fines and imprisonment for up to six months. Additionally, the Blue Eagle emblem was created in late July 1933 to serve as a symbol of compliance with the law—NRA violators would lose the right to display the emblem in their storefronts, advertisements, or directly on their products. This loss could be harmful, because President Roosevelt strongly encouraged Americans—especially the nation's housewives since they generally directed the family spending—to buy products only from Blue Eagle firms and essentially boycott those that were not in compliance with the NIRA.

The Blue Eagle was viewed as a powerful economic symbol, particularly in the late summer and early fall of 1933. Firms employed substantial resources to promote their compliance with the NIRA via the Blue Eagle, suggesting that the emblem did indeed carry significant economic weight. Furthermore, firms viewed the NIRA's Compliance Division, with its authority to prosecute violators and impose fines and jail time, as a formidable adversary that one would not wish to cross. As a result, firms viewed compliance with the NRA codes as being not only in the industry's collective best interest but in their individual best interest as well. Thus, compliance was initially very high.

Things began to change, however, in late 1933 and early 1934, when violations of the codes went unpunished. Complying firms, as well as patriotic consumers, vehemently protested the lack of action from federal authorities against violators. As defections continued without government action, enthusiasm for the Blue Eagle began to wane—the emblem was no longer viewed as an effective signal of who was complying with the program. By March and April of 1934, firms realized that the NIRA Compliance Division had far more bark than bite—thus, the classic prisoner's dilemma scenario returned and firms defected en masse from the codes. While some firms continued to comply, the achievement of cartel-oriented outcomes was less prominent after April 1934 than it had been in fall 1933 and winter 1934. The NRA tried to get industries back in step with its "mass compliance" drives in the fall of 1934, but the proverbial genie was already out of the bottle and compliance with the NIRA never returned to the level present in the last half of 1933.

When the NIRA was ruled unconstitutional in May 1935 via the Supreme Court's *Schechter* decision, the Roosevelt administration asked firms to continue to voluntarily comply with the codes. The Robert Committee surveyed forty-four industries in the summer and fall of 1935 to gauge the extent to which the codes were still being followed. The committee found a surprisingly large degree of compliance—specifically, it concluded that more than half of firms in 75 percent of all industries reported that they continued to voluntarily follow the codes' labor provisions. Still, there was a large industry-level variation in the degree of continued compliance—in some industries, massive "violations" had occurred. Additionally, just as the NIRA itself had heterogeneous effects on industries between 1933 and 1935, the removal of the program likewise had differential effects. Firms in industries such as cement and lumber, which had detailed and cartel-oriented codes, were far more affected by *Schechter* than firms in, say, the yarn industry, which were subject to very simple codes. In fact, I find that output rose faster in the two years after the NIRA in industries that had more complex codes than it did in industries whose codes were short and simple.

An Outline of the Book

The book proceeds as follows. Chapter 2 begins with the question of why policy makers thought a program of collusion, high wages, unionization, and reduced hours would promote recovery from the Great Depression. The views held by key architects of the NIRA are examined. To preview, many contemporary economists, including Roosevelt advisor Rexford Tugwell, felt that wages had not kept pace with the sharp productivity gains of the 1920s and this created the problem of "underconsumption." Underconsumptionists such as Tugwell proposed economic planning—both by the government as well as within industries through closer coordination—and the imposition of higher real wages as the means to put the economy on a sustainable high-growth path. The NIRA's reductions in the workweek were driven by a belief in the concept of work sharing—effectively spreading scarce work among more people by cutting each worker's ration of hours. This idea was not novel to the NIRA—in fact, it was a major focus of President Herbert Hoover's approach to the unemployment problem between 1930 and 1932. Hoover had also pushed for high wages as a means of boosting aggregate demand, consistent with the underconsumptionist doctrine, but whereas Hoover generally relied on moral suasion and voluntary compliance between 1929 and 1932, the NIRA would institute such policies into law. Chapter 2 also provides a time line of the NIRA's formulation and evaluates how it was received by the business community.

Chapter 3 provides a detailed investigation of the first six weeks after the NIRA's passage—what I call the code negotiation period. Industry representatives came together—generally in hotel conference centers in Washington DC, New York, Chicago, and other large cities—with the purpose of creating a code of fair competition for their specific industry. This process, which some industries began prior to June 16, in anticipation of the NIRA's passage, was open to any firm owner in the industry. Once an industry was ready to submit its proposal to the National Recovery Administration, a formal hearing would be held in Washington, DC, and the code would be put into a fairly standardized format. The law said that codes could not "promote monopoly"; thus, during these hearings, an industry had to carefully defend why its proposed code provisions would promote fair competition rather than being a pure profit grab. The code ultimately had to be approved by the Roosevelt administration, which sought the advice of representatives from labor, consumers, and the NRA's legal team. In some cases, these hearings took several days, and often recesses—which could last weeks or months—were called so that industry leaders could redraw provisions that the government deemed unacceptable. In other cases, the hearings lasted just a couple of hours. Still, code building and approval was a slow process. The first code, for the cotton textile industry, was passed on July 9, and codes in the shipbuilding and wool textile industries followed on July 26. Six weeks after the NIRA's approval, only three industries had approved codes.

Frustrated with the slow speed of the Act's implementation, President Franklin Roosevelt instituted the President's Reemployment Agreement (PRA), which took effect on August 1, 1933. Chapter 4 examines many important, but heretofore neglected, aspects of the PRA and considers the program's impact on wages, hours, and employment. The program, which is also responsible for the introduction of the Blue Eagle compliance emblem, was essentially a means to bring forward the implementation of the labor aspects of the NIRA while the collusive aspects of the Act were still being negotiated. Under the agreement, firm owners pledged to recognize the right of collective bargaining, to pay an hourly wage of at least 40 cents (35 cents in sales and clerical industries) and to cut the maximum workweek to thirty-five hours (forty hours in sales and clerical).

The Roosevelt administration sent canvassers door to door nationwide encouraging Americans to sign a pledge stating that they would only buy from

Blue Eagle firms that were in compliance with the PRA. Signers were given Blue Eagle buttons, posters, and pins designed to show firms that they risked losing business if they did not comply with the PRA wage and hours provisions. Firm-level compliance with the PRA was extraordinarily high even though at this point the only punishment for violators was the loss of the Blue Eagle—because codes were not in place, fines and jail time for violators were not yet on the table. The administration conducted a nationwide firm-level census to estimate the extent of compliance and the number of jobs the PRA had created through its work-sharing provisions. These employment gains were often reported in local in newspapers as a means of driving up patriotic compliance with the law.

The data reveal that a large spike in average hourly wage rates, as well as a sharp decline in average hourly workweeks, coincided with the introduction of the PRA in August and September 1933. But these wage movements varied dramatically among industries. High-wage industries such as chemical manufacturing and automobile production saw relatively little growth in hourly wage rates under the PRA. On the other hand, low-wage industries such as boot and shoe production saw sharp wage increases after the imposition of the 40-cent minimum.

Chapter 5 focuses on the attributes of the NRA codes of fair competition and the impact that they had on economic outcomes. Whereas the PRA's labor provisions were one-size-fits-all, industry-specific codes were extremely heterogeneous. The chapter demonstrates the extent to which industry-specific codes deviated from the PRA labor guideposts of a 40-cent minimum wage and a thirty-five-hour maximum workweek. In fact, many codes not only had industry minimum wage rates below 40 cents but also contained provisions allowing flexibility such as lower wages in the American South or lower minimum wage rates based on city population or even age and gender. The iron and steel industry code, for example, created a 40-cent minimum wage in Pittsburgh, Cleveland, Youngstown, Chicago, and Detroit—cities that together made up 60 percent of the industry—but it specified a minimum wage of only 25 cents an hour in the South. One would expect a "flexible" minimum wage program such as this to have less of a potentially negative impact on employment than a one-size-fits-all program.

Chapter 5 also details the variety of non-labor provisions that were contained in the codes. The heterogeneity from this perspective cannot be overstated. Industry success in achieving the collusive outcomes varied greatly based on how successful the industry was at negotiating its code internally and how successful it was at getting key provisions of its code approved by the government. I establish that industries with more complex codes were more successful than industries with simple codes at achieving collusive outcomes. Additionally, I examine how the presence of specific code provisions—such as those restricting the construction of new productive capacity, implementing production quotas, and mandating that all firms file data regularly with the cartel—affected an industry's ability to achieve collusive outcomes. I find that a particularly important predictor of cartel success was whether an industry had a trade association in place at the time of the NIRA's passage. The existence of an industry trade association greatly aided the cartel formation and negotiation process and apparently allowed industries to create codes of fair competition that were more in line with industry members' profit-maximizing interests.

Chapters 6 and 7 explore the NIRA's enforcement mechanism and how it largely broke down during the compliance crisis of spring 1934. These chapters explain that, although the NRA created what looked like an elaborate and effective mechanism for enforcement of the codes, the administration was effectively engaged in a game of smoke and mirrors—publicizing the relatively few cases where enforcement occurred in an attempt to make the compliance mechanism look credible. The late fall and winter of 1933/1934 saw a consistent trickle of violators who did not back down in the face of the NRA's threats of punishment. When the NRA did not follow through on its threats, this trickle became a steady stream of violators. Episodes of violations that were not met with government action made national news, encouraging still more defectors. By April 1934, compliance with the trade practice provisions in the codes was a shell of what it had been six months earlier.

Chapter 7 delivers empirical evidence that the compliance crisis occurred. Specifically, regression results suggest variables such as output, prices, wage rates, and hours worked were affected more between the month of code passage and March 1934 than they were in the months between April 1934 and the end of the NIRA in May 1935. This again suggests that treating the NIRA as a two-year cartel supply shock is a mistake. In short, although cartel outcomes did occur under the NIRA, they did not take place in every industry—many industry codes did not include provisions that would have directly led to cartel outcomes—nor did they generally last for two full years. Chapter 7 also outlines the government's attempts to bring industries back into compliance through the "mass compliance" drive of late 1934 and 1935.

Chapter 8 examines the impact of the Supreme Court's *Schechter* decision on May 27, 1935, which ruled the NIRA unconstitutional. The Roosevelt administration tried to keep aspects of the law in effect as the president asked firms to voluntarily abide by their industry's code provisions. Furthermore, the National Labor Relations Act, which was passed less than two weeks after the NIRA's demise, permanently codified the right to collective bargaining. The Fair Labor Standards Act (FLSA), implemented in 1938, brought back the 40-cent-per-hour minimum wage that was originally in the PRA and created a maximum workweek (with overtime pay for hours in excess) of forty hours.[5] However, unlike the NIRA codes, whereby industries could have their own specific minimum wages, the FLSA imposed a one-size-fits-all requirement. Chapter 8 also empirically examines whether the *Schechter* ruling brought about changes in wages, hours, employment, and output. In fact, the economy grew sharply in the two years after the NIRA was ruled unconstitutional. To what extent was this economic surge driven by the death of the NIRA as opposed to other potential tailwinds such as expansionary fiscal and monetary policy? Just as earlier chapters show that the NIRA had a heterogeneous impact on different industries, chapter 8 demonstrates that the demise of the NIRA also affected different industries differently. Specifically, industries that had more restrictive codes experienced growth after *Schechter* that was about twice as fast as the growth in industries with simple codes. Chapter 9 concludes the book with a summary and synthesis of the major findings. Overall, this book suggests a far more complex picture of the NIRA and its effects than those implied in the current literature.

Data and Methodology

Well-known articles dealing directly with the NIRA such as Cole and Ohanian (2004) and Eggertsson (2012) have employed macroeconomic-oriented models to assess the law's impact. Cole and Ohanian create a multisector dynamic general equilibrium model and simulate it for New Deal years. Their simulations suggest that the NIRA's cartelization and high-wage policies were key factors in what they describe as the "weak" recovery of 1934 to 1939. In the descriptive section of their article, they employ some industry-level data—for example, comparing the anthracite and bituminous coal industries, only one of which was covered by an NIRA code—however, their primary interest is on aggregate output, consumption, investment, employment, and wages. Eggertsson (2012) likewise uses a dynamic stochastic general equilibrium model with staggered price setting. He concludes that while Cole and Ohanian are correct that the NIRA's high-wage and cartelization policies would have been contractionary under normal economic conditions, these policies are shown to be expansionary in his model of emergency economic conditions because they help break a deflationary spiral.

Other research on the NIRA has performed industry case studies using establishment-level data. As mentioned earlier in this chapter, Chicu, Vickers, and Ziebarth (2013) use such data in the cement industry (collected in census years 1929, 1931, 1933, and 1935) to show that the costs of a firm's nearest neighbor affected a firm's price—suggesting competition—before the NIRA went into effect. However, after the implementation of the NIRA, there is no correlation between a neighbor's costs and a firm's price in this industry. In other work, Vickers and Ziebarth (2014) study the macaroni industry, which was also the subject of a case study by Alexander (1997). The authors use plant-level data from census years to examine changes in cost pass-through, cross-sectional dispersion in prices, and time-series persistence of prices, and they find evidence consistent with collusive outcomes occurring in the macaroni industry.

The empirical analysis in this book relies heavily on industry-level data employed in monthly panel regressions. Government agencies collected monthly data on output, prices, wages, employment, and hours worked for scores of industries during the 1930s. When macro-oriented data are employed, one must assume the NIRA codes turn on for the whole economy simultaneously, which is inconsistent with the historical facts. Industry-level monthly data allow researchers to better account for when a specific industry's code was in place. Additionally, having data disaggregated to the industry level allows us to examine how heterogeneity within the codes affected economic performance during the NIRA. For example, one can examine whether industries that had longer codes, or codes that contained specific trade practice provisions, performed differently than other industries.

This is not to imply that industry-level panel studies are the only way, or even the best way, to study the NIRA. The establishment-level data studies of Vickers and Ziebarth, among others, represent an exciting new approach that will undoubtedly continue to yield fascinating insights into firm behavior under the NIRA. At the other extreme, macroeconomic general equilibrium models and simulations can provide valuable insights into how the NIRA affected recovery from the Great Depression. The appropriate level of data aggregation and modeling *depends largely on the research questions being asked*. Given this book's focus on the heterogeneity of both the timing of implementation and the content of the NIRA codes, industry-level panel studies are the best fit.

What Is New in This Book?

This book builds off two decades of my research on the NIRA, but it is far from a simple summary of previously published articles. The book dives much deeper into the research questions that I have previously asked while also exploring several new ones. Like an onion, scholarly research on any topic has many layers. Journal articles in economics—which tend to focus heavily on quantitative methods and hypothesis testing—generally allow authors to peel back only a few of them. There are many additional layers to peel when it comes to the NIRA, and this book provides much deeper qualitative work than what has been previously done. In particular, this book dives systematically into the contents of the NIRA codes of fair competition as well as into archival evidence of how the codes truly affected firm and consumer behavior. It establishes the high level of heterogeneity within the codes and, more importantly, accounts for that heterogeneity while assessing the NIRA's impact. In short, the book deconstructs the NIRA monolith and shows that the program affected each industry uniquely.

The Underpinnings, Precursors, and Development of the NIRA

The National Industrial Recovery Act was passed on June 16, 1933. The Act was a fitting bookend to President Franklin D. Roosevelt's first hundred days of major reforms to the US regulatory system (see Alter 2006; Badger 2008; Cohen 2009). In a statement announcing the NIRA's passage, Roosevelt predicted that history would view it "as the most important and far-reaching legislation ever enacted by the American Congress." This statement appears not to be hyperbole when one considers just what economic changes the Act brought. The NIRA created the Federal Emergency Administration of Public Works (later renamed the Public Works Administration) and authorized $3.3 billion toward public works projects. The Act boosted hourly wage rates, cut workweeks, and required industry to recognize the right of collective bargaining. The Act suspended antitrust laws and facilitated intraindustry collusion.

The logic behind the creation of an agency providing funding for public works during a time of high unemployment is clear. But why did the Roosevelt administration think a policy of cartels, high wages, and reduced work hours would promote recovery from the Great Depression?[1] This question invariably comes up when NIRA scholars discuss the program in classrooms, conferences, and seminars. After all, economic theory suggests that cartels reduce, not expand, output (and hence employment) since the profit-maximizing monopoly output is below the perfectly competitive one. Furthermore, with unemployment already exceeding 20 percent in the spring of 1933, wage rates were clearly above, not below, their market-clearing level. From the perspective of economic theory, the NIRA would appear to be a contractionary policy rather than an expansionary one.

The framers of the NIRA appear to have been operating under different economic models and theories of output and employment than what are considered orthodox ones today.[2] There are three separate aspects of the NIRA—raising hourly wage rates, collusion (industrial planning), and reducing workweeks—that are worthy of discussion with respect to their theoretical underpinnings, and the first part of this chapter will address the development of each of these in the period leading up to the NIRA's formulation in late April 1933. In fact, these three policy approaches did not appear suddenly in spring 1933. Rather, each had been put forth in the 1920s (in some cases, earlier) as a means to addressing perceived structural economic problems. After the Depression began in 1929, these measures were advocated again as means of combating the economic downturn.

The Rationale for Higher Wage Rates

In the two decades prior to the NIRA's passage, a doctrine advocating increases in wage rates as a way to promote macroeconomic prosperity was steadily gaining intellectual ground.[3] The thrust of this doctrine is that when wages rise, workers have more purchasing power. This, the theory goes, induces more spending and hence increases the total demand for goods and services, which in turn encourages firms to hire more workers. Following this logic, higher wage rates could be used as a tool to reduce unemployment and bring economic prosperity.

Henry Ford's five-dollar day, first instituted in 1914—and the economic success of the Ford Motor Company in the years that followed—was a major data point that adherents of this doctrine pointed toward. Ford himself explained the logic behind his company's high-wage policy: "I believe [that] our own sales depend in a measure upon the wages we pay. If we can distribute high wages, then that money is going to be spent and it will serve to make . . . workers in other lines more prosperous and their prosperity will be reflected in our sales" (Ford 1922, 124). Twelve years after the five-dollar day's introduction, Ford (1926, 154–55) wrote that an employer's "own workers are among his best customers. . . . It is an ever-widening circle of buying . . . paying a high wages has the same effect as throwing a stone in a still pond."

Contemporaries pointed to the Ford Motor Company's success in the 1920s as evidence that high wages promoted industrial success. New England business magnate Edward Filene (1923, 415) noted that high wages were "a boon to the employer as well as the employee . . . I refer to Henry Ford. He has become the richest man in the world." William T. Foster and Waddill Catchings (1928, 175) likewise noted that "Mr. Ford has helped [employers] see that it is bad business to destroy customers by reducing purchasing power. . . . Mr. Ford is right: 'The best wages that have up to date ever been paid are not nearly as high as they ought to be.'" During the early stages of the Depression, one of the most respected economists of the time, Irving Fisher (1930, 25), wrote that "Henry Ford was substantially right when he suggested the need . . . of 'increasing the purchasing power of our principle customers—the American people.'" On the other side of the Atlantic, British economist John A. Hobson (1930, 88) wrote, "Increased purchasing power by high wages and low prices is seen to be essential . . . a wage-raising policy [would] redress the balance between producer and consumer and secure a general expansion of markets."

Such "underconsumptionist" views had been popularized a century earlier by Robert Owen ([1820] 1970) and Thomas Malthus (1827, 1836), who claimed that stagnation and depression were largely the result of workers' wages being insufficient to allow them to purchase the increased output that came with technological advances. Hobson (1909) sparked a resurgence in this literature in the early twentieth century when he argued for policies of income redistribution to overcome the problem of underconsumption. In his 1932 book, *The Way Forward*, Robert Brookings (founder of the Brookings Institution) provides an excellent example of the underconsumptionist/high-wage thinking as it stood just prior to the NIRA's formation: "We have now the anomaly . . . of a vast production of goods which cannot be distributed although there are millions of people needing them, and in some cases suffering acutely because of their lack. [We require] some modification in our system of compensation providing a more equitable distribution and so increasing the consuming power of the workers" (Brookings 1932, 2).

President Herbert Hoover was strongly influenced by this way of thinking about wages and their connection to aggregate demand. In his memoirs, Hoover (1952, 108) wrote that mass consumption can "only be obtained from the purchasing power of high wages" and that firms will not produce in mass unless there are buyers (quoted in Ohanian 2009, 2316). In fact, in late November 1929, a month after the stock market crash, Hoover held a conference with twenty-three industrial business leaders—Henry Ford, Alfred Sloan, Myron Taylor, Julius Rosenwald, and Pierre Du Pont, among others—in which he asked them to keep wages high rather than cut them, as had been common in past downturns. Hoover argued that cutting wages would make the downturn worse and that purchasing power had to be maintained to keep the economy afloat. Richard Vedder and Lowell Gallaway (1993) and Jonathan Rose (2010) establish that Hoover's pleas were impactful. Specifically, Rose shows that those companies whose executives were at the conference with Hoover generally maintained wage rates at their pre-Depression levels through October 1931, two years after the downturn began, despite the fact that the price level had fallen sharply, thus boosting average real wage rates.

Rexford Tugwell, an economist in Roosevelt's "Brains Trust" of advisors and a key architect of the NIRA, also embraced the high-wage logic outlined above. He argued that "income which is distributed as wages becomes immediate purchasing power. . . . A nation of well-paid workers, consuming most of the goods it produces, will be as near Utopia as we humans are ever likely to get" (Tugwell 1933, 183). Tugwell believed that the root cause of the Great Depression was that, despite the dramatic increase in worker productivity during the 1920s thanks to advances in technology, wages had not kept pace. Thus, workers did not have enough buying power to purchase the increased output. Boosting wage rates was the prescribed remedy, and Roosevelt, in his statement upon signing the NIRA into law, highlighted "the greatly increased sales to be expected from the rising purchasing power of the public. . . . The aim of the whole effort is to restore our rich domestic market by raising its vast consuming capacity."[4]

Lee Ohanian (2009) argues that the high-wage remedy was ineffective at preventing the Depression—in fact, he argues that the high-wage policy was the primary *cause* of the severity of the downturn. On the other hand, there is some support for the notion that a firm's labor demand curve can be upward sloping in some range of wages due to efficiency wage considerations. Raff and Summers (1987) argue that Henry Ford's five-dollar day is an excellent application of efficiency wage theory in practice, because it reduced turnover and boosted productivity. Eggertsson (2012) claims that the NIRA's high-wage policies raised inflation expectations. Still, the purpose here is not to evaluate the soundness or impact of the high-wage policies from the 1930s. Rather, this chapter strives to offer insight into what caused policy makers to advocate a large bump in wage rates in 1933. The simple answer is the development over the previous two decades of the high-wage doctrine, which tied wages to demand, output, and employment.

Economic Planning and Industrial Cooperation

Section 5 of the NIRA stated that, when a "code of fair competition" was in effect, firms in the affected industry were "exempt from the provisions of the antitrust law of the United States." Under the program, firms were encouraged to coordinate economic activity at the industry level. While this was a clear reversal from four decades of antitrust enforcement under the Sherman Act, which was geared toward preventing such collusion, Himmelberg (1976) and Kovacic and Shapiro (2000) note that antitrust enforcement had already begun to relax in the 1920s. Like the movement advocating higher wages as a way to fight economic downturns, the turn toward interindustry coordination was several years in the making, although it gained momentum after the onset of the Great Depression. A major inspiration for such industry-level planning was the purported success of the War Industries Board, which operated between July 1917 and December 1918. During these eighteen months, the War Industries Board made decisions on how to allocate the nation's resources in a way that was unprecedented in US history. The reported success of state planning in Russia was another data point that seemed to favor movement toward government coordination of industry. Journalist and social activist Lincoln Steffens, after returning from Russia in 1919, famously wrote, "I have seen the future and it works" (Hartshorn, 2011).

But more than simply viewing purported successes in planning, those who pushed for coordination also pointed toward what they saw as a systemic unfairness inherent in the competitive market system of the United States. Thus, the NIRA codes were created to promote what was called "fair competition" within industry. In fact, the word *competition* appears nineteen times in the text of the NIRA bill, and in all but one instance it is directly preceded by the word *fair*. (The one exception occurs where the bill refers to "an unfair method of competition.") Policy makers clearly believed that the state of the competitive markets was in need of intervention because competition in absence of coordination was inherently unfair. Members of the Roosevelt administration regularly used the terms *ruinous competition* or *cutthroat competition* and noted that the purpose of the NIRA was to eliminate this practice.

What exactly is ruinous competition, and what makes it different from the fair sort? Although no definition of fair competition was provided in the text of the NIRA, contemporaries generally evoked adjectives such as *destructive* or *dangerous* or *irresponsible* in front of the words *price cutting* and *overproduction* when discussing the topic of unfair competition. Essentially, it was widely believed that firms were producing too much output and hence driving prices down to a level so low that many could not stay in business. The heterogeneity of firms within each industry—some small scale, some large scale—certainly contributed to this problem. Firms that were using efficient mass production techniques involving modern power usage and assembly lines could be profitable at prices that would have smaller-scale, less efficient firms operating at a loss. In retrospect, many cases of actions that were considered unfair competition were simply a by-product of technological progress—the minimum efficient scale of operation rose in many industries, and, as a result, small firms could not survive long. Michael Bernstein (1987) notes that the effects of the Great Depression varied substantially by industry as the nation experienced major shifts in the composition of national output that accompanied the technological changes of the interwar era.

Importantly, when what the media initially called "the recovery bill" was in its infancy in late April 1933, its designers agreed that the meaning of fair competition would be hashed out at the *individual industry level* rather than having a one-size-fits-all definition for the macroeconomy. Firms in each industry would come together to form an agreement about fair standards of conduct within that industry. This idea was not as radical as it would have seemed a few years earlier because of the tremendous growth in trade associations in the late 1920s. In fact, some trade associations had implemented codes specifying an industry's rules of fair conduct that were in a similar vein to those of the NIRA.

In the decade before the NIRA, two important Supreme Court cases— *United States v. American Linseed Oil Company* (1923) and *Maple Flooring Manufacturers Association v. United States* (1925)—helped define what trade associations could and could not legally do. In the first case, American linseed manufacturers used a trade association to share business practice and statistical information about current and future business dealings. In their defense, they claimed their practice of openly communicating such information allowed them to "promote better and more safe, sane, and stable conditions in the linseed oil, cake, and meal industry and increase its service to the commonwealth."[5] However, the Court argued that the sharing of future pricing information was likely to drive up prices and profits for the linseed manufacturers—thus, the actions of the linseed trade association were in violation of the Sherman Antitrust Act.

Two years later, the Court heard a case against the Maple Flooring Manufacturers Association. The suit claimed that the trade association, by sharing past pricing information and other statistical industry data among members, was in violation of the Sherman Antitrust Act. However, in this case, the Court ruled in favor of the trade association. The key difference was that that maple flooring manufacturers were sharing old information, not information about the future. The Court said that trade associations that "openly and fairly gather information . . . without reaching or attempting to reach any agreement or concerted action respecting prices, production, or the restraining of competition, do not hereby engage in an unlawful restraint of commerce."[6] This 1925 ruling opened the door to a surge in trade association activity, both quantitative and qualitative, in the years that followed.

In 1925, a new appointment by President Calvin Coolidge to the Federal Trade Commission gave the commission a majority of business-friendly Republican members and brought a shift in the commission's polices toward trade associations away from strict antitrust enforcement. The Federal Trade Commission subsequently created the Trade Practice Conference Division

(TPCD). Members of individual industries could come together—via their trade association—and draft rules of fair competition. These "codes" were then to be submitted to the TPCD, and, if approved, they would have the force of law. Himmelberg (1976, 62) notes that the number of trade practice conferences designed to propose codes to the TPCD rose from only six in 1927 to fifty in 1929, suggesting that business felt that there were clear gains to taking such action. Each code dealt specifically with the key issues of that industry and outlined trade practices that were considered either illegal (Group I rules) or legal but unethical and undesirable in the eyes of the majority of industry members (Group II rules). According to Himmelberg (1976, 63), by 1928, the TPCD "was permitting the inclusion of rules in the codes which were intended to suppress competition, not merely make it 'fair.'" Viewed in this light, the NIRA's implementation of codes of fair competition in 1933 was not a dramatic departure from past practice, but rather a major extension of a 1920s program.

When Herbert Hoover began his presidency in 1929, his Office of the Attorney General came out against the TPCD's practice of approving trade association codes and took a more traditional stance of the Sherman Antitrust Act than had the Coolidge administration—specifically, it expressed the view that some of the practices specified by the TPCD-approved codes were illegal. Abram F. Myers, head of an organization of trade associations that had received Federal Trade Commission approval for codes, said in the fall of 1930 that the Hoover administration's actions "plunged the whole question of industrial cooperation through trade association activity into hopeless confusion" (Himmelberg 1976, 97).

While Hoover was less lax than Coolidge on antitrust, he was still quite conflicted on the issue of whether businesses should be left to their own devices. As secretary of commerce in the 1920s, Hoover had pushed for closer relationships between government and business—he believed that the Commerce Department should act as an agency in service of business rather than as an adversary. Hoover was an engineer by trade, and his Commerce Department worked with business to promote efficiency through "indicative planning"—pushing for industry standardization and avoidance of waste (Vedder and Gallaway 1993, 70). In an October 1930 speech to the American Federation of Labor, Hoover said that the economic system should not "produce a competition which destroys stability in an industry and reduces to poverty all those within it. . . . If our regulatory laws are at fault they should be revised."[7] Hoover went on to cite the voluntary labor agreements that he pushed in his meetings with industrial leaders shortly after the stock market crash in 1929, saying that the "demonstration of nation-wide cooperation and team play and the absence of conflict . . . have increased the stability and wholesomeness of our industrial and social structure."

The Depression created a renewed surge in calls for relaxation of antitrust laws in favor of government-supervised industrial planning. Among the most important advocates of such measures was Rexford Tugwell, who, as previously mentioned, was a key advisor to President Roosevelt. Tugwell (1933, 200) argued that the government's enforcement of competition through antitrust over the previous decades had failed to bring about an efficient economy—he cited the wide "disparity between our possibilities and our performance" as evidence of this failure. Tugwell wrote that the government should relax antitrust laws when such laws "interfere with planning for equilibrium," and he proposed that industries "set up their own planning boards and central management devices for maintaining standards of competition and form controlling maximum prices and minimum wages" (212). To enforce this system, a controlling body would have the power to impose fines on firms that were in violation of industry rules.

Scholarly reviews of Tugwell's book, *The Industrial Discipline and the Governmental Arts*, which was published May 9, 1933, just as the details of the NIRA were being hashed out in Washington (see below), noted that the book clearly had a major influence on the development of the NIRA. Charles Beard (1933, 833), in his fall 1933 review, wrote that "Professor Tugwell writes the philosophy of the New Deal." William Hopkins (1933, 502), in his review of the book, likewise stated the book's view "is in close harmony with President Roosevelt's policy [as evident by its similarity to the NIRA] which became law in the United States on June 16, 1933."

That the NIRA involved strict government oversight and planning, such as had occurred under the War Industries Board, is certainly a misnomer. Undersecretary of Commerce John Dickinson acknowledged that "a planned society is but a utopian dream." Instead, he claimed that the NIRA's brand of "planning means having in mind the broad outlines of a general picture of what we should be striving for. . . . Such planning involves no adherence to a blue print, but it recognizes the use of a compass and a map" (Berle et al. 1934, 41–42). The NIRA codes, like those approved by the TPCD in the late 1920s, were designed to provide a compass—one that could vary from industry to industry—to help create a system of fair competition throughout the economy.

Along these lines, President Roosevelt, in a May 4, 1933, speech to the chamber of commerce, said that the recovery bill in development would attempt to bring order out of chaos. "You and I acknowledge the existence of unfair methods of competition, of cut-throat prices and of general chaos . . .

order must be restored [and] the attainment of that objective depends upon your willingness to cooperate with one another . . . to prevent overproduction, to prevent unfair wages, and eliminate improper working conditions."[8] Furthermore, in Roosevelt's June 16, 1933, statement outlining the policies of the just-passed NIRA, he claimed that the Act "is a challenge to industry which has long insisted that, given the right to act in unison, it could do much for the general good which has hitherto been unlawful. From today it has that right."[9]

Rationale behind Hours Worked Reductions: Work Sharing

The standard workweek throughout the 1920s was forty-eight hours—eight hours per day, six days a week was typical. Of course, this was substantially below the average workweek throughout much of the nineteenth century, which was often sixty to seventy hours—essentially sunup to sundown, six days a week. Organized labor pushed aggressively for the eight-hour day throughout the nineteenth century, and Teddy Roosevelt made it a part of the Progressive Party platform in his unsuccessful 1912 bid for the White House. Generally, the rationale behind the shorter workweek was to provide more leisure time for workers, thus boosting their utility. But it was also recognized that firms would not necessarily cut back on their demand for total labor hours with a shorter workweek—they would instead hire additional workers, thus spreading scarce work among more laborers. The idea that shorter workweeks could boost the total number of people employed is broadly known as work sharing.[10] In 1887, Samuel Gompers of the American Federation of Labor became perhaps the first major figure to advocate for shorter workweeks as a means of spreading work (Best 1981). But it was not until the 1920s that US policy makers actively encouraged or incorporated work sharing as a means of reducing national unemployment. Once again, Herbert Hoover was a major player in its advocacy and adoption.

In response to the depression of 1920–21, Secretary of Commerce Hoover called a President's Conference on Unemployment, which first met in September 1921. Among the specific recommendations was the encouragement of manufacturing firms to reduce workweeks and implement a rotation of multiple workers to fill each scarce job (Hoover 1921, 21). The goal was not to create more work in aggregate but rather to spread scarce work around so as to increase the probability that each American could have some means of employment. This was particularly important given the scarcity of formal welfare or unemployment insurance programs at the time. Importantly, however, Hoover's policies were simply public recommendations and were in no way binding to firms. In fact, the economy began to recover sharply shortly after the committee's report, and hence there were no substantial changes to the workweek. The unemployment rate fell from 11.3 percent in 1921 to 8.6 percent in 1922 and 4.3 percent in 1923.[11] Rather than dropping after the president's recommendations, the average weekly hours worked *rose* from 46 in September 1921 to 47.7 in October 1921; one year after the commission's work-sharing recommendations were released, the average workweek was almost 50 hours.

The next time the economy faced a major economic challenge—in the fall of 1929—President Hoover again turned to work sharing as a potential cure. Hoover's efforts to promote work sharing began in earnest on November 21, 1929, when, as mentioned earlier in the section on high wages, the president held a conference with several leading industrialists at the White House. In addition to asking them to maintain high wages rates, Hoover asked them to spread available work among more employees by temporarily shortening the work week (Hoover 1952, 54). Following the president's lead, in May 1930, the Railway Employees Department of the American Federation of Labor (AFL) urged a forty-hour workweek as a way to reduce unemployment (I. Bernstein 2010, 476). The AFL's Executive Council likewise endorsed reductions in work hours as a way to alleviate unemployment at the union's October 1930 convention, and Standard Oil of New Jersey went to a forty-hour workweek shortly after.

Building on this momentum, in October 1930, Hoover created the President's Emergency Committee for Employment (PECE). Consistent with Hoover's general approach to the Depression, the committee encouraged local responsibility among and voluntary cooperation from employers to solve the "employment problem." Shorter workweeks were strongly encouraged by PECE as a means of keeping workers off relief rolls. Myron C. Taylor, head of US Steel's Finance Committee, went on the radio on behalf of PECE to announce that, in December 1930, US Steel was operating at only 38 percent of capacity but that it employed as many men as it did in December 1929 thanks to a reduction in the average workweek from 46.2 to 34.4 hours (I. Bernstein 2010, 306). Work sharing, it appeared, was lessening the burden of the Depression on the American worker, even if it may have meant less take-home pay.

PECE pamphlets provided suggestions for how companies could optimally cut hours and implement shorter shifts to promote maximum efficiency. Many companies followed PECE's guidelines, including American Telephone and Telegraph, Bethlehem Steel, Du Pont, General Electric, General Motors, International Harvester, and Westinghouse. Indeed, the average workweek in the manufacturing sector fell over 26 percent from 44.5 hours in June 1930 to 32.8 hours in June 1932.[12] Some of this drop would certainly have occurred anyway with the faltering economy, but Neumann, Taylor, and Fishback (2013) examine movements in hours worked across other downturns and suggest that a large portion of the decline was caused by Hoover's work-sharing programs.

In August 1932, with the Depression near its trough, Hoover once again called industrial leaders to Washington so that he could push for a new round of work-sharing-inspired cuts to the workweek. Hoover created a new committee headed by Standard Oil of New Jersey president Walter C. Teagle. The Teagle Committee, with its slogan "Job Security by Job Sharing," further encouraged companies to cut workweeks, and again provided models of how such measures could be accomplished. In early 1933, a survey by the Commerce Department suggested that 80 percent of the nation's employers had adopted some form of work sharing and that one-quarter of those Americans employed owed their situation to this policy.

Given that Hoover's work-sharing program was simply one of moral suasion—there were no legal requirements for firms to cut workweeks—why did so many industrial leaders follow Hoover's suggestions for work sharing? Neumann, Taylor, and Fishback (2013) suggest that firms may have felt that if they did not cut workweeks, the Hoover administration might shift federal policy in favor of unions. Although union membership and strike activity had waned dramatically since a brief spike a decade earlier, employers might well have feared that an irritated Hoover and Congress would respond to the economic emergency with pro-labor policies. In his meetings with industrialists, Hoover (1952, 54–57) emphasized that he wanted to prevent lockouts and strikes that would add to the turmoil. But Hoover also supported expanded opportunities for collective bargaining by signing the Davis-Bacon Act in March 1931 and the Norris-LaGuardia Act in March 1932.

After Roosevelt's electoral victory in November 1932, labor unions, which had long pushed for shorter workweeks in the United States, saw an opening to accomplish not just Hoover's push for firms' voluntary compliance in shortening the workweek but legislative action. Shortly after the election, AFL president William Green proposed a six-hour-per-day, five-day week, claiming it would have a dramatic positive effect on the unemployment problem. Three weeks later, Alabama senator Hugo Black introduced a thirty-hour-per-week bill, and the bill passed the Senate on April 6, 1933. Work sharing via shorter workweeks, it appeared, would soon be incorporated into law.

Formulation and Passage of the NIRA: April 30–June 16, 1933

In the four months between Roosevelt's election and his taking office on March 4, 1933, the president-elect had expressed some interest in plans that would boost purchasing power via wage increases—a course of action strongly favored by his secretary of labor, Francis Perkins. However, Roosevelt had resisted calls to relax antitrust laws, implement price and output controls, and more generally allow for increased industrial self-governance—actions that many business leaders and trade associations were advocating. In early April, any type of broad-based recovery program along the lines of what would become the NIRA was simmering far on the back burner of the president's active policy agenda. However, passage of Senator Black's thirty-hour-workweek bill caused Roosevelt to dramatically change course. The Black bill limited hours to promote work sharing, but it did not raise hourly wage rates, and Roosevelt feared a reduction in take-home pay would cause damaging drops in the purchasing power of labor. Politically, however, the president could not simply oppose the popular bill—he needed to present a viable alternative. Therefore, Roosevelt asked Raymond Moley, a key member of his Brains Trust, to review the various plans that had been proposed to the administration over the prior few months.

In mid-April, Moley met with New York senator Robert Wagner to develop the required alternative to Senator Black's recovery bill. On April 22, Wagner invited several individuals associated with recovery planning to meet and draw up a proposal—among these were Harold Moulton, James H. Rand, Fred Kent, and Malcolm Rorty. What emerged over the following days was a bill largely in line with the desires of business for cartel-driven recovery where industry was allowed self-governance but which also contained provisions to raise hourly wage rates and reduce workweeks.

The media was eventually made aware of these negotiations as the April 30 *New York Times* reported that "a 'national industry recovery act' modeled on the lines of the War Industries Board is being whipped into shape for submission this week."[13] On May 2, the *Times* noted that the Black thirty-hour-workweek bill was effectively dead because the administration was pushing a comprehensive bill that would include as much as $2 billion in public works spending along with a package of labor and industrial policies. According to the article, "Secretary Perkins has proposed that in order to make the Black bill ... workable, it should include a provision for minimum wages ... and a section permitting control of intra-industrial plants engaged in unfair competition."[14] A front-page headline in the May 5 *Wall Street Journal* noted that, "To Plan or Not to Plan No Longer Seems to Be the Question."[15]

On May 6, it was reported that "a rough draft of the national industrial recovery act, designed to achieve federal coordination and control of production, was completed today by experts who have been drawing up the plan."[16] The draft, which was subject to revision, was noted to also include a guarantee of the right to collective bargaining for labor as well as between $3 billion and $5 billion for public works. In terms of industry reaction, Henry Harriman, president of the US Chamber of Commerce, agreed with the spirit of the infant bill, saying that American businesses must "take the brutality of wage and price cutting out of competition . . . by the self-regulation of industry with the government acting as umpire and seeing to it that fair conditions prevail." But the media offered some skepticism; a May 7 *New York Times* column wrote that we must "see that business cooperation does not run away with its new freedom from trust law restraints and place additional burdens on the public in the way of exorbitant prices."[17]

While business interests were quite enthusiastic about the new bill, it was then made known that a second proposal had been simultaneously prepared by General Hugh Johnson. The Johnson proposal was to give the president, rather than business, the right to organize and control industry. On May 10, Roosevelt created a committee to reconcile the Wagner and Johnson proposals. Business leaders vehemently called for access to this committee's deliberations, and Roosevelt acquiesced. According to Johnson (1935, 204), this committee essentially locked itself in the office of Lew Douglas, director of the Bureau of the Budget. The participants included Douglas, Johnson, Wagner, Undersecretary of Commerce John Dickinson, one of Roosevelt's chief legal advisors, Donald Richberg, and occasionally a few of what Johnson called "horners-in," — the only one mentioned specifically by Johnson in his memoirs is Rexford Tugwell.

The final bill, which was submitted on May 17, was in line with the desire of business for the suspension of antitrust laws and industrial self-governance; however, it also contained provisions for raising wage rates, cutting work hours, and guaranteeing the right of collective bargaining. Roosevelt summed up the bill in a statement that accompanied its introduction to Congress, saying the NIRA was a "cooperative movement throughout all industry [to] obtain wide reemployment, shorten the workweek, to pay a decent wage . . . and to prevent unfair competition and disastrous overproduction."[18]

Reaction to the bill over the following days was largely enthusiastic. Raymond L. Collier, managing director of the Steel Founders Society of America—a trade association of steel foundries—called it "an advanced step in social evolution. . . . Industry best knows its troubles and shortcomings. It knows what it wants and needs to place itself on a profitable basis that will insure maximum employment and fair wages."[19] Leo A. Del Monte, head of the Industrial Council of Cloak, Suit, and Skirt Manufacturers, reported a resolution from the trade association supporting the bill, saying that "unfair competition has created demoralization in the industry" and that the NIRA "offers a practical and effective solution."[20] In fact, Del Monte noted that the industry had scheduled a meeting in Washington for May 22 in which firms representing over 70 percent of the men's clothing industry would discuss the outlines of a code of fair competition. Bernard Baruch, the former head of the War Industries Board, came out in support of the NIRA bill, but he warned that the codes would need an effective enforcement mechanism—"nothing is possible without distinct and adequate authority."[21] Harriman, president of the US Chamber of Commerce, met in New York with representatives for 250 trade associations on May 19 to gauge businesses' overall reaction to the bill. He reported that the group enthusiastically believed that implementation of the NIRA would mean that "many industries will soon be using black ink instead of red."[22]

Fortuitously, the National Electrical Manufacturers Association was scheduled to hold its annual spring meeting in Hot Springs, Virginia, on May 22 and 23. At the meeting, the 269 members approved via voice vote a motion that the industry would cooperate with the NIRA if the law was approved. The association's president, J. S. Tritle, general manager of Westinghouse Electric and Manufacturing Company, said that the association offered its "loyal support and sincere cooperation to the President."[23]

The NIRA bill passed the House of Representatives by a vote of 325 to 76 on May 26. Democrats voted overwhelmingly in favor of the bill, 266 to 25, while Republicans were more split, with 53 in favor and 50 opposed. In the wake of the bill's passage, the stock market rose over 7 percent on May 26 and 27. Interestingly, while the Act saw almost universal support from major industry groups leading up to its passage in the House, the National Association of Manufacturers reacted with a statement strongly against the bill. The group feared that the wage and price increases would make American products less competitive with imported goods—it suggested that the bill needed to include protections against foreign competition.[24] Some senators were also resistant to the impact that the $3.3 billion allocated to public works would have on the deficit and advocated raising additional taxes to help offset these expenditures.

On June 2, the American Federation of Labor formally endorsed the NIRA bill, saying that it was "the most advanced and forward looking legislation for recovery yet proposed." The AFL noted: "This depression is ample proof that our economic system of free competition has broken down. This bill points the way to a new order in which industry can regulate itself." The union approved strongly of the labor provisions of the NIRA, noting that the key to recovery was to promote "a steady flow of buying power" of labor.[25]

The debate in the Senate was quite contentious, with many opposing the industrial control portions of the bill. Debate on the bill began with the Senate Finance Committee. On Friday, June 2, Senator Bennett Clark (D-MO) proposed an amendment to strike out the entire bill less the public works provision and this amendment was defeated by the narrow margin of 10 to 8. Senator William McAdoo (D-CA) proposed an amendment essentially eliminating the enforcement mechanism behind the industrial control provisions—an action that Senator Wagner said "took the heart right out of" the bill—and this passed the Finance Committee 12 to 7 in what the New York Times called an "almost complete emasculation" of the bill. [26] Republican senator David Reed (R-PA) then proposed an amendment, which passed 10 to 8, to create an embargo against imports that would harm the operation of the bill. Together these amendments were called an "astonishing revolt" against Roosevelt. In response, committee chairman Pat Harrison (D-MS) adjourned the meeting, saying that he would fight to restore the bill to its former self when the committee reconvened. The media speculated that the revolt against Roosevelt by members of his own party may have been caused by "resentment by certain Democrats over Mr. Roosevelt's handling of appointments," as some felt they "had not been sufficiently consulted on important nominations made by the President."[27] On Monday June 5, the antiadministration revolt subsided; by a vote of 12 to 6, the industrial control provisions were restored to the way they had been passed in the House, and the bill was approved by the Finance Committee to be sent to the whole Senate.

On June 7, Wagner began discussion of the NIRA to the full Senate, saying that the legislation "would be a powerful factor in bringing order and health into the economic life of the American people." Senators William Borah (R-ID) and Huey Long (D-LA) spoke strongly against the NIRA. Borah expressed his concern about the law's promotion of monopoly: "You not only propose to let big business organize in to trusts and combines, but you propose to let them invoke the law [and] send to jail those who do not conform to their codes!" Senator Long dryly noted that the bill would eliminate the unemployment problem because everyone would "be in jail for violating this infernal thing."[28] Despite these misgivings, the bill passed the Senate on June 9, 1933, by a vote of 58 to 24; Democrats voted 47 to 4 in favor, while Republicans were 20 to 10 opposed.

The Senate version differed slightly from that passed by the House in the way the bill would be financed: Both bills had specified tax increases of

$220,000, but the bills varied in terms of how these would be administered. On Saturday, June 10, the bill was reconciled by joint committee, and the reconciled bill was quickly approved in the House. The Senate approved the reconciled bill by a vote of 46 to 39 on June 13. President Roosevelt signed the bill into law on June 16, 1933. The NIRA's passage was hailed by the chamber of commerce's Harriman, who said the law "constitutes a most important step in our progress toward business rehabilitation. . . . Some large industries are ready to submit their codes. Others should prepare to do so immediately." Robert Lund of the National Association of Manufacturers, which had been somewhat skeptical of the NIRA throughout its development, said, "I urge manufacturers to give their wholehearted cooperation to [the NIRA] and to the President in increasing employment and speeding up the business recovery which is already clearly under way."[29]

Legislative Prototypes of the NIRA in 1931 and 1932

That a bill changing the economic landscape the way they NIRA did could be formulated in about three weeks and then be approved by Congress in the same amount of time seems unfathomable. Of course, desperate times can call for desperate measures. But beyond this, another factor that helped the NIRA move relatively quickly through the legislative process is that variations of the ideas embedded in the program had been entertained in academic circles as well as by Congress in the two years prior to 1933. This chapter concludes with an examination of some major precursors to the NIRA that had not been approved by Congress.

In September 1931, with the Depression deepening, General Electric President Gerard Swope proposed what became known simply as the "Swope Plan." Swope proposed that firms should be required to administer life insurance, pensions, disability insurance, and unemployment insurance for their employees. However, in a world of perfect competition, firm owners would likely be unwilling or unable to unilaterally supply such benefits. Swope proposed that firms yield authority to industry trade associations, which would regulate industrial output and prices in addition to supervising employee insurance programs. The plan was clearly a quid pro quo proposal—industry would gain the ability to coordinate but would make concessions to workers. Hawley (1966, 42) notes that, although the plan was hailed widely by business, President Hoover called it "the most gigantic proposal of monopoly ever made in history." Still, Swope's idea of economic planning via trade associations was a major topic of discussion in policy circles, and conferences on some measure of antitrust reform as a means to ending the Depression began to blossom at universities (Himmelberg 1976, 127).

Following up on the Swope Plan, in December 1931, Senator Gerald Nye (R-ND) introduced a series of bills that would promote fair trade practices in industry and would have provided antitrust immunity from Federal Trade Commission–approved trade practice provisions. Essentially Nye's plan was to expand the Trade Practice Conference Division that had been active in the final three years of the Coolidge administration. In January 1932, Senator David Walsh (D-MA) submitted a bill that would have allowed industries to fix prices at "fair and reasonable" levels, and in June 1932, Walsh introduced a separate bill that would have suspended antitrust laws for two years—just as the NIRA would do for industries under codes of fair competition.

Whereas such plans dealt with revision of antitrust laws economy-wide, others were concerned with stabilizing conditions in specific industries. In January 1932, Senator James Davis (R-PA) and Representative Clyde Kelly (R-PA) introduced a bill specific to the bituminous coal industry. The Davis-Kelly bill proposed to grant the right of collective bargaining to workers in the bituminous coal industry while also giving producers the ability to co-operate on issues of production and prices. The Senate's Committee on Mines and Mining held hearings on the bill, but it failed to get past the committee level (Lauck 1936). On February 29, 1932, Representative David Lewis (D-MD) introduced a bill for the coal industry to create a Coal Operators Board that would have been charged with administering quotas for mine operators as a means of stabilizing prices and output in the industry (W. Fisher and James 1955). Because these bills for the coal industry were unsuccessful in Congress, president of the United Mine Workers of America, John L. Lewis, decided that rather than push for special legislation for one industry, it would be better to push for broad legislation covering all industries. On February 17, 1933, Lewis testified before the Senate Finance Committee, which was hearing testimony from leading industrialists on plans for economic recovery. He recommended the creation of a Board of Emergency Control, which would consist of rep-resentatives from labor, industry, agriculture, and finance. Workers would be given the right to collective bargaining while the board would be given broad powers to reduce workweeks and engage in "fundamental economic plan-ning . . . in accordance with the judgement of the Congress" (Lauck 1936, 132). Ultimately, this is not too far off from what the NIRA implemented four months later. When viewed in the light of proposals such as these, the NIRA looks far less like a radical idea hatched during an eventful six weeks in the spring of 1933.

Summary and Discussion

The policies put forth by the NIRA seem puzzling today. Why did the Roosevelt administration think that a combination of higher wage rates, shorter hours, and intraindustry collusion would boost output during a depression? All three of these policies would appear to be contractionary rather than expansionary. This chapter has outlined the logic behind these three policies. Higher wage rates were pushed as a way to boost aggregate demand. Shorter hours were promoted in the name of work sharing. Finally, intraindustry collusion was promoted as a way to eliminate the unfair competition that many firms increasingly blamed for their troubles. In all three cases, arguments in favor of policies such as those embedded in the NIRA had been brewing for over a decade.

The NIRA was formulated and signed into law in just over six weeks. This seems remarkable given how radical and far-reaching the law was. However, several precursor bills had been considered over the prior two years, and these certainly aided the bill's speedy formation and passage. When the NIRA is viewed in the full context of economic and political movements and debates of the prior fifteen years, and particularly of the prior three years, the legislation does not appear as radical as it does when viewed outside of that context.

3

The NIRA Code Negotiation Process

The National Industrial Recovery Act stipulated that each industry had to write a "code of fair competition." This code had to include minimum wage rates, maximum workweeks, and a statement recognizing the right of collective bargaining. Additionally, it could include specific trade practice provisions regulating firm behavior in the industry. Although the NIRA was officially signed into law on June 16, 1933, the Act would have no binding effect upon a firm's economic behavior until the government approved its industry's code. The text of the NIRA said that the code had to be explicitly approved by the president, and indeed through the end of 1933, every code was officially approved by Roosevelt upon the recommendation the National Recovery Administration's top administrator, General Hugh Johnson. Executive Order 6543-A (December 30, 1933) gave the NRA administrator the power to approve codes, or changes in codes, so that after this date codes were approved by the NRA rather than the president himself. The process of getting a code to the approval stage, however, was long and cumbersome. Each code was supposed to pass through seven formal phases of code making, which are described in detail below.[1] Although these were the formal guidelines of the NRA, not every industry followed each of these steps toward code formulation.

Phase 1: Preparation of the Code. Each industry was told to communicate under the umbrella of its trade association (or, in some cases, multiple trade associations) or, if no trade association existed, under some kind of ad hoc representative group made up of representatives from major firms in the industry. The text of the NIRA made it clear that the group formulating and presenting the code had to be representative of the industry and "that such association or groups impose no inequitable restrictions on admission to membership" to these bodies. In effect, any firm representative who wanted to participate in its industry's code preparation was to be allowed to do so. The first step the organizational body would take in its industry code formulation was submitting its information to the NRA Control Division—only after the NRA approved the representative body as truly reflecting the industry would the body be officially allowed to draft a code. The location of the industry code drafting meetings was left to the discretion of the industry itself. For example, the preliminary draft of the automobile code was written in Detroit, while the draft of the steel code was written in New York. When a proposed code was complete, it was sent back to the NRA Control Division.

Phase 2: Checking Proposed Codes. Upon receipt of a proposed code, the NRA Control Division would send it to one of the sixteen NRA deputy administrators, who would be assigned to steering the code proceedings of this industry. The deputy administrator would first make sure that the code contained the mandatory provisions—the right to collective bargaining, minimum wages, and maximum hours. The deputy administrator would then write a report making any suggestions to the industry group for revisions that he deemed proper and would send this back to the group. The industry group would then edit the proposed code, send it back to the administrator, and request a preliminary conference. The proposed code would be sent out to the following NRA subagencies: the Industrial Advisory Board, the Consumers Advisory Board, the Labor Advisory Board, the Legal Division, and the Research and Planning Division.

Phase 3: Preliminary Conference. An informal conference would then be held in Washington, DC, with a small representative group from the industry attending along with a staff member from each of the five NRA subagencies listed above. The NRA deputy administrator assigned to the case—or if that person was unavailable, then an assistant deputy—would chair the meeting. The purpose of this meeting was to finalize a code that was acceptable to all interested parties and would have a chance of being approved by the president. The code draft that came out of this conference was reported back to the entire membership of the industry so that it could suggest any final changes to the code prior to the public hearing.

Phase 4: Public Hearings. The proposed code would be made available to the public, and the date and time of a hearing in Washington would be set. These hearings were formal events and were presided over by an NRA deputy or assistant deputy administrator—preferably the same person who had chaired the preliminary conference. Anyone could testify at these hearings, but to do so, one had to file, at least a day before the hearing, a brief statement proposing to either eliminate or modify a specific provision of the code

FIGURE 3.1. Photographs from Code Hearings for the Electric Light and Power Industry (Top) and the Scrap-Iron and Nonferrous Waste Materials Industry (Bottom)
Notes: The power industry hearing was held on January 11, 1934, and the scrap-iron industry hearing took place on November 22, 1933, at the Commerce Building in Washington, DC.
Source: National Archives, Record Group 9, ARC Identifier 16703546, "Pictorial Materials" Entry Number PI 44–43, Box 3.

or to create a specific new provision. These hearings could last for as little as one hour or could go on for several days. Media often attended these meetings, particularly if they involved large industries, and newspapers and radio would report details of what transpired. Figure 3.1 reproduces two government photographs from the hearing of the scrap iron and nonferrous waste materials industry and the electric light and power industry. Figure 3.2 shows Robert P. Lamont, president of the American Iron and Steel Institute (and

FIGURE 3.2. Testimony at the Code Hearing for the Iron and Steel Industry
Notes: This hearing took place on July 31, 1933. Standing on the right is Robert P. Lamont, president of the American Iron and Steel Institute. Seated on the left is NRA administrator Hugh Johnson.
Source: Photo by ACME Newspictures, Inc.

former secretary of commerce) testifying at the public code hearing for the iron and steel industry while NRA administrator Hugh Johnson listens.

Phase 5: Post-Hearing Analysis and Conference. After the public hearing, the deputy administrator and the industry representatives communicated informally regarding potential amendments to the code that could satisfy any objections that were raised. These discussions could last for days or weeks depending on the nature of the changes requested. Ultimately, the industry group needed to obtain approval by majority vote of the amended final code—although in many cases, industry members simply voted early on to delegate authority for the code preparation to a smaller representative group, in which case only that subgroup's approval was required. When the deputy administrator was satisfied with the industry's revised code, he would submit the final draft back to each of the NRA advisory boards and divisions and ask for their final opinions of it in writing. A final report, which included written reports from each of these divisions as well as the deputy administrator, would then be sent to the NRA's chief administrator. Hugh Johnson served in this role between June 1933 and September 1934, and he approved, or recommended approval to Roosevelt, 522 of the 557 NIRA codes.

Phase 6: Final Amendments and Approval by NRA Administrator. After analyzing the reports, the NRA administrator could make further suggestions for revisions and send the code back to the industry group, or he could recommend approval of the code. Once he was ready to approve, the administrator would write a brief report about the details of the code and then apply his signature to the code recommending for approval. These reports were published alongside the approved code itself in the documents printed by the US Government Printing Office.

Phase 7: Presidential Approval. After December 30, 1933, the process would be finished with phase 6, but prior to this time, President Roosevelt himself also had to formally approve each code. The president could approve the code or he could approve it contingent on specific changes being made. For example, Roosevelt created thirteen contingencies for his approval of the cotton textile code on July 9, 1933. Among these were the creation of a provision requiring firms to maintain the amount by which the highest paid workers in the industry were making more than lowest paid workers. The code had noted that wages as low as six dollars per week were common at this time, but the new minimum wage would be twelve dollars per week for forty hours of work (i.e., 30 cents per hour). Roosevelt's suggested provision meant that a worker making ten dollars per week at a firm where a lower paid worker was making only six dollars would continue to make four dollars more than the lowest paid worker—that is, presumably sixteen dollars for the high-paid worker and twelve dollars for the low-paid one. The Cotton Textile Industry Committee, headed by George A. Sloan, submitted on July 15 a series of amendments to the code that met Roosevelt's contingencies so that the amended code went into effect on July 17.[2]

Industry Code Deliberations Prior to June 16, 1933

Despite the NRA's formal suggested process, many industries had begun to meet prior to the NIRA becoming law on June 16, and in these cases, the process was often much less organized and rigid. The earliest reference I found to such a meeting occurred on May 4, 1933, just five days after the first hints of the NIRA were made known. The Dress Institute of America, a trade association for the garment industry, met at the Garment Center Club on Seventh Avenue in New York City to discuss the formulation of an industry trade agreement. Marton Mandel, the trade association's lawyer, said that the group was acting on that week's news from Washington that the government was formulating a plan whereby "individual industries would be encouraged to engage in self-regulation."[3]

By the middle of May, it appeared highly probable that trade associations would be charged with drawing up industry-specific rules of fair conduct. On May 15, Raymond Collier of the Steel Founders' Society of America noted that "trade associations are getting the green light. They can proceed to lay out sound plans for their respective industries [and] draft industrial codes outlawing its unfair trade practices."[4] After May 17, when the NIRA bill was formally submitted to Congress, a flurry of industries began to meet to formulate codes. On May 19, the Institute of Leather Cloth and Lacquered Fabric Manufacturers held a meeting with representatives accounting for over 80 percent of the industry, and the group appointed a five-person committee, chaired by Rudolf Neuberger of the Zapon Company, to draft the industry's code.[5]

On May 22, executives representing firms that accounted for 70 percent of the production of men's clothing in the United States met in Washington, DC, to begin the process of drawing up a code. From Chicago, representatives from manufacturers Hart, Schaffner & Marx, Kuppenheimer, and Meyer & Co. attended. From Rochester, New York, representatives from the International Tailoring Company and Hickey-Freeman were in attendance. The Clothing Manufacturers Exchange sent a representative from its New York office. Because the text of the NIRA bill discussed the need to have input from organized labor, Sidney Hillman, president of the Amalgamated Clothing Workers of America, was invited to attend to represent the interests of labor.[6] Also during the week of May 22, the directors of the Associated Grocery Manufacturers of America, the Silk Association, the National Association of Hosiery Manufacturers, and Merchants Ladies Garment Association met to begin to discuss the formulation of their industries' respective codes of fair competition.[7]

The National Paperboard Association announced on May 22 that the paperboard industry had prepared a code that was ready to be submitted once the NIRA was signed into law. The association announced that its code would create a six-hour work day while providing hourly wage rates that gave workers the same purchasing power they had enjoyed under an eight-hour day in 1929. William Jeffrey, the association's chairman, noted that such provisions "will increase the cost of production somewhat, but through the stabilization of the industry by other features of the plan it is hoped that this increase in cost can be covered."[8]

It may be interesting to follow up on some of these codes that were formulated prior to the NIRA's passage and prior to the development of a formal process for code making. The public hearing for the paperboard code was held on September 14, and the code was approved on November 8, 1933. It did not, in fact, contain a six-hour day, but instead specified an eight-hour maximum. For wage rates, the code specified a minimum wage of 38 cents per hour for males (33 cents for females) in most of the country, and a minimum wage of 30 cents per hour in the South. Section 5 of Article 10 said that the code authority—that is, the Executive Committee of the National Paperboard Association—would conduct a study of the feasibility of a shorter working day and submit a report within three months of the code's passage. There was clearly division in the industry over the efficacy of a six-hour day. The code also required all firms to submit data to the code authority on plant capacity, production, sales, prices, wages, inventory, and other measures.

One challenge faced by many industries was the existence of multiple trade associations within that industry. Of course, such a situation is not uncommon today. For example, in the scholarly field of economic history, groups such as the Economic History Association, the Economic History Society, and the Economic and Business History Society have overlapping, or even competing, interests. In such cases, trade associations had to either unify or work together to bring the industry under one representative organization to draw up a code. To illustrate, on May 25, 1933, members of the American Association of Woolen and Worsted Manufacturers met at the Manhattan Club in New York and appointed a committee of five individuals to work with its rival association, the National Association of Wool Manufacturers, to try to unify the industry for the purpose of designing an NIRA code.[9] In another example of multiple trade associations working together to create one industry code, on May 25, a twenty-person committee—headed by T. M. Marchant, president of the American Cotton Manufacturers Association; Earnest Hood, president of the National Association of Cotton Manufacturers; and George Sloan, president of the Cotton Textile Institute—met with representatives of the Roosevelt administration to begin discussions of a code for the cotton industry.[10] The committee passed a resolution for a forty-hour maximum workweek, with two shifts allowed—that is, an eighty-hour capital usage maximum per week. There were disagreements about minimum wages between Northern and Southern concerns. Northern firms were in favor of a ten-dollar weekly minimum—that is, 25 cents an hour—however, representatives from Southern firms thought that this was too high and hence no agreement was reached at this meeting.

In the women's dress industry (the first group to begin to formulate a code), there were several trade associations, and many dressmakers were not members of any association. Hence, on May 26, members of the industry recommended the creation of a new organization to be known as the National Dress Manufacturers Association (NDMA), which would unify the industry.[11] According to the dress manufacturers' code of fair competition, which was approved on October 31, 1933, the NDMA consisted of about six hundred firms at the time of the code's formulation. Still, not all dressmakers agreed to join the NDMA. The Affiliated Dress Manufacturers, Inc., which consisted of about 125 firms that generally focused on the production of very high quality garments, remained an independent trade association outside of the NDMA, and these two trade associations worked together to create the dress code.[12]

The previous chapter mentioned that the 269 members of the National Electrical Manufacturers Association (NEMA) had given symbolic approval to the NIRA at its May 22–23 meeting. At that meeting, the membership also directed the thirty-member board of governors of the association to draft a proposed code. On May 28, the board sent two separate proposals to the membership. One of these looked a lot like the Swope Plan of 1931, which is not surprising since Swope had served as NEMA's president upon its founding in 1926. This plan not only specified the standard wage and hour provisions but also called on firms to offer life, disability, and unemployment insurance. The second proposal was more in line with other proposed industry codes, calling for firms to file data with a central board, standardize accounting methods throughout the industry, and implement the typical wage and hour provisions.[13] Ultimately, the electrical manufacturing code was the fourth code to be approved on August 4, 1933, and it did not contain any of the Swope-like provisions for worker insurance programs, but instead contained provisions in line with the second proposal.

The executive directors of the National Retail Dry Goods Association met in the Palmer House Hotel in Chicago between May 31 and June 3 to discuss the development of its industry's code. At the conclusion of this meeting, Lew Hahn, president of the association, was empowered to create a committee that would formally draw up a proposed code for consideration by the full membership before the end of June. The association's discussions provided input into the direction they wanted Hahn's committee to take the code. The code was clearly viewed by industry members as a quid pro quo "bargaining arrangement" whereby manufacturers were given immunity from antitrust law but in return had to boost employment, purchasing power, and make other concessions to labor. The group noted, however, that the code should not be viewed as an "open sesame" to fix prices and that the code should work to curb "sweatshop" working conditions. The group also discussed the creation of an insignia that would be placed on all dry goods produced under fair labor conditions.[14]

Ultimately, the dry good industry was covered by the broad wholesale or distributing trade code, which was approved on January 12, 1934, after the industry's formal hearing on November 13 in the ballroom of Washington's Mayflower Hotel. The dry goods industry sought provisions that would be more specific to its industry and hence pursued a supplementary code for the wholesale dry goods trade—this was approved on May 14, 1934. A supplementary code would expand upon the articles, or replace provisions, from the broader industry code. Interestingly, neither the regular code nor its supplement contained any language about the inclusion of insignia on dry goods made with fair labor practices, as was proposed at the Chicago meeting in June 1933. Of course, the NIRA's Blue Eagle emblem, which will be discussed in the next chapter, was just such an insignia and could be employed by any firm complying with the NIRA codes.

The Rubber Manufacturers Association hired Newton D. Baker, who served as secretary of war during World War I, to help the rubber industry formulate its code.[15] The industry was particularly concerned that too much entry and overproduction had driven prices to destructively low levels—of course, these types of complaints were common to many industries. Following up, the Rubber Manufacturers Association ultimately submitted its proposed code on September 26, 1933, and its hearing was held in Washington on October 25. Exceeding forty pages, the rubber manufacturers code was among the more lengthy and complex codes approved by the NRA.

On June 15, twenty-four oil-producing organizations sent representatives to a meeting in Chicago to develop the industry's code. The *Chicago Tribune* reported that 99 percent of the oil industry was represented at the Stevens Hotel, where industrialists, "long trained in the ways of laissez-faire were trying to discover just what you do when you suspend antitrust laws and join with your competitors in a love feast" that is the new planned economy.[16] At the same time, industry leaders from the bituminous coal industry met in Chicago's Drake Hotel. A committee of thirteen leading operators in the National Coal Association presented a preliminary draft of a code for the industry to more than five hundred delegates from the nation's coal producers.[17] Both of these summits continued over three days. The coal conference culminated with a code the industry felt was ready for submission.[18] In both of these cases, the meetings were closed to the media and secrecy was maintained regarding the contents of the discussions. It is interesting to note that these two industries were among the first wave of code approvals. Petroleum was the tenth code approved (on August 19, 1933), and bituminous coal was the twenty-fourth code approved (on September 18, 1933)—although in both cases, which will be discussed later, the road to code passage was quite bumpy.

The First Code: Cotton Textile Industry

Given that the cotton textile industry was the first industry to have its code approved—on July 9, 1933—it is worthwhile to explore more fully the development of this code. As mentioned earlier, the government held an initial meeting with industry representatives on May 24—more than three weeks before the law was enacted.

The Roosevelt administration was interested in moving quickly to bring this industry and its estimated 400,000 employees under the NIRA. George Sloan, president of the Cotton Textile Institute, stated that "healthy conditions in employment can never be realized until we correct overcapacity and . . . remove the threat of overproduction."[19] The cotton textile industry submitted its code for approval on June 16, just hours after Roosevelt signed the NIRA into law. The formal hearing for the code was held between June 27 and July 1, 1933, and it was presided over by Hugh Johnson and NRA deputy administrator William H. Allen. Also in attendance were members of the NIRA's Industrial Advisory Board, the Labor Advisory Board, and the Consumers Advisory Board as well as members of the Department of Justice and the Federal Trade Commission. About five hundred people attended the meeting, as did a full press complement, and "Every person who filed an appearance, whether as a worker, employer, or consumer, was freely heard in public, including a representative of a Communist organization."[20]

The proposed cotton textile code had set a maximum workweek of forty hours and ten dollars minimum weekly pay (i.e., 25 cents per hour) in the South and eleven dollars per week (27.5 cents per hour) in the rest of the country. At the public hearing, the regional wage differential was defended on the grounds that the cost of living was lower in the South because fuel and clothing costs were lower owing to the warmer weather.[21] Other witnesses disagreed, saying that no adequate statistics were available to determine the cost of living in one broad region of the country versus another. This argument against regional wage differences did not ultimately hold up, and the approved cotton code, as well as many other codes, contained different minimum wages for different regions. More importantly, labor representatives strongly objected to the industry's proposed minimum wages as being too low—they countered with a proposal of 50 cents per hour, which was double the initial proposal. The forty-hour minimum workweek was also objected to for not providing enough potential gains from work sharing. Suggestions were made to cut the maximum workweek to as little as twenty-seven hours. Still, Alexander Sachs, the head of the NIRA's Research and Planning Division, testified that the forty-hour workweek was the proper length to permit gains in employment of 100,000 people compared to its 1929 level, when workweeks were close to fifty hours; hence, the forty-hour workweek was maintained.[22] On minimum wages, the sides eventually agreed to 30 cents per hour in the South and 32.5 cents in the North.

Testimony was offered to add to the code the prohibition of employment of children under age sixteen. Johnson (1968, 233), in his memoirs, noted that when Sloan reported the next day that he had secured an agreement from the Cotton Textile Code Committee to outlaw the employment of minors under age sixteen, a "thunderous burst of applause" broke out in the public hearing. Although the text of the NIRA said nothing about minimum ages of employment, most codes followed the example of the cotton textile industry and either outlawed or dramatically limited employment for individuals under age sixteen. In fact, Secretary of Labor Perkins strongly encouraged Johnson not to recommend approval of any code that did not outlaw child labor.[23] Testimony was also given that the code should limit women to working only during daytime hours. This proposal was opposed via testimony from the National Women's Party, which claimed it would be detrimental to the position of women and violate their rights. No such provision was added to the code.

To address the industry's strong concern about overcapacity, the code added an amendment at the hearing stating that all firms in the cotton textile industry had to provide the Cotton Textile Institute, which was the code's organizing authority, a statement with its current capital and productive capacity. Furthermore, if a firm wanted to add new capital or productive capacity, it had to gain permission from the code authority in advance.

The hearing concluded with a statement from Johnson praising the events of the prior four days. "You men of the textile industry have done a very remarkable thing, a patriotic thing. . . . Today's proposed wage increases make a very profound increase in the money to be paid out." At the airport after the hearing, Johnson provided another formal statement to the press: "The textile industry is to be congratulated on its courage and spirit in being the first to assume its patriotic duty and in the generosity of its proposals."[24] Roosevelt, who was on vacation at the time of the hearings, formally approved the Cotton Textile Industry Code of Fair Competition on July 9, 1933, conditional to the changes that were mentioned earlier in this chapter. Many industries watched with great interest the proceedings of the cotton textile industry code as a model for how they should organize under the NIRA. After the public hearing ended on July 1, scores of industries requested a copy of the cotton textile code. The *New York Times* wrote that the cotton code "has blazed a trail in a way for the 7,000 other trades and industries" that will eventually come under the NIRA.[25]

Code Negotiations after the NIRA's Approval

Upon the NIRA's passage, the administration set a goal to have the vast majority of industries covered by codes within two months (i.e., by mid-August), which it estimated would help put three million Americans back to work. However, the NRA's examination of the wave of proposed codes that flooded its office in the hours after the bill's passage—most of which were done with no government input or direction (and certainly did not follow the rigid steps of code formulation outlined earlier)—revealed the broad challenges that were in store. The administration noted on June 17 that many of the proposed codes were "overburdened with detail and the thinly disguised aim was to write in the programs a guarantee of profits and freedom from competition."[26] Industries were told to dramatically simplify their codes and to focus more tightly on the wage and hour provisions as well a few issues of fair competition that were most important to industry. None of the codes as submitted—aside from the aforementioned cotton textile code—were deemed acceptable enough to be formally considered in a public hearing.

On June 20, the NRA released a bulletin titled "Basic Codes of Fair Competition" to provide industry with broad guidelines for code writing and submission. The document, which was published in newspapers nationwide, began by outlining the procedure for industries to submit their proposed codes by mail. It also discussed the desired scope of the agreements, including the required provisions such as maximum hours, minimum wage scales, and the boilerplate statements recognizing collective bargaining. The bulletin emphasized that the codes had to increase purchasing power to labor and acknowledged that this action would raise firms' costs; however, it noted that "greatly increased sales are to be expected from the rising purchasing power of the public." The bulletin wrote that, although it was not the function of the NRA "to prescribe what shall be in the codes," if industry could not agree to a code, then the president could impose a code upon an industry. Indeed, this was specified under Section 7(c) of the NIRA.

On June 22, the cast-iron soil pipe industry submitted what was reported by the *New York Times* as the second proposed code that the NIRA found acceptable enough to proceed to a formal hearing. This industry, which made cast-iron pipes for plumbing systems, consisted of about thirty firms and employed around ten thousand workers. Given its relatively small size, Johnson initially indicated that the proposed code would not likely receive a hearing until the other major industries codes were completed.[27] In fact, although this code was the second to be submitted, it was the eighteenth to be approved (on September 18, 1933). The approved code was only eight pages, just over half the length of the average code approved over the life of the NIRA (14.4 pages), and it was clearly along the lines of the basic code the NRA was looking for. Interestingly, the code created a twenty-seven-hour maximum workweek (forty hours for clerks and bookkeepers, and no limit for supervisors), which was among the shortest maximum workweeks of any approved code.

That smaller industries such as soil pipe would be given lower priority by the NRA is not surprising. In his statement following the signing of the law on June 16, 1933, President Roosevelt stated his hope "that the 10 major industries which control the bulk of industrial employment can submit their basic codes at once and this country can look forward to the month of July as the beginning of our great national movement back to work."[28] While Roosevelt and Johnson did not reveal what the ten major industries were for fear of giving the impression that industries were either "essential" or "nonessential," in his memoirs, Johnson wrote that these ten industries were cotton textiles, coal, petroleum, iron and steel, automobiles, lumber, garments, wholesale trade, retail trade, and construction.

As it so happened, the National Coal Association was in the final day of its annual convention in Chicago on June 16, the day the NIRA was passed. Given the long history of deep division in this industry, Johnson felt it important to travel from Washington to address the convention. However, poor weather forced his plane to land in Pittsburgh, so he addressed the coal convention—and American industry in general—publicly via a radio broadcast: "The simplest and most direct course for each industry is now to submit . . . what it would like to do, first . . . to put men back to work at decent living wages in the shortest possible time, and second, those provisions which you find it absolutely necessary to include to protect [your industry] from the racketeers and price cutters."[29]

On June 22, the petroleum industry formed a sixty-two-member committee to continue the work on the code that it had begun at the industry's June 15 meeting in Chicago.[30] The committee met intensively over the next two days and presented its proposed code, which included production quotas, to the full industry on June 24. A motion to include a provision to fix prices was made during the committee's discussion of the code. Specifically, the provision said that the industry's code authority could establish "minimum and maximum prices for motor fuel and any other products of petroleum . . . for the different localities of the United States in relation to such base points as the committee may indicate." E. B. Reeser of the Barnsdall Oil Company was a chief proponent of adding this provision, saying that "price control must be behind the mere fixing of quotations for crude oil."[31] On June 29, the oil industry sent its proposed code to the NRA; however, it was initially sent back because of deficiencies in the labor clauses. The code was resubmitted on July 14 with a proposed forty-hour workweek and hourly wage rates between 40 and 47 cents depending on geographic location.

Interestingly, oil was the only industry to have a section of the NIRA bill devoted to it. Section 9 gave the president the federal authority to enforce state quotas, which were already in effect, on oil production and to prohibit the transportation of so-called hot oil—or oil in excess of quota—punishable by a fine of $1,000 and up to six months in prison. On July 12, secretary of interior Harold Ickes estimated that 500,000 barrels of oil a day were being shipped in excess of state quotas. The administration had included this clause in the NIRA so that violators would be subject to the penalties established by the NIRA. Oil executives hailed this as the first tangible step the federal government had taken toward solving the problem of overproduction in the industry.[32] Article 2 of the proposed oil code further attempted to curtail production through more stringent quotas, saying "there shall be equitably allotted a maximum production to the various producers."

The public hearing on the oil code began on July 24, and the *Times* noted that "practically every provision [created] controversy between the major producers, the independent producers, and labor." Labor proponents felt that the proposed wage and hour provisions did not go far enough in promoting work sharing and higher purchasing power—they proposed a thirty-hour workweek with a weekly wage of $23.75—that is, 79 cents per hour, which was nearly twice the minimum wage proposed in the code. How to allocate production among firms, as well as whether to include a provision for price fixing, was another major point of contention. Johnson created a committee with one representative from the large oil producers, one from the independent producers, two from labor, and an NRA representative. He said that he would put them in a room and "lock the door until they reached an agreement."[33] Although some issues were agreed upon at this meeting, little progress was made on issues related to production quotas and price fixing. Thus, Johnson decided to carry out Section 7(c) of the NIRA, which stated that if industry could not come to a mutual agreement on a code, then the president could write one for the industry—Johnson wrote the oil code on behalf of President Roosevelt.

Johnson's oil code did not allow for price fixing, but it did create an administrative committee of nine individuals—six from industry and three from the government—which would determine quotas and otherwise oversee the administration of the code.[34] The code also set maximum workweeks that varied from thirty-six to forty hours and minimum wages that were between 40 and

55 cents depending on the nature and location of work—moving the initial industry proposals partway toward what labor representatives desired. In his memoirs, Johnson (1968, 246) said his writing of the oil code for the industry "was the nearest I ever came to meriting the frequently repeated charge of 'cracking down'" on an industry.

Johnson held off on formally recommending his oil code to Roosevelt to allow additional time for the oil industry to comment on the code or reach a breakthrough on its own. Harry F. Sinclair, one of the leaders of the large oil firm contingent, said that the "million dollars a day" increase in wages that the code imposed would bankrupt the industry unless a hard minimum price on oil was imposed and that any oil firm that signed the code "might as well sign a bankruptcy petition at the same time."[35] In response to the industry's concerns, the administration agreed to a ninety-day test trial during which President Roosevelt would set a base price for gasoline and it would be a violation of the code to buy or sell for less than this price. On the evening of August 19—eight weeks after the industry's initial code formulation meeting in Chicago and four weeks after the first public hearings—a majority of the industry voted to endorse the modified code, and Roosevelt approved it immediately. The code was thirty-four pages long and contained seven major articles—Article 5 alone (on marketing) contained thirty-one distinct rules— and two appendixes.

The Second and Third Codes: Shipbuilding and Wool Textile Industries

The shipbuilding and ship repairing industry submitted a proposed code on July 12 and asked the government for an immediate hearing in the hope that the code could be in place before July 26, which was the date that bids would begin for the navy's new $238 million construction program. This program was part of an overall expansion of public works under the New Deal, and it included the building of twenty-one new warships. The proposed code was relatively short and straightforward—it was short enough that the New York Times printed not only the proposed code in its entirety but also the letter (which was twice as long as the code itself) from the shipbuilding industry that accompanied and justified the proposed code.[36] The code would create a forty-hour maximum workweek and a minimum hourly wage of 40 cents, except for in the South, where it would be 35 cents. Industry noted that the typical workweek in shipbuilding had traditionally been forty-eight hours but that the industry had already voluntarily reduced workweeks to forty hours in response to Hoover's calls for work sharing over the prior three years. Thus, the code would essentially formalize the forty-hour week that was already in place.

The public hearings were held in Washington on July 19–21. Labor and industry representatives were extremely far apart on their vision of the code's wage and hours provisions, and on the second day of the hearings the American Federation of Labor presented a substitute code for the shipbuilding industry. Rather than imposing the 40/40 guideposts, the proposed AFL code called for a thirty-hour maximum workweek and an 83.3-cent minimum hourly wage (twenty-five dollars for thirty hours per week). In addition, it proposed that overtime hours not be permitted except in the case of "extreme emergency" and that overtime wages be double their regular rate. After the third day of public hearings with little compromise, the two sides spent a fourth day negotiating in private. After some concessions from both sides, a code was largely agreed upon late in the evening/morning of July 22/23 and an amended code was submitted on July 25. The minimum hourly wage rate was 45 cents per hour, with the exception of 35 cents in the South. The average hourly workweek would be thirty-six hours, and any hours over eight per day would be paid time and a half. However, for any projects that involved US government projects—such as the navy contracts, which were a large part of the industry's business, the maximum workweek would be thirty-two hours. The code was the second to be approved when it passed on July 26, 1933.

The wool textile code was the third to be approved by the NRA—also on July 26, 1933. The code's public hearing was held in Washington on July 24 and 25 under the supervision of A. D. Whiteside, deputy administrator of the NRA. As was the case with shipbuilding, labor and industry executives disagreed widely on wage and hour provisions. The industry-proposed code specified a forty-hour workweek with a fourteen-dollar minimum weekly wage (35 cents per hour) with a thirteen-dollar-per-week minimum wage in the South (32.5 cents per hour). Representing the National Textile Workers Union, Ann Burlack proposed a thirty-hour workweek with a minimum pay of eighteen dollars per week (i.e., 60 cents per hour) throughout the country.[37] Another major source of contention at the hearing was the industry's proposal to restrict hours of machine operation. The majority of members of the National Wool Manufacturers Association, which had submitted the proposed code, wanted to limit operations to two forty-hour shifts per week. A representative of the association noted that the current typical shift was fifty-three hours per week, and thus, other factors constant, a limit to forty-hour shifts would raise employment from the current level of 146,000 to 172,000.

However, the president of Botany Worsted Mills of Passaic, New Jersey, argued that no restrictions on machine hours should be included in the code.[38]

On the second day of hearings, the industry made a concession to labor by agreeing to a provision stating that "no employer shall, on or after the effective date, pay an employee a wage rate which will yield a [lower] wage for a work-week of 40 hours" than the employee was receiving under the longer work-week prior to the code's adoption. Additionally, the minority of industrial executives who opposed the forty-hour shift restriction withdrew their objections in favor of the majority. Whiteside called the day "the finest spirit of sportsmanship I have seen since I have been in Washington."[39] An amended code was submitted the afternoon of July 25, and Roosevelt signed the code the next day. The final code kept the fourteen-dollar (thirteen in the South) minimum pay for forty hours maximum workweek that was in the original proposed code and contained a limit of machine operation to two forty-hour shifts.

The Importance of Trade Associations: A Case Study of the Ice Manufacturing Industry

Those industries that had active trade associations clearly had an advantage in terms of effectively organizing and creating a code of fair competition in a timely and efficient manner. The development of the ice manufacturing code, which was the forty-third code to be approved (on October 3, 1933), nicely illustrates many of these advantages. The National Association of Ice Manufacturers (NAIM), headquartered in Chicago, took a very active role in organizing the industry and formulating the ice code as the association's secretary, Leslie C. Smith, sent regular updates to ice manufacturing concerns throughout the spring and summer of 1933. On May 11, Smith sent a memo outlining the latest news from Washington regarding the proposal for the NIRA. Smith followed this on May 22 with a letter stating that NAIM would begin the process of drawing up a proposed code and said that those ice concerns who were not currently members of NAIM should immediately join the organization "if they are to have a voice in establishing these rules for self-regulation."[40] On May 24, Smith wrote a memo to NAIM's board of directors expressing urgency in drawing up a code, stating: "We do not want to lose a day, yet we cannot act definitely until we know exactly what the law is to be." Thus, Smith wrote that, on the fourth day after the bill became law, NAIM's executive committee would meet at 10:30 a.m. in the Palmer House in Chicago, and two days later the entire board of directors would meet in the same venue.[41] On June 6, Smith sent another memo noting that General Johnson's office encouraged him to have the ice industry meet to formulate a code even in advance of the law's passage, and thus the Palmer House meeting of the executive committee would be moved up to June 12, with the meeting of the full board to follow on June 14. On June 19, Smith sent a memo to all members of the ice industry that summarized these meetings and included the draft of the proposed code, which was formulated by "104 men in this business from all sections of the country." Smith noted that thirty-six of these ice executives were not members of NAIM, but they "had equal voice in all that was done."[42]

On July 7, Smith went to Washington along with a representative from NAIM's southern district to gauge the attitude of the NRA toward the proposed ice code. On July 11, they met with NRA Deputy Administrator Whiteside. Smith reported that it "was a morning of turmoil with bells and calls sounding at every moment." The NRA felt that the ice code's wages and hours were out of line with the goals of work sharing and boosting purchasing power. Smith then met with NAIM executives, and the group hashed out some proposed changes to the code, which were sent out for consideration in a memo of July 17.[43] On August 1, NAIM formally submitted its revised code to the NRA for approval. On August 3, NRA deputy R. A. Paddock sent the ice industry a report in which he recommended some further alterations to the text of the code. A preliminary conference was held in Washington on August 28, and the public hearing was held on September 8 at 10:00 a.m. in the Mayflower Hotel, Washington, DC.

The proposed code set the minimum hourly wage for ice manufacturers at 32.5 cents per hour with a wage of 23 cents per hour in the South. Maximum hours were set at an average of forty-eight throughout the whole year, with fifty-six-hour weeks allowed during the peak season. Not surprisingly, labor representatives strongly opposed these standards as far too lax. Lucy Mason, general secretary of the National Consumers League, sent a memo in advance of the public hearing to NRA administrator Paddock, who was to preside over the hearing, in which she criticized ice executives for seeking to "perpetuate the evils of a long houred, low waged industry. . . . Please swat it!"[44] Likewise, Joseph Moreschi, president of the International Hod Carriers', Building, and Common Laborers' Union sent a letter to NRA administrator Johnson objecting to the labor provisions of the ice code. Moreschi recommended all workers in the ice industry have a minimum wage of 62.5 cents per hour and a maximum workweek of thirty hours.[45] Despite these protestations, Johnson recommended approval of the ice code on September 30, 1933, with the same labor provisions as those mentioned above, and Roosevelt approved it on October 3. Indeed, these wage and hour provisions were quite far (to the detriment of labor) from those of many other codes, and the impact of a powerful and active trade association such as NAIM certainly appears to have played a large role in the ice industry's success in this respect.

Summarizing the Code-Making Process through July 1933

When the NIRA was passed on June 16, 1933, Roosevelt expressed hope that all the major industries would be covered by codes within the next four to six weeks. In this way, he said, July would mark the "beginning of our great movement back to work." In fact, these hopes were wildly overoptimistic because the code negotiation process was far more time-consuming than expected. While the administration did see a flurry of proposed codes come in immediately after the NIRA was passed, it noted that these codes were "overburdened with detail" and were generally not drawn up in the spirit of recovery but of monopoly.[46] Roosevelt asked industries to focus on wage and hour provisions and a handful of major issues related to fair competition that were most important to industry. Proposed codes more along these lines began to come in and hearings were conducted, but, again, in many cases, industry, labor, and the government were often far apart on major issues such as minimum wages and maximum hours. Labor unions often proposed workweeks in line with the thirty-hour limit of the Black Bill of April 1933 and hourly wage rates that were as much as twice as high as those proposed by industry. As a result, code hearings sometimes stretched across several days, and in many cases, the NRA ended the hearings and asked industries to go back to the drawing board and send in a new proposed code in the future.

By late July, the NRA had approved codes for only three industries: cotton textile, shipbuilding, and wool textile. Together these industries employed about 550,000 workers — although this is not a trivial amount, NIRA codes would eventually cover 22 million workers. Given the slow speed of the code-making process, the Roosevelt administration had to consider alternative ways to bring firms into compliance with the NIRA's key provisions. This was the genesis of the President's Reemployment Agreement, which took effect on August 1, 1933.

4

The President's Reemployment
Agreement of August 1933

Naturally, it takes a good deal of organizing and a great many hearings and many
months to get these codes perfected and signed, and we cannot wait for all of them to
go through. The blanket agreements, however, which I am sending to every employer
will start the wheels turning now, and not six months from now.

PRESIDENT ROOSEVELT's radio address, July 24, 1933

Although the President's Reemployment Agreement has been widely neglected—or simply treated as being one and the same with the National
Industrial Recovery Act—the PRA's economic importance in its own right
cannot be overstated. For it is through the PRA that the NIRA's labor policies
were quickly implemented by the vast majority of firms across the nonagricultural economy. Additionally, the PRA brought forth the colossal Blue Eagle
publicity machine, accompanied by ticker-tape parades, rallies, and door-to-
door canvasses by government employees and volunteers encouraging compliance with the program. This chapter details the development and implementation of the agreement and examines the PRA's impact on wage rates,
average workweeks, and employment.

The "Blanket Code"

The NIRA was passed on June 16, 1933, but four weeks later, only one industry—cotton textiles—was covered by an NIRA code. Thus, more than twenty
million Americans who were supposed to be working under an NIRA code
remained unaffected by the program that was viewed as the heart of President
Roosevelt's economic recovery plan. A new approach would be needed to
more quickly get the key policies embedded in the NIRA into place. As NRA
chief administrator Hugh Johnson wrote in his memoirs, "unless something
were done at once to close the gap of code completion, the mere physical limi-
tation on the process of code manufacture would withhold the benefits of the
NRA indefinitely" (Johnson 1968, 253).

On July 10, a tentative plan for a so-called blanket code that would establish a thirty-five- to forty-hour workweek and a fourteen- to fifteen-dollar
minimum weekly wage was discussed by a group that included Mary Rum-

sey of the NRA's Consumer's Advisory Committee, General Electric's Gerard Swope, Alfred Sloan of General Motors, Leo Wolman of the NRA Labor Advisory Board, and president of the American Federation of Labor William Green.[1] The goal was to get the work-sharing and enhanced purchasing power aspects of the NIRA immediately into place while industries would continue the process of formulating their codes of fair competition. A week later, Johnson announced that the administration was formulating a program that would administer a temporary code for hours and wages. Johnson also noted that the "most intensive publicity campaign indulged by the government since the Liberty Loan drives of the World War" would accompany the program.[2] Charles Frances Horner, a key organizer of the patriotic wartime drives of fifteen years earlier, was recruited to reprise his promotional role. As the NIRA specified that mandatory codes could not be enacted without public hearings, adherence to the blanket code would have to be voluntary, and thus an effective publicity machine would be needed to achieve a high level of compliance.

On July 20, 1933, the President's Reemployment Agreement was unveiled. Section 4(a) of the NIRA authorized the president "to enter into agreements with, and to approve voluntary agreements between and among" businesses. Thus, under the PRA, Roosevelt asked firm owners—rather than entire industries—to voluntarily sign and abide by the agreement. The PRA would take effect on August 1, 1933, and was to remain in effect until December 31, 1933, or until the date of approval of the code of fair competition specific to the firm's industry. The December 31 closing date was created because the administration believed that by year's end nearly every industry would be covered by an industry-specific NIRA code. This was overly optimistic—in fact, only 195 codes were approved by year's end, while another 360 industries would have codes approved over the following seventeen months and hundreds of other industries submitted codes that were never approved. Therefore, as the initial date of termination approached, the agreement was extended to April 30, 1934. As that date approached, around 400 codes had been approved. But with many other industries still without an approved code, the PRA was extended indefinitely so that it held until the NIRA was ruled unconstitutional in May 1935. The agreement had fourteen parts, the most important of which are summarized below:

1. To restrict the employment of workers younger than age sixteen.[3]
2. To enact, with some exceptions, a maximum workweek of thirty-five hours for factory, mechanical, or artisan workers and a minimum rate of pay of 40 cents per hour for such workers.
3. To shorten workweeks for clerical and sales workers to no more than forty

hours and to pay such workers a minimum weekly wage of $15 (i.e., 37.5 cents per hour for a forty-hour week) in a city of more than 500,000 people; a wage of $14.50 per week in a city of between 250,000 and 500,000; and $14 in cities with a population between 2,500 and 250,000. For areas with populations below 2,500, firms had to either pay such workers a $12 weekly minimum or increase the current weekly wage by 20 percent.

4. To not reduce compensation for employees who were making more than the prescribed minimums prior to the PRA.

5. To support and patronize establishments that have also signed the PRA.

6. To try to the fullest extent to have an industry-specific code of fair competition related to their business submitted as quickly as possible.

The minimum wage and maximum hour provisions for white-collar workers in sales and clerical professions were particularly significant because this category of employee—largely unorganized—lacked political sway and hence was not generally a target for such government intervention. As Arthur Krock, Washington bureau chief of the *New York Times*, wrote, "the drug clerk, the ribbon salesman, the book keeper, and the stenographer will, for the first time in the history of their trades, be the direct beneficiaries of a government movement."[4]

The Blue Eagle Emblem

How could the Roosevelt administration get firms to voluntarily abide by an agreement that would clearly raise the cost of doing business? The key to the government's solution to this quandary was the creation of the Blue Eagle emblem, which was designed by artist Charles Coiner (Duvall 1936, 1). In a July 24 radio address, President Roosevelt said, "In war, in gloom of night attack, soldiers wear a bright badge on their shoulders to be sure that comrades do not fire on comrades. On that principle, those who cooperate in this program must know each other at a glance. That is why we have provided a badge of honor [the Blue Eagle] for this purpose . . . with a legend, 'We do our part.'"[5] It would be each American's patriotic duty to engage in commerce at stores that were in compliance with the recovery plan and hence displaying the Blue Eagle.[6] The administration predicted that the program would bring five to six million new employment opportunities by the first week of September.[7] Roosevelt's radio address was clearly effective, because the White House received more than twenty thousand telegrams and letters from businesses over the following forty-eight hours pledging compliance with the wage and hour mandates of the PRA to allow them to display the Blue Eagle.

Johnson, in his own radio address on July 25, explained how firms could obtain the Blue Eagle. Between July 27 and 29, mail carriers from the nation's forty-eight thousand post offices would deliver two documents to each place of business. One would be the agreement itself and was to be signed and returned to the government in the supplied envelope as an indication that the firm intended to abide by the rules of the agreement. The other document was to be signed by the firm owner once he or she had actually instituted the agreement by adjusting the wages and hours accordingly. This paper was to be taken directly to the local post office, which would verify receipt of the signed agreement by affixing a small Blue Eagle sticker to it. The postmaster would then record the name of the business on an "honor roll" of PRA signers, which was to be publicly displayed at the post office. The agreement itself, with the sticker from the postmaster, would be kept by the business and could be displayed if the business so chose. The postmaster would also provide at least one large poster or window sticker with the Blue Eagle so that it could be displayed prominently in the place of business. Just how much Blue Eagle paraphernalia was distributed varied by city. In New York City, each employer who brought in the signed document announcing compliance with the PRA received one large Blue Eagle placard; two smaller ones that were one foot square; five stickers that were six inches square; four automobile stickers; and ten oval stickers, one and a half inches in diameter, which could be used on stationery or packages.[8] Figure 4.1 shows an example of a Blue Eagle poster that would have been hung in a firm's window.

While the government had produced two million "employer sets" of Blue Eagle materials to be distributed by post offices by August 1, additional Blue Eagle paraphernalia could be purchased by a firm that had signed onto, and was complying with, the PRA, and it could be displayed in any manner connected with its business—on packaging, communications, transportation vehicles, and so on (Duvall 1936, 2). The printing of this extra Blue Eagle paraphernalia was largely left to the private sector; however, printers and lithographers who wanted to create and sell Blue Eagle emblems had to apply to the government for explicit permission to do so. Naturally, to gain federal consent to supply Blue Eagle printing service, these firms had to sign and comply with the PRA. Additionally, they were authorized to sell Blue Eagle items only to businesses that first showed them the signed the agreement with the sticker of verification. Finally, the manufacturer of Blue Eagle paraphernalia had to sell materials at "reasonable prices." In the August 1, 1933, issue of *New York Times*, the Ever Ready Label Corp. advertised its sale of Blue Eagle stamps to be affixed to packages, letters, or window displays—three dollars could buy one thousand large stickers measuring nine square inches, or one dollar could buy five thousand postage stamp–size Blue Eagle stickers. Private

FIGURE 4.1. Blue Eagle Poster
Source: The author's personal collection.

printers would often customize the Blue Eagle paraphernalia to be specific to the firm or purpose. To illustrate, figure 4.2 displays a tag that was attached to merchandise of the Air-Way Electric Appliance Corporation of Toledo, Ohio, announcing the firm's compliance with the NRA.

On July 27, post offices across the nation reported being "overrun" with demand for blank copies of the PRA as well as with returns of the signed forms. In San Francisco, the postmaster reported that more than 3,500 copies of signed agreements had been received before noon that day. In many cases, firm owners were simply typing up the agreement as it had appeared in the newspaper and signing this handmade document rather than waiting for the official copy to show up in the mail. In the meantime, PRA-related telegrams continued to arrive for the president, including one from a government offi-

FIGURE 4.2. Blue Eagle Tag
Source: The author's personal collection.

cial in Bay City, Michigan, who reported that the city would hold a parade featuring all the PRA-signing merchants in the city to celebrate their adoption of the agreement. Additionally, West Virginia governor H. G. Klump announced that his state would become the first to formally adopt and come into compliance with the PRA with respect to the labor conditions of all state employees.[9]

To further spread the Blue Eagle movement, the NRA sent telegrams to the chambers of commerce and other civic leaders in all 12,500 US cities with a population over 2,500. Johnson asked them to quickly form local recovery organizations with volunteers who would canvass local businesses to make sure they had signed, and were complying with, the PRA. Members of these local recovery boards were encouraged to speak to local community organizations to discuss the importance of compliance with the program. To help coordinate and oversee the work of these local organizations, an NRA State Recovery Board was created for each of the forty-eight states.[10]

The Blue Eagle drive was not just targeted toward businesses. Consumers were also encouraged to go to their local post office and sign the "Consumer's Statement of Cooperation," whereby the person pledged to support Blue Eagle–bearing firms by shopping at them. Signers would receive Blue Eagle stickers, posters, buttons, or other various paraphernalia declaring "NRA Consumer." An estimated seventy-two million consumers stickers were printed, "of which a large proportion found their way to private automobile windshields and the windows of private homes" in August and September 1933 (Duvall 1935, 4). A copy of the Consumer's Statement of Cooperation as well as examples of the stickers, pins, and buttons given to signers are reproduced in figure 4.3.

Later in August, rather than passively waiting for citizens to go to post offices, local canvassing drives were enacted whereby volunteers went door to door encouraging the signing of the Consumer's Statement of Cooperation. Service-minded groups such as Boy Scout troops engaged in the drive to obtain signatures. For example, in Utica, New York, Boy Scouts acquired 25,000 of the total of 36,000 signatures to the statement in that city.[11] Figure 4.4 shows a Boy Scout troop in Boise, Idaho, participating in the Blue Eagle campaign.

To better attract patriotic NRA consumers, firms often displayed the Blue Eagle in their newspaper advertisements. By September and October, nearly half of all advertisements contained the Blue Eagle emblem (Taylor and Klein 2008). Figure 4.5 shows examples of two advertisements that incorporated the emblem.

Parades were a regular staple of the Blue Eagle drive. For example, the local recovery committee in Detroit organized a parade on the evening of August 31, in which fifteen thousand people participated, most of whom were workers claiming to have owed their employment to the PRA. The first five hundred marchers consisted of young women who had found work as sales clerks in the prior four weeks. Other sections of the parade consisted of reemployed barbers, bakers, brewers, and automobile factory workers. The parade also featured capital that was supposedly newly employed thanks to the PRA— for example, floats contained office equipment representing the new surge in clerical business. Speakers such as Mrs. Frederick Alger, who was on the local recovery committee and was charged with getting women to support the

IN THE NATIONAL EFFORT TO BRING SECURITY
TO ALL, I WILL ENCOURAGE AND PATRONIZE
THOSE BUSINESS ESTABLISHMENTS IN WHICH
THE BLUE EAGLE OF NRA CODES IS DISPLAYED

CONSUMER'S STATEMENT OF COOPERATION

I will cooperate in reemployment by supporting and patronizing employers and workers who are members of N. R. A.

_____

(Name)

_____

(Street)

_____

(Town or city)   (State)

FIGURE 4.3. (*Opposite and above*) NRA Consumer's Cooperation Sticker, Buttons, and Statement of Cooperation

Sources: Sticker is from National Archives, Record Group 9, ARC Identifier 16703546, "Pictorial Materials" Entry Number PI 44–43, Box 3. Buttons and Consumer's Statement of Cooperation is from the author's personal collection.

FIGURE 4.4. Boy Scouts and the Blue Eagle Drive

Source: National Archives, Record Group 9, ARC Identifier 16703546, "Pictorial Materials" Entry Number PI 44–43, Box 3.

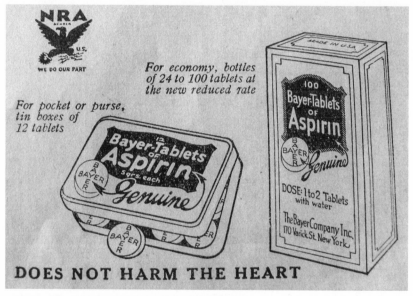

FIGURE 4.5. Advertisements Incorporating the Blue Eagle
Source: Both of these ads were in the November 1933 issue of the *Christian Herald* magazine. The Bayer ad was on page 41, and the Jonteel ad was on page 40.

NRA, said, "Now it is the duty of all women to buy from Blue Eagle stores."[12] The largest NRA parade took place in New York City on September 13, 1933. An estimated 1.5 million people lined the streets to watch the nine-hour-and-thirty-seven-minute parade, which included workers from seventy-seven different trade and industry divisions that were covered by the NRA/PRA. Governor Herbert Lehman called the parade, a scene from which is shown in figure 4.6, "an inspiration. . . . Nothing of its kind has ever been seen before."[13]

Exceptions to the PRA Provisions

It was acknowledged that the provisions of the PRA could potentially create extreme hardship for some business owners. Initially petitions for exemptions or substitutions of PRA provisions were handled by NRA deputy administrators. But because these administrators were already heavily occupied with helping industries prepare their codes or arranging and conducting code hearings, a PRA policy board was created on August 7 to review and rule on these petitions (Dearing et al. 1934, 66). This board consisted of five members, three of whom were representatives from the NRA Labor, Legal, and Planning Divisions, respectively. Section 13 of the PRA said that the NRA could allow industries to replace the PRA wage and hours provisions with those in their submitted code, even if the code was not yet approved by the NRA. Thus, the board established as a requirement that no substitution would be considered unless it was included in the industry's proposed code of fair competition, which had already been submitted for government approval. This provided an incentive for industries that desired provisions more lax than those of the PRA to quickly submit a proposed code. Additionally, the substitution had to be in line with the spirit of the PRA—that is, it would still spread work and raise purchasing power (Dearing et al. 1934, 68). All petitions had to be submitted by September 30, and the board was terminated on October 26, 1933, at which time its functions were largely replaced by the newly created NRA Compliance Division, which will be discussed in detail in chapter 6.

The first such exception to the PRA actually predated the formation of the policy board and instead was approved directly by Johnson. On July 31, the day before the PRA was to go into effect, the NRA approved a modified PRA code for the two million retail stores in the United States. Retailers had already submitted a proposed code to the NRA, but it would not be approved until December 30, 1933. Members of the retail trade argued that the PRA's mandate of a forty-hour workweek would be overly burdensome for small shops that only employed a handful of workers since these shops tended to be open for more than forty hours per week. The administration agreed to

FIGURE 4.6. NRA Parade in New York City
Source: Photo by ACME Newspictures, Inc.

allow grocers and pharmacies to employ workers for up to forty-eight hours per week rather than the forty specified by the PRA and still display the Blue Eagle. Additionally, minimum weekly wages for employees of retail stores, including hardware clothing, furniture, shoes, and mail order supplies, could be one dollar lower than those specified for the PRA and could be two dollars lower in stores south of the Mason-Dixon Line. Even with these exceptions, the NRA estimated that when the nation's retailers adhered to these new guidelines, it would create 1.1 million new jobs through work sharing and would increase annual payrolls by $900 million.

The rayon and synthetic yarn production industry provides another example of an approved exception to the PRA. This industry had quickly submitted a code, and its public hearing was held on July 27; however, the code was not formally approved until August 26, 1933. On August 2, the government granted PRA-signing firms in the yarn industry an exception whereby they could implement a thirteen-dollar-per-week minimum wage and a forty-hour workweek—in line with those in the proposed code—in lieu of the slightly more restrictive PRA guidelines. As a final example, the electrical manufacturing industry, whose public code hearings were concluded on July 21, was granted a special PRA code exemption whereby its maximum workweek would be the thirty-six hours proposed in its code rather than the thirty-five in the PRA.[14] By October 14, 1933, the government had approved 350 such exceptions (Martin 1935, 160).

Part 4 of the PRA also noted that exceptions for the thirty-five- to forty-hour workweek could be made for "very special cases where restrictions of hours of highly skilled workers on continuous processes would unavoidably reduce production." On July 31, the NRA clarified that this meant that newspaper reporters and editors, nurses, hospital technician and interns, and research technicians were exempt from the PRA maximum hour restrictions. Additionally, owners of small businesses who hired no employees could also display the Blue Eagle even if they were the residual claimant of the firm's profits and hence not earners of a regular wage—they simply had to sign the PRA.[15]

The Effectiveness of the Blue Eagle Drive of August 1933

The take-up rate of firms signing onto the PRA was extremely high, although it was not necessarily immediate. In the state of New York, for example, by August 6, 100,000 firms had reportedly signed onto the agreement, and this number rose to 148,813 on August 10. Looking at specific cities, by August 7, 80 percent of the businesses in Schenectady, New York, had signed on to the PRA. In Detroit, by August 5, around 13,000 employers had signed onto the PRA, and by August 14, this number had risen to 17,659.[16] By September, 7, 31,686 Detroit firms with 266,903 employees had signed the agreement, supposedly bringing the city close to full compliance.[17]

Newspapers in many smaller cities regularly—sometimes even daily—printed an honor roll of local firms that had signed the PRA. For example, on August 17, 1933, the *Midland Republican* (Michigan) printed the name of all eighty-eight area businesses that were on the honor roll. In larger cities, where a complete honor roll would be too large to reproduce, it was common to list the new additions to the roll each day. For example, every day throughout the month of August, the *Lansing State Journal* published a list of firms signing the PRA over the prior twenty-four hours. Newspapers from large metro areas, such as the *Chicago Tribune* and the *Washington Post*, would often report the aggregate number of new firms signing the PRA each day. For example, the August 15 *Chicago Tribune* noted that 908 additional Chicago firms, which employed 11,780 workers, had signed the PRA the day prior, bringing the city's total to 17,425 firms employing 601,004 workers.[18] By August 19, the *Tribune* reported that the number of PRA-covered employees in the city had surged to 1,192,829.[19] The *Tribune* also often listed the names of specific large companies that signed on in the past twenty-four hours. For example, on August 20, the *Tribune* listed Goss Printing Press with 400 employees, J. Greenbaum Tanning with 1,236 employees, and Gordon Baking Company with 450 employees as being among the three largest area firms to sign in the past day.

The Ford Motor Company of Detroit was the highest-profile business that did not sign onto the agreement. Not only did the company not sign the PRA, but it also did not agree to participate in or abide by the automobile industry code of fair competition, which was approved on August 26, 1933. Lewis (1976) and Gelderman (1981) note that Henry Ford objected strongly to the NIRA's Section 7(a), which required firms to recognize the right to collective bargaining, and he objected to the automobile code's provision requiring firms to share data with other auto manufacturers. In terms of labor policies, Ford, who began paying workers five dollars for an eight-hour day (i.e., 62.5 cents per hour) as early as 1914, noted that his company's wage and hours policies were already far more generous than the NRA's. Ford said, "If we tried to live up to it, we would have to live down to it" (Lewis 1976, 241). Throughout August and September, Ford was vilified in editorials in newspapers across the nation for his refusal to sign onto the PRA. In an attempt to capture market share, Chevrolet and Chrysler took out advertisements touting their proud compliance with the NRA. Still, Biles (1991) notes that Ford did not lose much, if any, market share as a result of his refusal to participate in the NRA. Consumers may not have boycotted the Ford Motor Company because they knew that the company was in fact meeting or exceeding the wage and hour restrictions of the automobile code even if Ford refused to sign the code for other reasons.

Many of the large firms that signed the PRA publicly touted their dramatic cuts to hours and increases to wages. For example, the Great Atlantic and Pacific Tea Company, better known as A&P grocery stores, announced on that on August 1 it had put into effect the stipulations of the blanket code at all of its 15,700 retail stores, offices, warehouses, and food plants across the United States, which together employed more than ninety thousand people. Two weeks later, A&P took out advertisements across the country noting that, through its compliance with the PRA, "8,300 men had been put back to work" and the company had seen "an increase in annual payroll of $8,246,000." Interestingly, many grocers around the country had been cutting store hours so that they would not have to hire additional employees while cutting work-weeks to a maximum of forty hours. The NRA declared this to be against the spirit of the PRA, and on August 5, the government was considering how to respond to such "cheating on the Blue Eagle." Thomas S. Hammond, the executive director of the PRA, said about the allegations of grocers' limited hours of operation, "If we find anyone hitting below the belt, the Blue Eagle will come down from his store front."[20] An A&P ad in the August 15, 1933, issue of the *Chicago Tribune* noted in response that, unlike some of its competitors, the company "continues to operate under regular grocery store hours for your convenience."

Violations of the PRA

Not every firm that signed the PRA abided by its policies. New York City's volunteer recovery committee was headed by Grover Whalen, and it worked in coordination with the New York State committee headed by Averell Harriman—both the city and state organizations were headquartered at the Hotel Pennsylvania in Manhattan. The committees noted instances as early as August 9 of New York City employers failing to follow through on the agreements they had signed and cases where firms that had not signed an agreement were displaying Blue Eagles that were purchased illegally from the black market. Still, Henry Wolff, head of complaints and compliance for the New York City organization, maintained that the vast majority of firms in the city were in compliance and that most violations were due to ignorance or misunderstanding of the program rather than mischievousness. Wolff said, "In investigating, reporting, and acting on complaints, we will proceed on the assumption of good faith on the part of both the complainant and the business being complained against."[21] Between August 26 and 29, the New York State organization received 968 complaints, most of which were from workers alleging that their employer was displaying the Blue Eagle while not paying wages stipulated by the agreement.[22] Issues of compliance with the Blue Eagle, or lack thereof, are discussed in chapter 6.

During the second week of August, the Roosevelt administration, while explicitly avoiding the word *boycott*, continued to ask consumers to shop at Blue Eagle firms to pressure firms that had not signed on to do so. In an August 7 speech, Johnson said, "Where should you spend? . . . You should spend under the Blue Eagle. If you spend there you are spending for increased employment. If you spend elsewhere you are hurting the chance" for recovery.[23] Wolvin (1968) notes that the Blue Eagle campaign focused on women since they generally directed family spending. An August press release from the NRA wrote, "If the women who control the purse strings of the nation use this mighty instrument of mass buying power to support the Blue Eagle, they can [help] to achieve security for themselves and build a better and happier America" (quoted in Wolvin 1968, 132–33). The administration tried to make firms believe that noncompliance would cost them dearly. On August 11, Johnson said, "the time is coming when someone is going to take one of those Blue Eagles off of someone's window in a clear cut case and that is going to be a sentence of economic death."[24]

The President's Reemployment Agreement Censuses

On August 28, the NRA began a door-to-door census of firms and households. The goal was to not only determine what percent of firms had signed onto the PRA—as well as what percent of consumers had signed the pledge to shop at Blue Eagle firms—but also to estimate how many employees had been added to payrolls since the PRA had begun. These censuses were conducted in every locale by the aforementioned volunteer NRA organizations. Throughout September, newspapers across the country reported the results of the surveys. For example, the September 21 *Syracuse Herald* reported that the PRA was responsible for 2,700 jobs in the city and a total of 51,808 in all of upstate New York. Given the 1930 populations (209,326 in Syracuse and around 4.5 million in upstate New York) and an assumption of a 40 percent labor force participation rate, this implied around 3 percent of the labor force obtaining employment in just over a month. In Tulare, California, it was reported that "through NRA compliance 97 jobless Tulareans have been given regular employment." Given Tulare's 1930 population of 6,207, and again under an assumption of a 40 percent labor force participation rate, ninety-seven workers would represent approximately 4 percent of Tulare's labor force. It is interesting to note that the article also reported that an additional sixty-nine Tulareans had gained employment through New Deal work relief programs. This suggests that the PRA work-sharing program was responsible for nearly 50 percent more jobs in Tulare than the better-known work relief aspects of the New Deal with respect to reemployment. In Fitchburg, Massachusetts, the September 2 *Sentinel* reported that 1,100 of the city's firms had signed the PRA and that this had led to the creation of 688 new jobs. The September 3 *Bee* reported that 2,030 Fresno firms had signed on, creating 1,914 jobs. Furthermore, the Fresno County Welfare Board reported a 50 percent drop in requests for food aid since August 1 and attributed this to PRA job creation.[25]

Rather than focusing on the number of signing firms or jobs created, newspapers sometimes reported the percentage of firms that had signed the PRA and/or the percentage of consumers who signed the Consumer's Statement of Cooperation. The September 10 *Journal and Star* of Lincoln, Nebraska, reported that 94 percent of the city's 2,015 employers had signed the PRA. In Jefferson City, Missouri, the September 15, 1933, issue of the *Post Tribune* noted that "practically all local employers are operating under the president's re-employment agreement or special codes" and that 75 percent of the city's households were displaying the emblem in their windows. The September 21 *Chronicle-Telegram* reported that 99.32 percent of Elyria, Ohio, households canvassed had signed the Consumer's Statement of Cooperation—only sixty-eight households out of ten thousand had refused to sign.

In terms of the tally for the nation as a whole, the NRA periodically released a running score from its reemployment censuses. The first figures on the PRA's effects were announced on August 30, when the NRA declared that the reemployment program had created two million new jobs in just one month. On September 13, the NRA estimated that 85 percent of employers nationwide had signed onto the PRA or were covered by an NRA code. By October 14, the administration had tallied three million jobs created by the PRA (Taylor 2011, 138).

In late October, the administration decided to conduct an additional "postcard census" in which a form was distributed by mail carriers to all businesses along their route. The form asked firm owners how many employees they had and how much they had paid in total payroll to these employees for the two pay periods ending on June 17 and October 14. The NRA received 900,000 of these returned forms; however, only 643,000 were usable because the others were illegible or had other problems such as not reporting data for both periods. The final results of this census showed an increase in employment of 1,697,819—a 15.6 percent jump between June and October—and an increase in payroll of $44,158,823—an increase of 18.5 percent. Of course, this was an incomplete sample, and selection bias probably led to an overstate-ment of the true percentage increases in employment and payrolls. Over the twenty-two-plus months that the PRA was in existence, 2.3 million separate agreements were signed between a firm owner and the president. Together these firms covered approximately 16.3 million employees (Martin 1935, 168). If we employ the 15.6 percent change in employment to a sample of 16 million employees, this would be around 2.5 million jobs, which is a bit less than the 3 million the administration had estimated from its door-to-door census be-tween August and September.

Movements of Wages, Hours, and Employment under the PRA

Another way to estimate the PRA's effects is by looking at aggregate govern-ment data for the manufacturing sector. Figure 4.7 shows that a dramatic rise in wages began in August 1933, the month the PRA was instituted, and continued in September, before beginning to level off. In manufacturing in-dustries, average hourly earnings rose from 45.6 cents to 53.6 cents between July and September—a rate of 17.5 percent. A broader measure of wage rates, which also includes workers outside of manufacturing such as teachers, cleri-cal workers, and sales clerks rose less quickly but still jumped 10 percent dur-ing these two months.

Figure 4.8 shows the sharp decline in the average hours worked per week that accompanied the PRA. For males in manufacturing, the average work-week fell 15.6 percent, from 42.9 hours to 36.2 hours, between July and Sep-tember. For females, the decline was a slightly steeper 17 percent, from 42.9 to 35.6 hours. It is notable that the wage and hour changes that accompanied the PRA in August 1933 were maintained—or, in the case of wages, augmented further—throughout the NIRA period. By May 1935, when the legislation was ruled unconstitutional, the average hourly wage in manufacturing stood at 60 cents, 31.3 percent higher than the July 1933 rate, and the broader measure of wage rates was 19.9 percent above its pre-PRA level. The consumer price index rose only 1.1 percent between July 1933 and May 1935, so almost all these gains in wage rates were real. With respect to the average workweek, the number of hours for females in May 1935 was 21.4 percent below its July 1933 level, and for males, it remained 15.6 percent lower than it had been before the PRA was instituted.

Figure 4.9 examines the change in employment, measured two ways: (1) the number of people employed and (2) aggregate hours worked. The raw data suggest that the PRA work-sharing provisions were effective because the total number of manufacturing workers employed continued the rise it

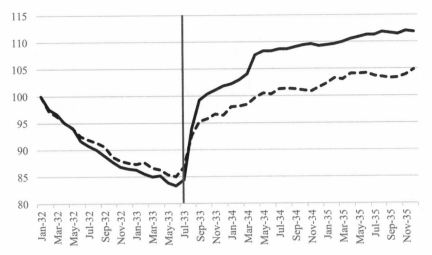

FIGURE 4.7. Nominal Wage Movements, 1932–1935

Notes and Sources: The vertical line at July 1933 marks the month prior to the President's Reemployment Agreement. The solid line represents "Average Hourly Earnings, Twenty-five Manufacturing Industries, National Industrial Conference Board" (NBER series 8142). The dashed line is a broader wage index, "Index of Composite Wages" (NBER series 8061), which includes manufacturing, railways, clerical, teachers, building, farms, road construction, retail trade, bituminous coal mining, telephone and telegraph, power and light, hotels, and laundries. Both measures are indexed so that January 1932 = 100.

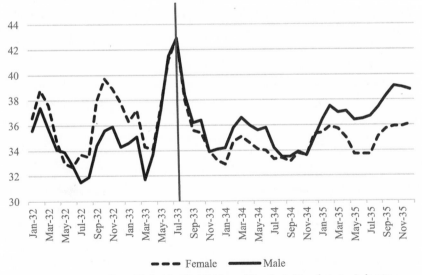

FIGURE 4.8. Average Hours Worked Per Week, Males and Females in Manufacturing Industries

Notes and Sources: The vertical line at July 1933 marks the month prior to the President's Reemployment Agreement. "US Average Hours of Work per Week per Wage Earner, All Male, Twenty-Five Manufacturing Industries" (NBER series 8030) and "US Average Actual Hours of Work per Week per Wage Earner, Female, Twenty-Five Manufacturing Industries" (NBER series 8033).

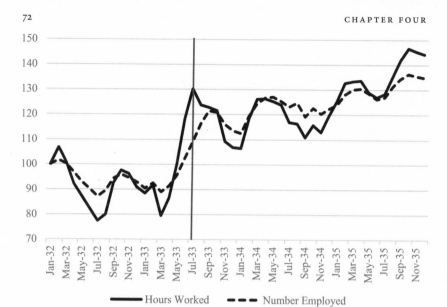

FIGURE 4.9. Changes in Employment Measured Two Ways

Notes and Sources: The vertical line at July 1933 marks the month of data prior to the President's Reemployment Agreement. "Hours Worked" is computed by the total number employed times the average workweek. Number employed is "US Production Worker Employment, Manufacturing, Total" (NBER series 8010b). Average workweek is "US Average Hours of Work per Week, Manufacturing Industries, Total Wage Earners, NICB" (NBER series 8029).

had enjoyed since spring, climbing from 6.15 million to 6.86 million between July and September—an increase of 11.5 percent. However, aggregate hours worked in manufacturing industries peaked in July at 264 million hours and fell 5.7 percent to 249 million hours by September. By December 1933, total hours worked in manufacturing were nearly 18 percent *below* where they had been before the PRA was enacted even though the total number of people employed was 4.2 percent higher.

Industry-Level Analysis of Wage Rates and Hours Worked

While analyses of sector-level data are informative, industry-level data can also be employed to provide insight into the PRA's impact and, perhaps more importantly, into the extent that the PRA was indeed responsible for movements in wage rates and hours. Average hourly earnings data are available by month for fourteen manufacturing industries. Because the PRA created a specific minimum wage of 40 cents per hour in manufacturing, we would expect the PRA to have had its largest effects on industries where this 40-cent minimum wage was most binding. Specifically, the PRA would be expected to have had a larger impact on the wage rates of industries that, on average, paid well below 40 cents an hour prior to the agreement and to have less of an impact on industries whose average wage rates were already above 40 cents. For example, the average hourly wage in the cotton manufacturing industry was only 29.7 cents in the month prior to the NIRA's passage, but the average wage was 56.7 cents per hour in the automobile manufacturing industry; hence, we would expect the PRA to raise the wage rates in the cotton industry more substantially than in the auto industry.

Data on average hours worked per week are also available for thirteen of these fourteen industries. Because the PRA set a maximum workweek of 35 hours in manufacturing, we would again expect the agreement to have a larger effect in industries whose average workweeks were far in excess of 35 hours than in those whose average workweeks were already close to or below this level. For example, average hours worked in the rubber products manufacturing industry was 34.7 hours in the month prior to the NIRA's passage, whereas average hours worked per week in the meatpacking industry was 49.3 hours. Again, if the PRA was, in fact, responsible for the observed decrease in hourly workweeks (rather than some macroeconomic factor boosting aggregate demand, which would impact all industries' workweeks simultaneously), then we would expect to see a larger drop in the meat packing industry workweek than in the rubber industry workweek. Table 4.1 reports the average hourly earnings and average workweek for available industries in May 1933

TABLE 4.1. Average Hourly Earnings (Cents per Hour) and Average Workweek in May 1933 and May 1934 in Selected Industries

Industry	Hourly earnings May 1933	Hourly earnings May 1934	Percentage change 1933 to 1934	Workweek May 1933	Workweek May 1934	Percentage change 1933 to 1934
Chemical manufacturing	45.7	56.3	23.2	40.1	38.4	−4.2
Cotton	29.7	44.4	49.5			
Electrical manufacturing	53.5	65.5	22.4	35.5	34.6	−2.5
Furniture	37.9	53.0	39.8	33.2	32.9	−0.9
Leather	40.6	55.2	36.0	45.0	37.3	−17.1
Machinery	54.5	62.2	14.1	31.8	37.9	19.2
Meatpacking	39.5	52.4	32.7	49.3	40.2	−18.5
Paper production	41.5	50.4	21.4	41.2	37.7	−8.5
Passenger cars	56.7	72.4	27.7	33.4	31.9	−4.5
Rayon	33.4	49.9	49.4	40.9	29.0	−29.1
Rubber products	55.8	75.3	34.9	34.7	33.1	−4.6
Iron and steel	47.7	64.6	35.4	35.4	36.6	3.4
Boot and shoe	40.3	56.6	40.4	40.5	37.4	−7.7
Wool	34.3	51.9	51.3	41.6	32.8	−21.2

Source: National Bureau of Economic Research, NBER Macrohistory Database, chap. 8, http://www.nber.org/databases/macrohistory/contents/.

and May 1934. The rationale for using May to May is to avoid any potential seasonal impacts on the workweek or wage rates.

All industries saw average hourly earnings rise in the twelve months after the NIRA was enacted. However, the seven industries with the lowest wage rates in May 1933 saw rates rise 42.7 percent, while the seven industries with the highest wage rates in May 1933 saw rates rise by only 25.6 percent. In hours worked, seven of the thirteen industries had workweeks that were above forty hours prior the NIRA, and these industries experienced hourly workweek declines averaging 15.2 percent over the next year. In the remaining six industries, where average workweeks were already below forty hours in May 1933, the average workweek actually *rose* by an average of 1.7 percent. This increase was driven by one industry, machinery, whose workweeks jumped dramatically. But even if we omit that industry, the remaining five saw their workweeks decline by only an average of 1.8 percent. This analysis strongly suggests that the movements in wages and hours were indeed caused directly by the PRA/NIRA rather than some other factor that would have caused all wages and hours to move in unison.

In earlier work (Taylor 2011), I employed an industry panel to address the specific question of whether the PRA, in fact, promoted reemployment. My results suggested that the PRA labor provisions increased employment by over 1.3 million in the late summer and early fall of 1933. However, in examining only the work-sharing provisions of shorter workweeks, my estimates suggest that these raised employment by nearly 2.5 million. I found that the higher wage rates that accompanied the shorter hours had a negative effect on employment that offset around half of the work-sharing aspect's gains. In the following chapters, I will employ industry-level panel data to estimate the extent to which the NIRA impacted output, prices, employment, take-home pay, and other variables. I will also employ the NIRA in an attempt to gain insight into the theory of cartels. Because this chapter has demonstrated that the PRA is an important, but distinct, part of the NIRA, this program will be accounted for in subsequent empirical analysis as an entity that is separate from the NIRA as whole.

Summary and Discussion

The President's Reemployment Agreement has been largely neglected by economic historians of the New Deal. This is unfortunate. The economics literature highlights the NIRA's twin policies of collusion and higher wage rates, and it generally treats these as being implemented simultaneously upon the Act's passage. The literature typically ignores the work-sharing aspects of the reduced workweeks. In fact, because the code approval process was long and cumbersome, the collusive aspects of the NIRA were not implemented in most industries until the fall of 1933 or later. As this chapter has shown, the wage and hour aspects of the law, however, were implemented in the late summer of 1933 under the PRA.

In return for signing and abiding by the PRA's labor provisions, firms could display the Blue Eagle emblem. What gave this emblem strong economic weight was the Roosevelt administration's consistent encouragement of the nation's consumers — through parades, door-to-door canvasses, and speeches — to shop only at firms displaying the Blue Eagle. In fact, the take-up rate of signing onto the voluntary agreement was extraordinarily high. Later in the book, I will empirically demonstrate that the Blue Eagle was indeed economically significant in maintaining compliance with the recovery program. Newspapers printed daily updates on which firms joined the honor roll of PRA signers as well as tallies of how many employers had signed on and how many new jobs had been created through the PRA's share-the-work program of reduced hours. By mid-September, the government reported that 85 percent of the nation's employers had signed the PRA or were covered by an NRA code, which would have superseded the PRA. In total 2.3 million firms, which together employed 16.3 million workers, signed the agreement with the president.

The issue of compliance will be discussed in detail in chapter 6, but the data suggest that firms generally did raise wage rates and reduce workweeks. The average hourly earnings in manufacturing industries jumped over 17 percent between July and September of 1933, from about 46 to 54 cents an hour. The average number of hours worked per week also dropped sharply, from around 43 hours in July to around 36 hours in September. Upcoming chapters detail industry-level panel analysis that attempts to hone in on the precise impact of the PRA wage and hour provisions as a separate program from the NIRA's collusive aspects.

Codes of Fair Competition: Industrial Planning and Collusion under the NIRA

When the President's Reemployment Agreement took effect on August 1, 1933, only three industry-specific codes of fair competition had been approved. By the end of that month, seventeen industries had approved codes. Thirteen more codes were accepted in September. Then, on October 3, seventeen codes were approved in one day as the avalanche of code implementation had finally begun. By the end of 1933, almost two hundred industries had an NIRA code in place. By the time the program was ruled unconstitutional in May 1935, 557 industry codes had been approved, as had around two hundred supplementary codes.[1] This chapter explores the degree of heterogeneity within these codes, and it analyzes the impact of this heterogeneity on economic outcomes.[2] Past studies of the NIRA, including Brand (1988) and Alexander (1997), have discussed how firm heterogeneity *within* industries—that is, some large, some small—affected the success of the NIRA. The focus here is on code heterogeneity *between* industries. Some industry codes were scores of pages long and contained dozens of provisions directing various aspects of business—production, pricing, capital usage, productive capacity, packaging, shipping, sales techniques, and so on—within that industry. Other codes were just a couple of pages long and simply contained the required rules pertaining to wage rates, hours, and the recognition of the right of collective bargaining.

The heterogeneity of code contents has not generally been acknowledged in literature of the NIRA as widely cited studies such as Cole and Ohanian (2004) and Eggertsson (2008, 2012) largely treat the NIRA as a monolithic program of cartels and high wages spread evenly across the industrial economic board. In addition to the heterogeneity of the contents of the codes, there was also wide heterogeneity in the timing of code passage, and this aspect has also been largely ignored in the NIRA literature. If the objective is to empirically estimate the potential impact of the cartel-oriented aspects of the codes of fair competition, then the precise timing of when an industry's code was in effect must be examined. Furthermore, industries with highly complex and detailed codes may be expected to perform differently than those with short and simple codes, and thus the heterogeneity of code contents must also be considered. After establishing the wide heterogeneity within the codes, this chapter offers an industry-level panel analysis exploring how the attributes of the codes affected economic outcomes under the NIRA.

Heterogeneity of the Timing of Code Passage

Figure 5.1 shows the number of codes of fair competition approved by month during the NIRA. The cotton textile code—which, excluding reports and perfunctory statements from the administration, was four pages long and contained ten sections—was the first one passed on July 9, 1933. The bowling and billiard equipment industry and trade code was the final code passed on March 30, 1935. It was ten pages long and had twelve broad articles, most of which contained between six and ten subsections of provisions. The median code in terms of timing of passage—number 279—was the steam heating equipment code of February 12, 1934. This code was eleven pages long (again, excluding perfunctory statements and reports) and contained eleven articles. Article 9 itself specified twenty distinct rules of trade practices for the industry.

Importantly, code provisions would not have any legal impact until after the code was approved.[3] With this in mind, the notion that NIRA-enabled collusion (leaving the wage and hours provisions out of the equation) could have had much macroeconomic impact prior to at least October or November of 1933 seems dubious. The administration gave priority, in terms of code hearings, and assistance in general with code formulation to "major industries" that had 50,000 employees or more, and thus the median employee was certainly covered by a code sooner than the date of median code passage in February 1934. The cotton textile industry itself had 400,000 workers, which represented nearly 2 percent of the twenty million Americans employed outside of agriculture in 1933. Electrical manufacturing and wool textiles, the third and fourth codes passed, respectively, each had well over 100,000 employees. The lumber and iron and steel codes, which were both passed on August 19, had half a million employees between them. But there were also plenty of codes passed in the early days of the NRA in industries with very few employees. The lace manufacturing industry, whose code was the sixth to be passed on August 14, had 6,043 employees. Three codes passed on Sep-

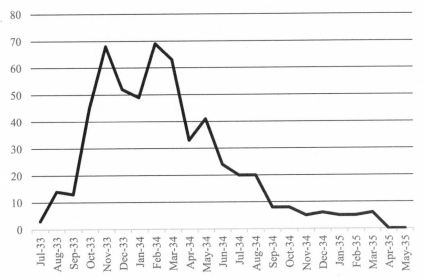

FIGURE 5.1. Number of Industry Codes of Fair Competition Approved by Month

Notes and Sources: A total of 557 codes were passed between July 9, 1933, and March 30, 1935. US National Recovery Administration, *Codes of Fair Competition*, 23 vols. (Washington, DC: US Government Printing Office, 1933–35).

tember 7, 1933—wallpaper manufacturing, salt producing, and motion picture laboratory—each had between 3,500 and 4,400 workers. I estimate that around half of the twenty million or so workers in the nonfarm economy were in an industry covered by a code of fair competition by December 1, 1933.[4] The best—perhaps only—way to account for the heterogeneity of the timing of code passage in empirical work on the NIRA is to use industry-level monthly data whereby the code dummy is turned on in the precise month of code passage for that industry. This empirical approach is employed in the remainder of this book.

Empirical Analysis: Which Types of Industries Were Codified Faster?

This section analyzes the factors that may have influenced the speed of industry code approval under the NIRA. The discussion above suggests that industries with more workers may have had codes approved more quickly, ceteris paribus, since the NRA was pushing these industries into action and moving them up in the code-hearing queue. At the same time, cartel theory suggests that collusive agreements are easier to form in concentrated industries with few firms because the coordination costs are lower (see, e.g., Levinstein and

Suslow 2006; Posner 1970; Hay and Kelley 1974). With this in mind, we would expect the level of coordination involved in completing a proposed code of fair competition would have been lower in industries with fewer firms, ceteris paribus. The presence of a trade association could likewise have helped speed the code formulation and approval process, as suggested above. At the same time, the homogeneity of firms within the industry with respect to costs could also have played an important role in how quickly an agreement could be reached on a code. If an industry was strongly divided between high-cost firms employing traditional production methods and low-cost firms that had adopted modern mass-production techniques, it would be much more challenging to reach agreements on labor and trade practice provisions than it would be in an industry where most firms had the same cost structure. Alexander (1997) notes that cost heterogeneity contributed to a breakdown in collusion under the NIRA, but it could also have slowed code adoption.

The 1933 *Census of Manufactures* provides some industry-level data on factors such as the number of firms, the number of workers, output, and aggregate wages paid. For the dependent variable in the regressions reported below, I have obtained the date of NIRA code passage for each industry and calculated the *number of months it took past June 1933 for the industry's code to be approved*. For example, the dependent variable takes on a value of 1 for the cotton textile industry (approved July 9, 1933), a value of 2 for the automobile industry (approved August 26, 1933), and a value of 8 for the book publishing industry (approved on February 17, 1934), and so on. The independent variables include the number of workers in the industry, the number of firms in the industry, whether the industry had a trade association helping formulate its code, and the average annual earnings of each worker in the industry (total wages paid in the industry divided by number of workers). I also include Alexander's (1997, 339) proxy for cost heterogeneity within each industry.[5] The results are reported in table 5.1. Note that a negative coefficient means fewer months passed between the NIRA's passage and the implementation of the industry's code.

The results suggest that, as expected, industries with more workers saw their codes passed more quickly than firms with fewer workers, ceteris paribus. Likewise, high-wage industries saw faster code passage than low-wage industries. A potential reason for this is that it may have been easier for actors in these industries to agree on labor provisions that would conform to the NRA's guidelines since wage rates were already fairly high. Low-wage industries likely faced contentious debate regarding how much they could concede to labor and still remain in business. The results also suggest, consistent with cartel theory, that those industries with more firms generally took longer to

TABLE 5.1. Determinants of Speed of Industry Code Passage

	Months Past June 1933 until Code Passage
Constant	3.576
	(.00)
Number of workers in industry (thousands)	−0.00974
	(.04)
Number of firms in industry	0.0003
	(.05)
Trade association dummy variable (1 if present)	−0.183
	(.50)
Average annual earnings per worker	−0.0015
	(.04)
Alexander's cost heterogeneity proxy	0.0013
	(.99)
R^2	.367
Number of observations	15

Notes: Poisson estimation is employed since the dependent variable is count data. The *p*-values (in parentheses) are computed using robust standard errors. Industry data are from the *Census of Manufactures*. Trade association dummy variable was created by examining whether the code specifically mentioned a trade association that helped in its formulation.

attain an approved code. It is somewhat surprising that the presence of a trade association did not significantly affect the speed of code passage—although the sign of the coefficient is as expected with faster passage in those industries. Alexander's proxy for cost heterogeneity had no effect on the speed of code passage.

The Heterogeneity of the NRA Codes' Labor Provisions

The President's Reemployment Agreement was relatively homogeneous in terms of the wage and hour mandates that it imposed as well as the timing of its beginning. Most firms signed the PRA in early August, and 85 percent of firms had signed on by mid-September. Although some wage and hour exceptions were approved, the PRA said that all signing firms in manufacturing industries had to pay at least 40 cents per hour and have a maximum workweek of thirty-five hours. Sales and clerical workers were to be paid at least 35 cents per hour for no more than forty hours of work per week. Not surprisingly, the NRA codes of fair competition were much more heterogeneous than the PRA in terms of labor policy. In fact, the Roosevelt administration hoped that the

PRA would encourage industries to more quickly propose codes since these codes could potentially provide relief in terms of lower minimum wages and longer maximum hours than those stipulated in the general agreement. To examine the extent to which approved code wage and hour provisions differed from the PRA, I sampled the first fifty-seven codes (all passed on or before October 11, 1933) and summarize their labor provisions in table 5.2.

Many codes contained different wage and hour requirements for different classes of workers within the industry or for different geographic regions. Because the goal is to determine how much relief or flexibility the codes gave industries in comparison to the 40-cent/thirty-five-hour guidelines of the PRA, the lowest minimum wage and highest maximum hour rules stipulated in the code are reported in the table. For example, the lumber and timber products code said that the standard maximum workweek was forty hours; however, it allowed forty-eight hours per week during seasonal peak times, so I report forty-eight hours in table 5.2. The lumber code also reported sixty-six different minimum hourly wage rates depending on the type of wood and the location of the work. These minimums ranged from a high of a 50-cent minimum for workers in zone two of the Special Woodwork Subdivision, which included New York City and Chicago, to a low of 23 cents per hour in the Southern Rotary Cut division. I report the 23-cent minimum in table 5.2, because it is the lowest in the code. The table also reports whether the code contained regional wage differentials—thirty-five of the fifty-seven industries (61 percent) specified different minimum wages by region. The most common of these was a lower minimum wage for workers in the South. For example, the boiler manufacturing code stipulated a minimum wage of 40 cents per hour generally, but 34 cents per hour in the South. Some codes specified different minimum wages for many different geographic regions beyond simply North versus South. For example, the iron and steel code contained minimum wage rates for twenty-one different districts—the minimum was 40 cents in the Cleveland district but 37 cents in the Canton, Massillon, and Mansfield district just south of Cleveland. The lowest minimum wage of 25 cents per hour was in the southern district.

The final column of table 5.2 reports the number of pages of each code.[6] The three shortest codes among these, each at 6 pages, were fishing tackle, rayon and synthetic yarn producing, and optical manufacturing. The longest codes were for lumber and timber products at 52 pages and iron and steel at 38 pages. Of these first fifty-seven codes, the average was 11.94 pages, and the median code was 10 pages. The standard deviation on page length was 7.5. The 557 codes totaled 8,046 pages; thus, the average code was 14.4 pages long.

It is interesting to note that longer codes belonged to industries that were

TABLE 5.2. Summary of Labor Provisions in First Fifty-Seven Approved Codes of Fair Competition

Industry	Date in 1933 code passed	Minimum hourly wage (cents)	Maximum hours per week	Regional wage difference	Number of pages
Cotton textile	July 9	30.0	40	Yes	24
Shipbuilding and ship repair	July 26	35.0	36	Yes	8
Wool textile	July 26	32.5	40	Yes	10
Electrical manufacturing	August 4	40.0	36	No	8
Coat and suit	August 4	21.0	35	Yes	8
Lace manufacturing	August 14	32.5	40	No	10
Corset and brassiere	August 14	35.0	40	No	12
Dramatic and musical theatrical	August 16	30.0	40	Yes	14
Lumber and timber products	August 19	27.0	48	Yes	52
Petroleum	August 19	45.0	40	Yes	24
Iron and steel	August 19	25.0	40	Yes	38
Photographic manufacturing	August 19	35.0	40	No	8
Fishing tackle	August 19	35.0	40	No	6
Rayon and synthetic yarn producing	August 26	32.5	40	No	6
Men's clothing	August 26	36.1	40	Yes	10
Hosiery	August 26	20.0	40	Yes	12
Automobile manufacturing	August 26	40.0	35	Yes	8
Cast-iron soil pipe	September 7	32.0	40	Yes	8
Wallpaper manufacturing	September 7	32.5	40	No	10
Salt producing	September 7	25.0	54	Yes	10
Leather	September 7	32.5	40	Yes	12
Motion picture laboratory	September 7	37.5	40	Yes	10
Underwear and allied products	September 18	32.0	40	Yes	14
Bituminous coal	September 18	30.0	40	Yes	16
Oil burner	September 18	37.5	48	No	10
Gasoline pump manufacturing	September 18	40.0	40	No	12
Textile bag	September 18	24.0	48	Yes	10
Transit	September 18	30.0	48	Yes	10
Artificial flower and feather	September 18	37.5	40	No	8
Linoleum and felt base manufacturing	September 18	35.0	48	No	8
Lime	October 3	30.0	40	Yes	14
Knitting, braiding, wire machinery	October 3	35.0	40	No	6
Lumber products/building materials	October 3	35.0	48	Yes	20
Laundry machinery manufacturing	October 3	35.0	40	No	12
Textile machinery manufacturing	October 3	35.0	40	No	8
Glass container industry	October 3	30.0	48	No	12
Building supplies trade	October 3	40.0	48	Yes	12
Boiler manufacturing	October 3	34.0	40	Yes	8
Farm equipment	October 3	30.0	48	Yes	10
Electric storage and battery	October 3	31.3	48	No	12
Women's belt	October 3	30.0	40	No	8
Luggage and fancy leather goods	October 3	30.0	40	Yes	10
Ice	October 3	32.2	56	Yes	12
Boot and shoe	October 3	30.0	40	Yes	10
Saddlery manufacturing	October 3	32.5	40	No	12

(continued)

TABLE 5.2. (continued)

Industry	Date in 1933 code passed	Minimum hourly wage (cents)	Maximum hours per week	Regional wage difference	Number of pages
Motor vehicle retailing	October 3	29.6	44	Yes	12
Bankers	October 3	30.0	40	Yes	12
Silk textile industry	October 7	30.0	40	Yes	12
Optical manufacturing	October 9	25.0	40	No	6
Automatic sprinkler	October 9	28.0	56	Yes	8
Umbrella manufacturing	October 9	32.5	40	Yes	10
Mutual savings banks	October 9	30.0	40	Yes	6
Handkerchief	October 9	30.0	45	Yes	14
Throwing	October 11	30.0	40	Yes	10
Compressed air	October 11	35.0	40	No	10
Heat exchange	October 11	35.0	40	No	10
Pump manufacturing	October 11	35.0	40	No	9

Notes: Nine codes (shipbuilding, rayon, leather, textile machinery, boiler manufacturing, luggage, saddlery, optical manufacturing, and umbrella manufacturing) allowed for overtime at higher pay—often 1.33 times—for short periods of time (e.g., "emergencies") where workers could generally work an extra four to eight hours per week. I did not factor this into the maximum hours in the table. All information is from US National Recovery Administration, *Codes of Fair Competition* (1933), vol. 1.

able to pass wage and hour provisions that were generally further away from the 40-cent/thirty-five-hour guidelines of the PRA. I subtracted the minimum wage reported in the table from 40 in each industry and regressed that against the number of pages of the code. Likewise, I subtracted the maximum hours in the table from the 35 specified in the PRA and regressed this against the number of pages of the code. The results of these simple regressions are reported below with *p*-values in parentheses:

(1)   Deviation of wage from 40 cents = 6.43 + 0.12 * code length in pages

(.00)   (.05).

(2)   Deviation of maximum hours from 35 = 5.96 + 0.09 * code length in pages

(.00)   (.13).

Equation (1) suggests that holding the number of pages at zero, the average code's minimum wage was 6.43 cents below 40 cents. Additionally, for every page the code was in length, the minimum wage fell by 0.12 cents. Because the standard deviation in the number of pages in a code was 7.5, a one standard deviation increase in length caused the minimum hourly wage to fall around a penny. Equation (2) suggests that for a code of zero pages, the average maximum workweek was 5.96 hours longer than the 35 stipulated in the President's Reemployment Act. For each additional page of the code, the maximum workweek rose by 0.09 hours — a one standard deviation increase in code length would raise the maximum workweek allowed by around 40 minutes; however, this result is only marginally significant with a p-value of .13.

The Heterogeneity of the NRA Codes' Trade Practice Provisions

While the labor provisions of the codes differed from industry to industry, that degree of heterogeneity was not even close to that which existed in the codes' trade practice provisions. To fully explore this aspect, one must analyze the contents of the codes with respect to what they required of industries. In Taylor (2007b), I explored this heterogeneity quantitatively by examining whether the code of fair competition matched to sixty-six industries for which monthly industry-level output was available contained some specific trade practice provisions, such as production quotas, constraints on new productive capacity, requirements to file data, and requirements to file price changes in advance. I will return to that quantitative analysis shortly, but first I will present a more qualitative look at code heterogeneity.

To give this analysis some randomness of selection, I will briefly report the details of codes 50, 100, 150, 200, 250, and 300. Code 50 covered the automatic sprinkler industry, which applied to industries "in the business of the manufacture of automatic sprinklers and devices and the fabrication and installation of automatic sprinkler equipment." The code was only seven pages long. As was standard in most codes, a code authority was created to "make investigations as to the functioning and observance of any provisions of this code." Articles 2 through 5 dealt with the perfunctory labor provisions of the code. Article 6 listed nine unfair methods of competition that would now be outlawed — including the use of anything but the standard forms of contract "adopted by the National Automatic Sprinkler Association" as well the giving of rebates, credits, or other special services. The code also forbade charging prices below cost; Pearce (1939, 46) notes that about 55 percent of all codes approved by the NIRA contained prohibitions against selling below cost.

Code 100 was for the paperboard industry. It was approved on November 8, 1933, and was ten pages long. The code began as many did by defining precisely the industry covered by the code — in this case, it consisted of makers of cardboard, sheathing paper, ham wrappings, and sulfate boards, to name a few. The specifications for hours worked was over a page long and specified maximum hours for six different classifications of employees — for example, watchmen could work up to fifty-six hours per week, but forty hours was the maximum week for most common laborers. Minimum wages were broken down by northern, central, and southern zones and differed between men and women. A person "whose earning capacity is limited because of physical or mental defect, age, or other infirmity" could be paid 80 percent of the applicable minimum wage. For trade practice provisions, the code required firms to follow a standardized method of accounting and cost. It also required firms to submit to the code authority data on "plant capacity, volume of production, volume of sale in units and dollars, orders received, unfilled orders, stocks on hand, inventory" as well as the number of employees and wages paid. Moreover, it stated that the code authority could verify these numbers by checking the firm's books upon request. As was common in codes that had such data filing provisions, these data were said to be for the eyes of the code authority and/or the government only and were not to be shared with other firms in the industry.

Code 150 covered the asphalt and mastic tile industry and was sixteen pages long. In the code's introduction, Johnson noted that this industry had only about four hundred employees. Like the paperboard industry code, it set more lax minimum wages for those limited by age or "physical or mental handicap" but said that not more than 5 percent of all employees at a firm could fall into this category. With respect to the code authority, firms had to join the industry's trade association if they wanted to have a vote for who would comprise this group. Industry members would be required to submit data "from time to time" to the code authority, and, like the paperboard code, these data were not to be shared with other members of the industry. When it came to terms of sale, however, firms had to file their prices with the code authority, and in this case, the information would be shared with all members of the industry. Furthermore, firms had to notify the code authority—which would in turn notify all other firms—of any change in prices at least ten days in advance. Such "open-price filing" provisions were common; Pearce (1939, 66) notes that nearly two-thirds of all approved codes included provisions for the enactment and administration of price filing. Article 11 of the asphalt tile code contained fourteen specific provisions related to fair competition— among these were provisions outlawing false advertising; commercial bribery; the giving of prizes, premiums, or gifts; espionage against competitors; and selling for a price below the cost of production. It was also a violation of the code if a firm told a customer about a future price change in advance— that is, firms could not tell their customers that they had filed for a price reduction that would take place a few days in the future.

Code 200 was for the sanitary napkin and cleansing tissue industry, which had twenty-six firms and around 1,200 employees. This code, approved January 12, 1934, was ten pages long. The code established a minimum wage of 41.66 cents per hour for men and 33.33 cents per hour for women and a maximum workweek of forty hours. As was the case in every code I have seen that contains a separate minimum wage for men and women, the code said that when women were doing the same work as men, they were to be paid the same wage as men. The code also stipulated that women could not work between the hours of 8:00 p.m. and 6:00 a.m. The sanitary napkin code authority was to have seven members, voted on by members of the industry, and firms could be asked by the code authority to send in data from time to time on number of employees, wages, and so on, but there was no open-price filing stipulation as there was for the asphalt tile code. Article 7 contained eleven trade practice provisions, including those outlawing "false marking or branding," secret rebates, commercial bribery, defamation of competitors by imputing them to dishonorable conduct or falsely disparaging the quality of their goods, false advertising, and selling below the cost of production. The article also forbade "chain purchases" whereby a firm required customers to buy one product in order to buy another.

Code 250 was for the wire rod and tube die industry, which consisted of twenty-one firms that had around $2 million in combined revenue in 1933. This code was ten pages long and was approved on February 1, 1934. It mandated a 40-cent minimum wage and forty-hour maximum workweek for all employees. This code had an open-price filing provision very similar to that of the asphalt tile industry—prices had to be filed seven days in advance of any change. Article 13 stipulated twelve unfair trade practices that would be forbidden. These included commercial bribery, procuring of trade secrets from competitors, imitating any exclusive mark or brand used by another firm in the industry, spreading false information about competitors, giving customers protection against future price changes, false advertising, mislabeling, granting secret rebates, and selling used goods unless they are clearly stated as such. One provision forbade a firm from enticing the employee of another firm with a job offer—although employees were permitted to initiate inquiries toward changing firms.

Code 300, approved on February 19, 1934, covered the lye industry. The code was ten pages long and set up a standard forty-hour workweek, although it did stipulate some exceptions when hours could exceed this. The minimum wage was 35 cents; however, learners and apprentices could be paid a minimum of 28 cents for the first sixty days of employment. Similar to some of the codes discussed above, firms were asked to send information on their business to the code authority, and these data would remain confidential. In

terms of specific trade practices, the lye code had an open-price filing provision—any change in price had to be sent to the code authority ten days in
advance, and the authority would mail notification of the price change to all
members of the industry immediately upon its receipt. Among some trade
practice provisions that were different in this code from the others examined
was one that said firms could not provide free shipping—prices had to incor-
porate shipping costs, and prices to destinations that cost more to ship to had
to be higher than those that cost less. Additionally, the code specified detailed
product standards. For example, lye could not be sold with less than 74 percent sodium hydroxide. Furthermore, lye could not be sold in cans larger than
thirteen ounces, and cases of lye had to be sold in quantities of either twenty-
four or forty-eight cans of lye—no more or less.

Although the analysis of the six codes above was a random one, it turns out
that each of these codes represented a small industry. This is not surprising,
because only 8 percent of the approved codes were for industries with more
than 100,000 employees—though these large industries employed almost
three-quarters of all workers under the NIRA (Marshall 1935, 4). Seventy-
eight percent of the codes represented industries with fewer than 20,000 employees, and 55 percent of the codes were from industries with fewer than
5,000 workers. To ensure that these large industries are represented in this
analysis, I will examine two early codes from major industries—lumber and
iron and steel, both of which were passed on August 19, 1933.

The lumber and timber products industry code was fifty-two pages long,
which put it in the top 10 percent in terms of length. The code began by
breaking the industry into sixteen divisions, such as southern pine, red cedar
shingle, and oak flooring. The vast degree of heterogeneity of the labor provisions of this code were discussed earlier, so I will focus here on trade practice provisions. Article 8 of the lumber code dealt with control of production.
The code authority established production quotas, and it could revise them
from time to time depending on market conditions. Each firm would be given
a three-month allotment of lumber that it could produce. These allotments
would be determined based on each firm's maximum output during any three
years since 1924 so that those that had produced more in the prior decade
would get a higher allotment. In the case of a young firm, for which three
years of prior data did not exist, the code authority would evaluate its capital
and try to compare it to a similar established firm to determine its percentage
allotment. If a firm needed to exceed its allotment to fulfill an order, it could
do so, but that excess would be deducted from its next three-month allotment.
Any other production in excess of allotment was forbidden. Article 9 of the
lumber code gave the code authority the ability to establish minimum prices

for each lumber division—that is, it essentially fixed prices. The article went onto specify the factors involved in the determination of the minimum prices below which firms could not sell. The code's Schedule B included four full pages of "Rules of Fair Trade Practice" for the industry, which were similar in spirit to the types of rules detailed in other codes above.

The iron and steel industry code was thirty-eight pages long. The industry had employed 421,000 in 1929 but had only 272,000 employees at the end of July 1933. Overcapacity was cited as a major problem in this industry (as was true of many others). Article 5 of the code said that there were no immediate plans to institute production quotas; however, the code authority would collect data periodically from industry members and if it was determined that overproduction continued to be a major problem, it could, subject to approval by President Roosevelt, impose output quotas. The article did, however, say that because of the problem of overcapacity in the industry, "none of the members of the code shall initiate the construction of any new blast furnace or open hearth or Bessemer steel capacity." Pearce (1939, 91) notes that thirty-two codes had such limitations on the installation of new productive capacity. In terms of pricing restrictions, the iron and steel code employed a "basing point pricing" system whereby the prices charged are standardized and include transportation costs from a base point regardless of where the shipment was actually made. The code contained several pages of rules and explanations for how the pricing system worked and where the base points were. Of course, basing point price systems are treated in the economics literature as potentially enhancing the ability to collude, because firms can simply agree to a base price that is charged regardless of how near or far the customer is from the firm. Additionally, it prevents producers who are more favorably located to buyers from charging lower prices so as to gain market share, since they must include in their price an amount exceeding their actual transportation costs.

The lumber and steel codes were certainly at the more complex end of the spectrum of industry codes in terms of how much businesses were affected by the NIRA. To conclude the qualitative discussion of heterogeneity of the trade practice provisions, I will briefly examine two other codes passed on the same day as those two (August 19, 1933): photographic manufacturing and fishing tackle. The photographic manufacturing code was eight pages long—half of this included statements of introduction by Roosevelt and Hugh Johnson. The code contained the required labor provisions on wages, hours, and collective bargaining, and set up a seven-member committee to run the code and collect data (rather than calling it a code authority, as most did, it was called the Code Committee of the Photographic Manufacturing Industry). However, the code contained no trade practice provisions dealing with fair competition, prices, or output. The code was effectively no different than the PRA, with a 35-cent minimum wage and a forty-hour maximum workweek. The fishing tackle code was six pages long. Like the photographic manufacturing code, it had the basic labor provisions and set up a committee to administer the code. However, it did go a little further in that Article 3 contained a handful of trade practices, including those forbidding sales below cost, deceptive advertising, and tie-in sales where customers had to buy one item as a condition of buying another. Still, to view these two codes alongside iron and steel and lumber, passed on the same day, illustrates nicely the large degree of heterogeneity among the 557 codes of fair competition.

Did Industry-Specific Factors Drive the Heterogeneity of the Codes?

Tremendous industry-level variation was evident in the complexity of the codes of fair competition with respect to the regulation of trade practices. This section asks whether any industry attributes systematically contributed to how simple or complex an industry's code was. For example, did industries with trade associations end up with codes whose reach went much further in directing economic activity than those without them? Were industries with fewer firms able to agree to more complex codes since there were fewer actors who had to come to an agreement on each provision? Or, alternatively, did industries with many firms end up with longer codes since they had more competing interests and hence needed to include more detailed information on various contingencies and exceptions in order to bring about an agreement?

I begin by duplicating the regression reported in table 5.1 on the timing of code passage, but rather than employing the number of months until code passage as the dependent variable, I employ the length of the code in pages. Code complexity can be reasonably proxied by each code's number of pages since all codes were published in a standardized format with the same spacing, font size, layout, and so on—in general, the more pages a code was, the more it could be expected to affect firm behavior. The results reported in table 5.3 suggest that industries with trade associations did indeed have more complex codes, ceteris paribus. On the other hand, industries with more workers and those with higher-paid workers generally had shorter codes, ceteris paribus. Perhaps the most interesting result is that industries with more firms had significantly longer codes than industries with fewer firms. For example, the lumber industry had 3,179 firms, and its code was fifty-two pages long—about four times longer than the average code. In contrast, the glass industry had 18 firms, and its code was only twelve pages long. The results here suggest that

TABLE 5.3. Factors Affecting Code Complexity

Constant	3.913
	(.00)
Number of workers in industry (thousands)	−0.0061
	(.01)
Number of firms in industry	0.0005
	(.00)
Trade association dummy variable (1 if present)	0.394
	(.10)
Average annual earnings per worker	−0.0013
	(.01)
Alexander's cost heterogeneity proxy	−0.214
	(.31)
R^2	.828
Number of observations	15

Notes: Dependent variable is number of pages of industry code. Poisson estimation is employed since the dependent variable is count data. The p-values (in parentheses) are computed using robust standard errors. Industry data are from the *Census of Manufactures*. Trade association dummy variable was created by examining whether the code specifically mentioned a trade association that helped in its formulation.

industries with more firms generally had to include more rules about conduct in order to obtain the buy-in of all the various competing interests. With more players in the negotiating process, the stew had more ingredients.

In the next section, I employ data on specific code attributes such as whether an industry code required firms to regularly file data (on output, costs, and other information) with the code authority, whether firms were required to notify other members of the industry before changing their prices, or whether the code forbade sales below the cost of production. These were three of the most common trade practice provisions in the NRA codes. I reran the regression in shown in table 5.3, but this time I employed a probit analysis in which the dependent variable was whether the industry's code contained one of the specific provisions mentioned above (data filing, price filing, no sales below cost). The results, which are not reported in the interest of space, were generally insignificant, suggesting that these specific code attributes were largely exogenous to industry factors such as number of workers, number of firms, and so on. This is consistent with what I found in my prior work (Taylor 2007b, 612). Still, three coefficients in these regressions were significant at the 10 percent level. First, industries with more firms were more likely than industries with fewer firms to have imposed a price filing provision whereby firms had to notify industry members in advance of any price change. Second, industries that had more cost heterogeneity (using Alexander's proxy) were also more likely to have imposed a price filing provision. Third, high-wage industries were less likely to have had a provision in their code requiring firms to regularly file data with the code authority.

The Empirical Effects of the NIRA Codes of Fair Competition

Some research has focused on whether the NIRA helped or hindered the nation's recovery after 1933. The sharp divergence of conclusions to these questions is startling. To illustrate, consider the three most influential articles on the NIRA since the early 2000s: Cole and Ohanian (2004) and Eggertsson (2008, 2012). Cole and Ohanian attribute much of the "weak" recovery of the 1930s to the NIRA's cartelization and high-wage policies. They employ a general equilibrium model that incorporates the NIRA's wage and cartel polices and show that simulations of this model come closer to actual economic performance than do simulations of a competitive model; thus, they conclude that the NIRA harmed recovery. Eggertsson (2008), on the other hand, attributes what he views as the very strong recovery of the 1930s to Roosevelt's policy actions—including those embedded in the NIRA—which brought higher inflation. Following up on his earlier work, Eggertsson (2012) argues that, even though the NIRA cartel and wage policies created a negative supply shock, the legislation led to higher output and economic recovery because it raised inflation expectations and thus helped the nation escape a deflationary spiral.[7]

Of course, the empirical literature on the NIRA goes back much further than these three articles. In the first detailed econometric study of the program, Weinstein (1980) employs monthly wage and price data in a two-equation Phillips curve system. He specifies June 1933 to December 1935 as NIRA dummy variable months and concludes that the NIRA created a negative supply shock that caused substantial increases in wages and prices. Weinstein claims that the negative supply shock offset a positive demand shock from monetary expansion between 1933 and 1935 and thus slowed recovery. Vedder and Gallaway (1993) likewise provide evidence that the high-wage policies embedded in the NIRA slowed recovery.

These studies have been subject to the weakness that they either used macro-oriented time-series data, which cannot take into account the heterogeneity in the contents of the codes, or they used industry-level data but did not account for the exact timing of when each industry's code took effect. For example, in Taylor (2002)—an article drawing from my dissertation—I employed a time series of manufacturing sector-level output and created a dummy variable for the NIRA cartel codes that turned on in July 1933, when the first codes were approved. My findings suggested that output fell under the NIRA codes—at least in the first eight months of the program—even when wage rates are held constant, and I presented this as evidence of successful collusion under the NIRA. Still, we can do far better at addressing the precise impact of the codes with industry-level panel data by accounting for exactly when industries were under the codes and by controlling for how complex their codes were in terms of their length or the presence of specific provisions.

Some earlier empirical studies, such as Alexander (1994) and Krepps (1997), have focused on the microeconomic question of whether the NIRA codes facilitated collusive outcomes. Alexander (1994) uses price-cost margins from the 1933, 1935, and 1937 *Census of Manufactures* as a proxy for collusion. She finds a significant correlation between an industry's four-firm concentration ratio and its price-cost margin in 1933, but this relationship ceased in 1935, when firms were under the NIRA. She offers this breakdown in the Cournot-implied relationship between concentration and profits as evidence that the NIRA facilitated collusion in the 1935 data. In a step forward in accounting for the heterogeneity within the NRA codes, Krepps (1997) expands Alexander's study by including an industry-level dummy variable for the presence of an open-price filing provision (firms had to file price changes in advance) in their codes. He finds that industries with such provisions had higher price-cost margins in 1937 than industries that did not have such provisions. The assumption in both Alexander's and Krepps's studies is that one could analyze whether the NIRA codes promoted collusion by examining post-NIRA data collected in either 1935 or 1937 and comparing it to pre-NIRA data from 1933 or 1931. But the NIRA ended in May 1935—and furthermore, as will be discussed in the next chapter, it has been widely contended that the NRA codes underwent a "compliance crisis" in the spring of 1934 whereby collusion was lost in many industries. Thus, it is not clear to what extent the 1935, much less 1937, census observations can tell us about whether the NIRA codes promoted collusion. Still, if one wants to examine industry-level price-cost margin data from the 1930s, then biannual census data are the only option. Also employing census data, Chicu, Vickers, and Ziebarth (2013) and Vickers and Ziebarth (2014) offer fascinating cases studies of the cement and macaroni industries, respectively. These studies employ establishment-level data obtained from the 1929, 1931, 1933, and 1935 census manuscripts—and both offer evidence that collusion did indeed take place in these two industries.

An alternative approach, which I employed in Taylor (2007b, 2011) and Schuldt and Taylor (2017), is to use monthly panel data with dummy variables

for the NIRA codes that turn on during the month that the industry's code
is passed and turn off after May 1935, when the legislation was ruled unconstitutional. The output data I used in the 2007 and 2011 studies were not seasonally adjusted—in retrospect, they probably should have been since many
of the industries saw strong seasonal variation in output. Therefore, for the
analysis that follows, I seasonally adjusted the output data using a multipli-
cative adjustment moving average procedure following Schuldt and Taylor
(2017). Additionally, in my earlier work, to obtain as many industry-level observations as possible in the panel, I included output of every industry available. However, in many cases, several different output series were covered by
the same code and there was some clear overlap in the output for, or strong
correlations between, some of these industries. For example, I included data
from men's shoes, women's shoes, and total shoe production. Although it is
true that total shoe production is greater than men's shoe production plus
women's shoe production, and, hence, it does include additional information, there is still clearly a great deal of overlap. I also employed output data
on both tire pneumatic casings and tire tubes. Both of these industries had
unique output data and they were covered by the rubber tire manufacturing
code, but the output movements of these two industries are strongly correlated with each other. In some specifications, I also included data from eleven
foodstuffs industries such as ice cream, beef, and milk, whose sale, but not
production, was covered by the wholesale grocery code.

    Without conceding that one set of analysis is superior to the other, in the
analysis here I will err on the side of less overlap in terms of output and code
coverage by examining fewer industries. Specifically, to examine how code
heterogeneity impacted industry outcomes, I employ output data for thirty-
eight industries that were covered by a code of fair competition. The thirty-
eight industries are listed in table 5.4 along with the date the code was passed
and the number of pages of the code—the codes are ranked in order of length.
Additionally, the table specifies other attributes of the codes, such as whether
a trade association was present in the industry to help with the code's formulation as well as whether the code had specific types of rules such as requirements to file data or production quotas.

    I will begin by presenting some regressions whose methodology broadly
follows my 2007b study. The dependent variable is the monthly growth rate
(log difference) in seasonally adjusted industry output minus the growth rate
in a seasonally adjusted index of business activity.[8] The purpose of measuring
industry growth in relation to a broad index of business activity is to help control for macroeconomic factors aside from the NIRA that could have impacted
output. The independent variables include a dummy variable for the months

that the industry was covered by the President's Reemployment Agreement (August 1933 until the industry's code of fair competition was passed) and a dummy variable for NIRA code months (the month of code passage until June 1935, since the NIRA was ruled unconstitutional on May 27, 1935).[9] I also include a measure of the industry's capacity utilization—computed by dividing each month's production by its maximum level between January 1927 and December 1929. This is included to account for the likelihood that an industry operating near capacity will have slower percentage output growth than one operating well below capacity, ceteris paribus. I also include the dependent variable lagged one month. Finally, I employ industry fixed effects and cross-section weights, which allow for the presence of cross-section heteroskedasticity. The regressions include 132 months of observations, from January 1927 through December 1937.

Specification (1) of table 5.5 suggests that industry output grew 1.1 percent faster during the months when the firms in that industry were to be covered by the President's Reemployment Agreement; however, industry output was not statistically different when the industry was covered by an NIRA code. The capacity utilization control acts as predicted—industries further below capacity saw faster growth than other industries. Specification (2) adds the growth rates in industries' average hourly earnings and average hourly workweeks. While wage rates and hours are generally thought of as endogenous with output, a case can be made that the NIRA labor provisions should be treated as exogenous shocks. Hourly wage rates did not spike in August and September 1933 because output was booming (in fact, wage rates were stagnant between March and July, when the economy experienced its sharpest four-month upswing in history); instead, they spiked because the PRA mandated that firms dramatically raise wage rates. Likewise, workweeks plummeted in August and September 1933 not because the economy was contracting but because the PRA required firms to cut hours in manufacturing to thirty-five per week. The logic of adding these variables to specification (2) is to better isolate the impact of the non-labor provisions of the NIRA by holding these labor variables constant. Unfortunately, the sample size falls sharply because wage and hour data are available for only fifteen of the thirty-eight industries.

Interestingly, the magnitude of the positive effect of the PRA more than doubles when wage rates and hours worked are held constant. This suggests that the exogenous increases in hourly wage rates and cuts in the workweek harmed output, ceteris paribus, although other aspects of the PRA, such as the psychological boost to patriotism that came with the Blue Eagle and the "buy now" campaign, raised output sharply. The coefficient on the NIRA codes of fair competition remains statistically insignificant. Because a reduc-

TABLE 5.4. NIRA Code Details by Industry

Industry	Date passed	Number of pages	TDA	MFD	OPF	MACH	IB	NSBC	PQ	NNC
Book	February 17, 1934	68	0	0	1	0	0	1	0	1
Paper and pulp#	November 17, 1933	60	0	1	0	0	0	0	0	0
Lumber*	August 19, 1933	52	1	1	0	0	0	1	1	0
Rubber*#	December 15, 1933	50	1	1	0	0	0	1	0	1
Pig iron*#	August 19, 1933	38	1	0	1	0	0	0	0	0
Steel ingot#	August 19, 1933	38	1	0	1	0	0	0	0	1
Steel sheet*#	August 19, 1933	38	1	0	1	0	0	0	0	1
Crude petroleum*	August 19, 1933	34	0	0	1	0	1	1	1	1
Lubricants*	August 19, 1933	34	0	0	1	0	1	1	1	1
Cement*	November 27, 1933	28	1	1	1	0	0	1	0	1
Copper*	April 21, 1934	28	0	0	0	0	0	0	1	0
Lead ore*	May 24, 1934	26	1	1	1	0	0	0	0	0
Cotton*	July 9, 1933	24	1	1	0	1	0	0	0	1
Large cigars	June 19, 1934	23	1	1	1	0	0	0	0	0
Slab zinc	March 26, 1935	23	1	0	0	0	1	0	0	0
Zinc ore	March 26, 1935	23	1	0	0	0	1	0	0	0
Cheese	February 2, 1935	22	0	0	0	0	1	0	0	0
Solid and cushion tires	December 21, 1933	20	1	0	1	0	1	0	0	0
Construction	January 31, 1934	18	1	1	0	0	0	0	0	0
Fertilizers	October 31, 1933	18	0	0	1	0	1	1	0	0
Bituminous coal*	September 18, 1933	16	1	0	0	0	1	0	0	0

Industry	Date									
Machinery#	March 17, 1934	16	1	1	0	0	0	0	0	0
Woodworking machinery#	May 14, 1934	16	1	1	0	1	0	0	0	0
Asphalt*	November 6/, 1933	14	0	1	1	1	0	0	0	0
Brick*	March 26, 1934	13	0	1	1	1	0	0	0	0
Auto parts*	November 8, 1933	12	1	0	1	1	0	0	0	0
Glass*	October 3, 1933	12	0	1	0	1	1	0	0	1
Leather*#	September 7, 1933	12	0	0	0	0	0	0	0	0
Metal*	November 2, 1933	12	1	1	0	0	0	0	0	0
Newsprint*#	November 17, 1933	12	0	0	1	1	1	0	0	0
Raw silk*#	October 7, 1933	12	1	1	0	1	0	1	1	0
Chemicals*#	February 10, 1934	10	1	1	0	0	0	0	0	0
Small cigarettes	February 9, 1935	10	0	1	0	0	0	0	0	0
Shoes*#	October 3, 1933	10	1	1	0	1	0	1	0	0
Wool*#	July 26, 1933	10	1	1	1	1	1	0	0	0
Passenger cars*#	August 26, 1933	8	0	1	0	0	0	0	0	0
Trucks	August 26, 1933	8	0	0	1	0	1	0	0	0
Rayon yarn*#	August 26, 1933	6	0	0	0	0	0	0	0	0

*Industry for which price data are available.

#Industry for which wage and hours data are available.

Notes: TDA = presence of a trade association, MFD = firms had to file data regularly with cartel board, OPF = open-price filing, MACH = machine hours restrictions, IB = allows inspection of firms books, NSBC = no sales below cost of production, PQ = production quotas, NNC = restrictions on new capacity.

Source: US National Recovery Administration, Codes of Fair Competition (1933–35), 23 vols.

TABLE 5.5. Fixed-Effects Panel Analysis of Growth in Industry Output under the
NIRA Codes

	(1)		(2)	
	Coefficient	p	Coefficient	p
Intercept	0.0230	.00	0.0185	.08
President's Reemployment Agreement	0.0111	.03	0.0230	.00
(August 1933 to code passage)				
Industry-specific NIRA code	−0.0014	.58	−0.0029	.46
(code passage to June 1935)				
Capacity utilization (−1)	−0.0375	.00	−0.0272	.07
Dependent variable (−1)	−0.0928	.01	0.0006	.99
Growth rate in workweek			0.3319	.02
Growth in wage rates			0.2205	.14
Cross-sections	38		15	
Number of observations	4,792		1,902	

Notes: Dependent variable is growth rate in industry output minus growth rate in index of
general business activity. In this and all subsequent empirical tables, the column labeled
"p" reports the p-value associated with the coefficient. The p-value indicates at what
percentage the coefficient is statistically significant—for example a p-value of .03 indicates
that the coefficient is significant at the 3 percent confidence level. Regressions employ
robust standard errors, industry fixed effects, and cross-section weights, which allow for
the presence of cross-section heteroskedasticity. The regressions include 132 months of data,
from January 1927 through December 1937. Output data are seasonally adjusted.

tion in industry output would be consistent with a finding that collusion occurred under the codes, specification (2) offers no support for the notion that
successful collusion occurred when industries were covered by their codes of
fair competition.

But based on the qualitative examination of the sharp heterogeneity of
industry-specific codes performed above, it is not surprising that a full sample
of industries yields statistically insignificant results regarding the impact of
the NIRA trade practice provisions. After all, some codes specified nothing
more than the required labor provisions while others contained detailed production quota schemes or other anticompetitive rules. To explore this further,
I broke the sample into two groups: the twenty industries whose codes were
eighteen or fewer pages and the eighteen industries whose codes were twenty
or more pages. The results are shown in table 5.6.[10]

Specification (1) employs the subsample of industries with long codes. The
coefficient on the NIRA codes of fair competition is now negative and statistically significant—output fell by 0.63 percent per month when this sample of
industries was covered by their NIRA code of fair competition. Since the average industry in this subsample was covered by a code for 16.7 months, out-

TABLE 5.6. Analysis of Growth in Industry Output in Short and Long Codes

	(1) Eighteen longest codes		(2) Twenty shortest codes		(3) Eighteen longest codes		(4) Twenty shortest codes	
	Coefficient	p	Coefficient	p	Coefficient	p	Coefficient	p
Intercept	0.0263	.00	0.0202	.06	0.0299	.00	0.0116	.42
President's Reemployment Agreement (August 1933 to code passage)	0.0057	.31	0.0174	.01	0.0244	.04	0.0282	.00
Industry-specific NIRA code (code passage to June 1935)	-0.0063	.03	0.0038	.23	-0.0147	.00	0.0052	.16
Capacity utilization (-1)	-0.0400	.00	-0.0355	.04	-0.0400	.00	-0.0190	.37
Dependent variable (-1)	-0.0675	.20	-0.1171	.00	0.1163	.14	-0.0775	.14
Growth rate in workweek					0.5387	.00	0.1279	.21
Growth in wage rates					0.3141	.06	0.0149	.92
Cross-sections	18		20		5		10	
Number of observations	2,510		2,282		638		1,264	

Notes: Dependent variable is growth rate in industry output less growth rate in index of general business activity. Regressions employ robust standard, industry fixed effects, and cross-section weights, which allow for the presence of cross-section heteroskedasticity. The regressions include 132 months of data, from January 1927 through December 1937. Output data are seasonally adjusted.

put fell by around 11.1 percent under the codes, ceteris paribus. This finding is consistent with industries being able to successfully collude under the NIRA. Specification (2) shows the results for the subsample of industries with short codes. The coefficient on the NIRA is positive—suggesting output rose when industries in this subsample were covered by their NIRA codes—although the result is not statistically significant. Thus, there is no evidence that industries with short codes were able to achieve cartel outcomes. Specifications (3) and (4) duplicate the regressions but again add growth rates in wages and hours worked as independent variables to better isolate the non-labor effects of the NIRA. In fact, when I hold these factors constant, output in industries with long codes fell even more sharply—by just under 1.5 percent per month. Again, industries with short codes saw no statistically significant output effects under the NIRA.

My 2007b article used (like the analysis above) industry output minus an index of business activity as the dependent variable, but an alternative is to simply examine the growth rate in industry output and include additional independent variables to control for other factors that may have affected output. As a robustness check to the results reported in table 5.6, table 5.7 includes six regressions that employ this alternate methodology by including the growth rates in the money supply, government revenues, and government spending as control variables. I also include a pre-NIRA dummy variable for June and July 1933—these months include the six weeks between when the NIRA was passed and when the PRA was implemented, and the dummy variable may capture any anticipation effects of the program's implementation. In addition, to control for inflation expectations and bank health, I include the spread between AAA and BAA bonds, and the S&P 500 stock index. Specification (1) suggests that output fell around 0.7 percent per month when industries were covered by an NIRA code of fair competition. Compounded over the entire NIRA code time period, this implies a 12 percent decline in output, ceteris paribus, under the codes. Specification (2), however, suggests that much of this decline in output is driven by the NIRA's labor provisions; when wage and hour movements are held as exogenous—and thus better isolating the NIRA's collusive aspects—the coefficient on output diminishes by half, and it is no longer statistically significant.

Specifications (3) and (4) divide the sample into industries with short and long codes. The results suggest that industries with short codes did not see output decline under the NIRA codes; however, those with long codes saw output fall by 1.1 percent per month under the codes, implying a 20 percent decline in output under the entire code period. Because declines in output are consistent with collusion, this again suggests that cartel outcomes occurred in

TABLE 5.7. Analysis of Growth in Industry Output under the NIRA Codes

	(1) All codes	(2) All codes	(3) Short codes	(4) Long codes	(5) Short codes	(6) Long codes
Intercept	0.033	0.027	0.033	0.035	0.022	0.035
	(.00)	(.00)	(.00)	(.00)	(.08)	(.00)
June/July 1933 dummy variable	0.078	0.054	0.070	0.085	0.054	0.069
	(.00)	(.00)	(.00)	(.00)	(.00)	(.00)
PRA	−0.013	−0.003	−0.011	−0.016	0.004	−0.013
	(.01)	(.74)	(.15)	(.01)	(.65)	(.22)
NIRA code	−0.007	−0.004	−0.002	−0.011	0.001	−0.013
	(.02)	(.17)	(.50)	(.01)	(.61)	(.00)
Capacity utilization (−1)	−0.055	−0.040	−0.056	−0.055	−0.035	−0.048
	(.00)	(.00)	(.00)	(.00)	(.06)	(.00)
Dependent variable (−1)	−0.045	0.079	−0.065	−0.025	−0.015	0.215
	(.32)	(.19)	(.20)	(.71)	(.81)	(.01)
Growth money	0.614	0.318	0.678	0.578	0.411	0.289
	(.00)	(.00)	(.00)	(.00)	(.00)	(.01)
Growth in government spending (−1)	0.000	0.005	0.000	−0.000	0.005	0.006
	(.96)	(.09)	(.88)	(.98)	(.17)	(.02)
Growth in government revenues (−1)	−0.001	−0.000	−0.000	−0.001	−0.000	−0.000
	(.24)	(.91)	(.79)	(.24)	(.85)	(.95)
Growth in S&P stock index	0.085	0.095	0.126	0.052	0.101	0.097
	(.00)	(.00)	(.00)	(.01)	(.00)	(.00)
Growth in AAA-BAA spread	−0.026	−0.023	−0.022	−0.029	−0.012	−0.038
	(.03)	(.10)	(.13)	(.13)	(.99)	(.14)
Growth in wage rates		0.223			0.117	0.263
		(.13)			(.47)	(.10)
Growth in workweek		0.494			0.361	0.639
		(.00)			(.00)	(.00)
Cross-sections	38	15	20	18	10	5
Number of observations	4,792	1,902	2,542	2,250	1,264	638

Notes: Dependent variable is growth rate in industry output; *p*-values are reported in parentheses. Regressions employ robust standard errors, industry fixed effects, and cross-section weights, which allow for the presence of cross-section heteroskedasticity. The regressions include 132 months of data, from January 1927 through December 1937. Output data are seasonally adjusted.

industries with longer codes but not in industries with shorter codes. Specifications (5) and (6) hold constant movements in wages and hours to hold constant the NIRA's labor provisions and better isolate its cartel provisions. Again, industries with short codes saw no statistically significant change in output under the NRA codes, but those industries with long codes saw output fall sharply, by 1.3 percent per month, holding constant changes in wage and hours. This suggests that industries with long codes were able to successfully collude.

TABLE 5.8. Effectiveness of Specific Code Provisions upon Collusive Outcomes

	(1)	(2)
Intercept	0.0216	0.0212
	(.00)	(.00)
Inspect the books	0.0290	0.0400
	(.19)	(.07)
Must file data	−0.0119	0.0088
	(.08)	(.55)
No sales below costs	0.0020	0.0049
	(.91)	(.78)
Open-price filing	−0.0062	−0.0051
	(.78)	(.83)
No new capacity	−0.0339	−0.0320
	(.41)	(.42)
Production quotas	−0.0307	−0.0393
	(.30)	(.14)
Machine hour restrictions	0.0198	0.0015
	(.72)	(.79)
Capacity utilization (−1)	−0.0356	−0.0350
	(.00)	(.00)
Dependent variable (−1)	−0.0958	−0.0972
	(.00)	(.00)
Trade association		−0.0292
		(.05)
Cross-sections	38	38
Number of observations	4,792	4,792

Notes: Dependent variable is the rate of change in industry output minus rate of change in index of overall business activity; *p*-values are reported in parentheses. Regressions include industry fixed effects and employ White standard errors. Following Taylor (2007), a dummy variable for NIRA months is employed as a cross-section-specific coefficient to control for the legislation's general institutional effects. Sample runs January 1927 through December 1937.

In Taylor (2007b), I explored the impact on output of specific categories of provisions contained in the codes. I found that industries that had rules requiring firms to file data at regular intervals, had production quotas, and had constraints on new productive capacity saw output fall more than industries that did not have these rules—suggesting that these provisions were important in enabling successful collusion. Table 5.8 repeats this analysis, but employs the seasonally adjusted data and the thirty-eight-industry sample used in this chapter. Specification (1) shows that only the finding suggesting that data filing provisions differentially promoted collusion survives when the sample size is cut and the data are seasonally adjusted. The coefficients on production quotas and new capacity constraints are negative and large, but they fall short of being statistically significant.

In work with Robert Schuldt (Schuldt and Taylor 2017), I found evidence suggesting that the presence of an industry trade association played an important role in whether industries were able to attain collusive outcomes. Trade associations could have helped industries better formulate effective cartel rules—the roles played by trade associations such as the National Association of Ice Manufacturers in the code formulation process were documented in chapter 3. Trade associations could also have enabled more effective monitoring once the rules were in place. Specification (2) adds a dummy variable that turns on during code months if the code mentioned a trade association.[11] Twenty-four of the thirty-eight industries (63 percent) examined here had a trade association. The coefficient on the trade association dummy variable is negative and statistically significant at the 5 percent level, suggesting that industries with trade associations saw output fall significantly more than industries without trade associations while they were covered by an NIRA code. In fact, Schuldt and Taylor (2017), which goes into far more detail on the issue than I do here, find evidence suggesting that *only* those industries that had trade associations in place were able to successfully collude under the NIRA. This finding again suggests that outcomes under the NIRA were not one-size-fits-all.

Analysis of Prices and Timing of Code Adoption

While the analysis thus far has examined the impact of the NIRA codes on output, monthly price data exist for twenty-four of the thirty-eight industries in the sample. To control for economic factors aside from the NIRA that could have affected prices, I include all the controls that were used in table 5.7; however, the coefficients on these controls are not reported in table 5.9 to save space. Specification (1) suggests that prices rose, but only by 0.19 percent per month, during NIRA code months. Compounded over the seventeen months that the average industry in the sample was covered by a code, this adds up to only a 3.3 percent price rise. But again, we must account for industry heterogeneity. In this analysis, I take a different tack. I drop the NIRA code dummy variable and replace it with a series of seven dummy variables that turn on for only one month—the first turns on during the month of adoption, the second the month right after adoption, the third the following month, and so on. Because I am examining growth rates in prices rather than levels, the largest jumps in prices would be expected in the months immediately following code adoption.

TABLE 5.9. Analysis of Growth in Industry Prices in Short and Long Codes

	(1) All codes	(2) All codes	(3) Long codes	(4) Short codes
Intercept	−0.0041	−0.0038	0.0007	−0.0056
	(.00)	(.00)	(.48)	(.00)
President's Reemployment	0.0080	−0.0087	−0.0298	−0.0003
Agreement (August 1933	(.00)	(.10)	(.00)	(.96)
to code passage)				
Industry-specific NIRA code	0.0019			
(code passage to June 1935)	(.01)			
Month code adopted		0.0069	0.0018	0.0074
		(.16)	(.72)	(.37)
Code adoption + 1 month		0.0220	0.0427	0.0144
		(.00)	(.00)	(.02)
Code adoption + 2 months		0.0251	0.0486	0.0146
		(.00)	(.00)	(.02)
Code adoption + 3 months		0.0196	0.0505	0.0099
		(.02)	(.02)	(.06)
Code adoption + 4 months		0.0183	0.0221	0.0153
		(.00)	(.01)	(.02)
Code adoption + 5 months		0.0061	0.0214	-0.0000
		(.27)	(.19)	(.99)
Code adoption + 6 months		0.0058	0.0109	0.0039
		(.07)	(.24)	(.14)
Macro controls	Yes	Yes	Yes	Yes
Cross-sections	24	24	10	14
Number of observations	2,976	2,844	1,158	1,686

Notes: Dependent variable is growth rate in industry prices; *p*-values are reported in parentheses.
Regressions include industry fixed effects and employ White standard errors. Following Taylor (2007),
a dummy variable for NIRA months is employed as a cross-section-specific coefficient to control for
the legislation's general institutional effects.
Sample runs January 1927 through December 1937.

Specification (2) suggests that prices did not rise significantly during the month of adoption. In some cases, codes did not go into effect until a week or ten days after the code was passed; also, monthly price data reflect a sample taken in the middle of the month, so it is likely that, in many cases, the data from that month are not entirely reflective of a period when the code was in effect. In the month after code adoption, industry prices rose 2.2 percent. They rose another 2.5 percent the following month, and then the growth rates in prices diminish. Specifications (3) and (4) break the sample into long codes (eighteen pages or more) and short codes (sixteen pages or fewer), as before. Long codes see much larger increases in prices—4.3, 4.9, and 5.0 percent in the first three months after code adoption, and then the growth in prices quickly diminishes. Short codes see statistically significant increases in prices during the first four months after code adoption; however, the magnitude is much smaller—ranging between 1 and 1.5 percent per month—before diminishing to zero after month four.

Why did industries with short codes see any price increases? After all, the contention earlier was that short codes were unlikely to have contained cartel-oriented provisions such as production quotas or restrictions on capacity. While shorter codes did not generally contain such dramatic departures from competition, many of them did contains provisions forbidding sales below cost of production or open-price filing provisions. This likely put upward pressure on prices even if it did not have effects on industry output that were large enough for the earlier regressions to have classified as being statistically significant. Incidentally, I did try the monthly adoption dummy variables in the regressions that employed output as the dependent variable, such as those in tables 5.5 through 5.8. The results in some cases were consistent with those found in the price regressions, but the adoption dummy variables did not typically perform as well in the output regressions as they did in the price regressions. One possibility for this result is that the provisions that led firms to reduce output and productive capacity to raise price and profits took a little longer to administer so that the coefficient on any one month was not strongly different from other months in the sample.

Summary and Discussion

Past research has generally treated the NIRA as a monolithic twenty-three-month program, but this chapter has discussed the vast heterogeneity found within the industry-specific codes of fair competition. The President's Reemployment Agreement of August 1, 1933, was indeed a monolithic program. It asked all firm owners to simultaneously pay a minimum wage of 40 cents per hour (35 cents for clerical and sales) and cut workweeks to no more than thirty-five hours (forty hours for clerical and sales). But the NIRA codes of fair competition did not affect all industries in the same manner—this heterogeneity applies to both the timing for when industries were covered by codes as well as the rules under which industries operated. Some industries, such as cotton manufacturing and shipbuilding, were covered by the NIRA beginning in July 1933. But other industries, such as paper and pulp production, auto parts manufacturing, and cement, were not covered by an NIRA code until November 1933. Still others, such as copper, lead, and woodworking machinery, were not covered until the spring of 1934 or later. If one wishes to estimate the economic effects of the NIRA codes of fair competition, it is important to account for the heterogeneity of the timing of when industries were indeed covered by them.

Perhaps more importantly, the contents of the codes themselves varied dramatically from industry to industry. Some codes, such as those for rayon yarn and photographic manufacturing, were just a couple of pages long and contained nothing more than the required maximum hour and minimum wage provisions—there is no reason to think that codes such as these would have effectively fostered collusion. On the other hand, codes such as those for the lumber and steel industries were dozens of pages long and contained scores of detailed provisions restricting prices, output, and productive capacity. In this chapter, I have presented empirical evidence suggesting that the simple presence of a code of fair competition did not generally lead to collusive outcomes in an industry. However, those industries with long and complex codes experienced declines in output under the NIRA codes—a finding consistent with the achievement of cartel outcomes—and furthermore, this result holds even when the NIRA's effects on wages and hours (which likely caused their own negative supply shock) are held constant.

Clearly some industries were more effective than others in formulating detailed codes and pushing them through the government's approval process. In previous work I have shown that the presence of an industry trade association to help formulate and administer the code was an important factor in the achievement of collusive outcomes. One could argue that this may create an endogeneity problem for the empirical analysis—perhaps the industries that were already more prone to collusion were able to pass more complex codes. But the point of this chapter has not been to examine the effects of longer or shorter codes on cartel outcomes per se, but rather to highlight the vast heterogeneity of the codes and to show that the effects of the NIRA varied from industry to industry.

My findings here further "cement the case for collusion" having occurred under the NIRA, as Chicu, Vickers, and Ziebarth (2013) playfully noted in their study of the Portland cement industry. However, my results also suggest it is a gross simplification to say that collusion occurred under all industries between June 16, 1933, and May 27, 1935, when the NIRA was in effect. In the next chapter, I turn to issues of compliance and enforcement in the codes. This is also a very important part of the heterogeneity story—in this case, with respect to the heterogeneity of the program's impact over time—because it appears that even if some industries approached cartel outcomes in the fall and winter of 1933/1934, the collusive result was fleeting as many of the cartels broke down in the late winter and early spring of 1934.

The NIRA Compliance Mechanism
in Theory and Practice

The NIRA imposed rules and regulations on economic behavior. But, as the saying goes, rules are meant to be broken. In fact, firms — particularly as time went on — often flaunted the labor and trade practice requirements embedded in the codes. Around 166,000 cases of alleged violations of the program were investigated by the NRA. According to NRA records, more than three-quarters of these were successfully "adjusted" whereby the violating firm was brought into acquiescence through the actions of government compliance officials. This chapter focuses on the NIRA's compliance mechanism in terms of how it was supposed to work in theory. It also explores several examples of how it actually worked in practice.

The NIRA's Section 2(a) left the program's administration exclusively to Roosevelt, stating that the president "is hereby authorized to establish such agencies [and] to appoint . . . officers and employees . . . as he may find necessary" to carry out the program. To this end, on June 16, just after signing the NIRA into law, Roosevelt issued an executive order appointing Hugh Johnson as Administrator for Industrial Recovery, and he issued a document titled "National Recovery Administration Bulletin No. 1," which outlined the policies embedded in the NIRA. This bulletin contains the first official mention of the term National Recovery Administration, which became (and still is among New Deal historians) a ubiquitous synonym for the NIRA itself.

On July 15, 1933, Roosevelt issued another executive order, which gave Johnson sweeping powers "to appoint the necessary personnel on a permanent basis, to fix their compensation, and to conduct such hearings and exercise such other functions as are vested in me [Roosevelt] except the approval of codes, or making of agreements."[1] Thus, Roosevelt had effectively transferred to the NRA administrator much of the power that the NIRA had vested in the office of the president. Lyon et al. (1972 41) note that under Johnson the NRA assembled its army of personnel without any hearings or even formal calls for applications for positions; "It did not issue circulars describing the duties to be performed [or] qualification standards that would be applied in making selections." For better or worse, the whole system of compliance and enforcement under the NRA was appointed by Roosevelt and Johnson without any congressional oversight.

The NIRA compliance mechanism evolved dramatically over time as Roosevelt took advantage of the powers given him in Section 2(a) to create compliance and enforcement agencies. For instance (as detailed in chapter 4), the Blue Eagle emblem was created in late July 1933 as a symbol of compliance with the NIRA. No such plan for a compliance emblem was included in the text of the law itself, nor was the emblem mentioned in the text of the President's Reemployment Agreement for which it was created. Still, the Blue Eagle became a key part—perhaps even *the* key part—of the NIRA's enforcement mechanism. Coincident with the institution of the PRA, Roosevelt established the Blue Eagle Division to oversee the program's imposition. Frank Healy was the division's executive director and Charles Horner was the division's director of publicity and education. In the Blue Eagle Division, district recovery boards (generally comprised of seven members) were set up in each of the twenty-six districts of the Department of Commerce. Additionally, a state recovery board generally consisting of nine members was set up in each of the forty-eight states. Most cities also set up their own volunteer local recovery boards, which were to promote compliance through education and publicity. As outlined in chapter 4, these boards played a major role in convincing firms to sign the PRA and consumers to sign the Consumer's Statement of Cooperation saying that they would shop at firms that were in compliance with the NRA/PRA and hence displaying the Blue Eagle.

Allegations of violation of the NRA/PRA were to be sent to these state and local recovery offices, and the local office would be the first bureaucratic level to investigate such complaints. It would also be responsible for making the NRA's first attempts to resolve the issue. Local compliance officials were instructed to exploit every possible avenue of obtaining a resolution to the issue before calling a formal hearing. If these means of conciliation were unsuccessful, the accused employer would be offered the opportunity to present his or her case formally to the local board. Still, the board had no real authority—the accused was not required to appear, and if the accused did appear, he or she could not be required by the board to answer any questions or submit any evidence. If the local board felt that the issue was still unresolved, it could report the incident to the complaints section of the Blue Eagle Division—or, after October 1933, the NRA Compliance Division—and send the case further up the bureaucratic line. Although the NRA had the authority to take the Blue Eagle away from firms, other legal penalties such as fines and jail time—Section 10(a) said that violations "shall be punishable by fine of not to exceed $500, or imprisonment for not to exceed six months, or both"—could only be imposed after a formal trial brought about by the Federal Trade Commission or the Department of Justice.

Despite the fact that the state and local recovery boards had received tens of thousands of complaints of violations, no Blue Eagles were taken away in the first ten weeks of the emblem's existence. The Roosevelt administration consistently implied that almost all the violations were simply "misunderstandings" and that after a friendly conversation or two with the local compliance board, the business owner generally realized his or her mistake and quickly rectified it. Of course, it was important for the administration to portray near universal enthusiasm and compliance, whether this was true or not, since the NIRA was largely operating under a system of voluntary compliance with no real enforcement. As Johnson wrote in his memoirs (1968, 255), for the program to work, "we had to have an aroused, militant, and almost unanimous opinion" in favor of the NIRA. Firms had to believe that the Blue Eagle was an important emblem—and specifically that consumers would indeed boycott them if the emblem were lost. And consumers had to believe that any firm displaying the Blue Eagle was patriotically complying with the program. If firms felt that they could cheat and continue to display the Blue Eagle emblem, there would be no expected losses to defecting from the wage and hours provisions embedded in the program. And if consumers felt that the Blue Eagle was being displayed by firms regardless of whether they were abiding by the NRA, they would be unlikely to allow the emblem to influence where they shopped.

By October 1933, there were concerns that the nation was on the precipice of an avalanche of noncompliance. At the beginning of the month, Charles Mynatt of Knoxville, Tennessee, voluntarily sent his store's Blue Eagle emblems back to the NIRA after he stopped complying with the grocer's code. Mynatt said that many Knoxville grocers were "chiselers" who were not abiding by the code and that the lack of punishment against these firms left him with no other choice than to cut his wages in order to compete in his market. Memphis district NRA director, W. B. Henderson, and chairman of the Knoxville Recovery Board, C. F. Holland, asked Mynatt's grocery store to display a "provisional" Blue Eagle even though he was not in compliance. Mynatt said that he put the Blue Eagle "back because I was asked to do so in the name of patriotism," but he continued to pay wages below the code level.[2] Episodes such as this one, where it was perceived that honest employers had to defect from the NRA/PRA to stay competitive with recalcitrant—and unpunished—firms, created bad public relations that ate away at the perception of an effective NRA enforcement mechanism.

The fact that volunteer local compliance boards were given such a prominent role in ensuring compliance also meant that there was a great deal of heterogeneity in these boards' actions. Leighton Peebles, liaison officer of the NRA district offices, visited local and district recovery boards across the nation to see how effectively they were maintaining compliance with the NIRA. Peebles noted in an October 17 memo to NRA assistant director Alvin Brown that in some parts of the country, "patriotic and able citizens have actively taken over the work" of effective compliance boards; however, in other cases, it was clear that Washington needed to send in help to give these boards direction.[3] Between October 5 and 10, Peebles visited recovery boards on the West Coast, and he expressed his impression of a highly effective organization in most Western cities. For example, Portland, Oregon, was reported to "have a fine organization and Compliance Boards are set up and running smoothly." Likewise, Peebles noted that compliance was high in Washington State, except for a "few sore spots" in Tacoma and Bellingham.

After his West Coast visit, Peebles flew to Chicago and found an entirely different situation. On October 13, he met with representatives of the Chicago district office and discovered that, unlike most other cities where local volunteer boards were active, Chicago's city board had not yet even met. Fortuitously, the seven members of the board were to have their inaugural meeting that afternoon so Peebles attended. He reported that the board "did not appear to have a full realization of their responsibilities. Most members seemed to feel that the position was one from which they would get favorable publicity." Peebles noted that "the Chicago situation is one of apathy . . . which has brought about a bad psychological effect. There has been no consumer check-up and no employer check-up. The situation has gone so far that a popular song has been paraphrased as 'Who's Afraid of the N.R.A.'"

By early October, it was clear that the NRA needed to add some bite to its bark. On October 10, use of the Blue Eagle emblem was stripped from Theodore G. Rahutis, owner of a restaurant in Gary, Indiana. Johnson announced that every one of Rahutis's forty employees had complained that the restaurant was violating the NRA's wage and hour provisions—one employee noted that he was being paid only 14 cents per hour.[4] The next day, the Blue Eagle was similarly taken from Betty Wilmer, owner of the Crystal Beauty Shop, and Marice Rapaport, manager of the Shop-Town Market, both in New Rochelle, New York. The NRA did all it could to make sure that these three actions were front-page news—and, indeed, stories appeared in newspapers across the nation. The government claimed that each of these employers had flagrantly violated the PRA and had ignored repeated warnings from state and local compliance boards. Wilmer was allegedly paying her two beauty salon employees only nine dollars per week, well below the program's minimum. Rapaport was said to have failed to maintain both the PRA's minimum wage and maximum hour provisions. Some of Rapaport's employees alleged that they were compelled to work twelve to thirteen hours per day during the week, and sixteen to seventeen hours on Fridays and Saturdays. Rahutis was likewise said to be violating the wage and hour provisions of the PRA.

Hugh Johnson's letters to the three alleged violators stated: "You will immediately cease displaying the Blue Eagle and surrender any NRA insignia in your possession to the postmaster. . . . You will refrain from using the Blue Eagle in any advertising or in any other manner."[5] Rather than come into compliance, Wilmer simply handed over her Blue Eagles the following day. Rapaport responded that he was "happy to cooperate." The Shop-Town Market was essentially a minimall that leased areas to nine concessions, and Rapaport said that he was under the impression that each concession in Shop-Town was individually responsible for abiding by the PRA. Now that things had been clarified, he said he would "make it my business to make sure that each concessionaire lives up to his agreement."[6] Rahutis likewise he said he would "take immediate steps to regain our status with the administration," suggesting that he feared economic losses from not being allowed to display the Blue Eagle.[7]

In response to the first wave of Blue Eagle removals, the Detroit Free Press editorial page predicted that the Blue Eagle would continue to "give its claws some exercise in the next few weeks." The editorial continued: "Code violations have ceased to be a joke and can no longer be attributed to misunderstandings or good intentions gone wrong. . . . The time has come when the NRA must either prove its authority or admit that the chiselers will be allowed to get away with anything."[8] In fact, the editorial was correct; these three cases of the Blue Eagle's removal were but the opening salvo in a crackdown on noncompliance. Over the next twenty months, the NRA Field Division records suggest that the Blue Eagle was ordered removed 2,914 times—that is, an average of five emblems per day between October 1933 and May 1935 (Duvall 1936, 41). Furthermore, on October 14, Roosevelt issued an executive order that made the false display of the Blue Eagle punishable by fines or imprisonment.[9] Additionally, on October 25, the NRA created a new Compliance Division. The Blue Eagle enforcement mechanism was attempting to demonstrate that it indeed had claws.

The Role of Code Authorities in Compliance

The Blue Eagle Division (and after October 24, 1933, the NRA Compliance Division) under which the district, state, and local recovery boards operated, had total responsibility for the enforcement for the PRA. However, when an industry had a code of fair competition in place, the first line of compliance with respect to trade practice provisions was to be the code authority—that is, the group that was (in the vast majority of approved codes) set up to administer the code. Alleged violations of trade practice provisions were to be directed first to the code authority and that body would attempt to bring "adjustment"—the term the NRA used for settling the dispute between the complainant and the accused—to the situation through education and "the pressure of opinion within the industry" (Galvin, Reinstein, and Campbell 1936, 14). If the code authority was unable to adjust the situation, then the NRA compliance infrastructure would become involved, and the NRA made it clear that the code authorities were to be "adjustment agencies," not enforcement agencies. Alleged violations of labor provisions were supposed to fall under the purview of the NRA rather than the code authorities; however, in practice, code authorities sometimes did try to bring about adjustments for violations of wages and hours provisions as well.

As an example of the role code authorities played in compliance issues, consider the case of the Adamstown Hat Company. The hat manufacturing code stated: "Each member of the Industry shall furnish properly certified reports" on wages, hours, number of employees, production, stocks on hand to the code authority. It also vested the hat manufacturing code authority the right to make "investigations . . . in order to determine whether or not any member of the Industry is violating any provision of this Code."[10] To this end, on April 12, 1934, the code authority sent Max Pollack to investigate Adamstown Hat in Adamstown, Pennsylvania. Pollack was given access to company records on payroll and hours for the two weeks ending April 10.[11] In an affidavit, Pollack noted that the records he observed showed every employee worked exactly forty hours per week—the maximum allowed by the code. Pollack asked the company's secretary, H. N. Redcay, several follow-up questions and took detailed notes, during which time Redcay "acted very nervous." Pollack noted that he laid his portfolio down and asked if he could use the company's bathroom—his intention was to allow Redcay to see his notes documenting his strong suspicions in hopes of bringing forth a confession.

When Pollack returned, he said that his notes appeared to have been disturbed and that Redcay was very agitated. Pollack asked the secretary whether he had any other records to share, and Redcay "went to a filing cabinet and took out a soft-cover book . . . as if to say I plead guilty and let us get this over with." The company had been working its employees more hours per week than the code allowed and had been keeping double records for the purpose of concealing this action. The code authority sent a memo on April 18, 1934, to Vincent Powers of the NRA office in Philadelphia documenting fifteen specific cases of employees of the Adamstown Hat Company who worked in excess of eighty hours for those two weeks, including six who had worked over one hundred hours. The memo said, "It appears beyond dispute that this company was violating the code [and] that the violation is deliberate and willful as it was attempted to be concealed by keeping false records." The memo concluded with the hope that these records and the enclosed affidavit from Pollack would "be sufficient for the purpose of any action you may desire to take against this company."[12] After these actions, the Adamstown Hat Company came into compliance and paid back wages to all its affected employees. On June 22, 1934, the NRA Compliance Division closed this case.

The NRA Compliance Division State Offices and Some Examples of Complaints Received

The twenty-six NRA district offices (corresponding to Department of Commerce districts) were the main compliance authority in fall 1933, but a 1936 report on the history of compliance under the NIRA noted that they were "greatly undermanned . . . [sometimes] there were but two people actually handling the complaints which were pouring in at a rate of 70 to 80 per week" (Galvin, Reinstein, and Campbell 1936, 17). Therefore, beginning in January 1934, a "state director" system was formed whereby each state set up an Office of the State Director of the National Emergency Council; some large states such as California and New York were divided into multiple regions and so had more than one state office. Each state office would have a labor compliance officer and a trade practice compliance officer as well as a legal advisor and an office manager—although the positions of office manager and trade practice compliance officer were often filled by the same person. State offices regularly employed field adjusters who were tasked with visiting firms to attempt to bring about compliance. The state compliance directors had the authority to order the removal of the Blue Eagle emblem, and they could choose to send a case along to the national Compliance Division in Washington, where litigation could potentially be pursued involving fines and imprisonment.

Citizens or employees wishing to submit allegations of violations of the NRA/PRA could find official complaint forms at post offices. The forms were to be sent by mail to the appropriate state (or, prior to 1934, regional) office.

However, many complaints were simply letters or post cards addressed to "NRA, Washington," or even to President Roosevelt. As an example of one of these complaints, on November 22, 1933, James Brady of Waterloo, Iowa, wrote, "I wish to report the Waterloo Steam Laundry, Park Ave. and Jefferson St of Waterloo, IA, and the Rather Packing Company of East Waterloo, Iowa as not abiding in the NRA rules in hours, pay, or no. of employees. They both are displaying the NRA emblem." In another example, on September 3, 1933, Clarita Adams of 142nd Street, New York City, wrote that her husband was employed as an elevator operator at 235 Fort Washington Avenue, New York, and that he was working nine hours a day, seven days a week for a wage of forty-five dollars per month—an hourly wage of 17 cents. Adams asked that "my name be withheld for it would mean he would be discharged" if the employer found out the source of the complaint.[13]

Daryl Williams of Columbus, Ohio, submitted a complaint on September 6, 1933, on the letterhead of the Dixie Laundry Company of 196 East State Street. "I am a laundry truck driver for the above company and I work between 53 and 60 hours every week at the salary of $8 per week. They have signed the NRA code and have regulated every salary but mine. At the Columbus NRA headquarters, they told me to write my complaint to Washington which I am doing. Waiting for results." Williams was sent a reply two weeks later from John Moore, chief of the complaints section of the Blue Eagle Division in Washington. Moore's reply stated: "Local NRA Compliance Boards are being organized in every community. The Board for Columbus will be ready to hear complaints very shortly—it is probably ready now . . . the subject of your letter should be placed before your local board."[14] Correspondence such as this—local boards instructing complainants to write to Washington and then Washington writing back to complainants instructing them to take the case to their local board—certainly contributed to the NRA being given the nickname "National Run Around."

The state or local compliance office was to handle complaints as follows: If the office felt that the complaint had validity, the first step was generally to mail a letter to the alleged violator outlining the allegation and including a copy of the industry code, noting the specific provision that the firm was said to be violating. The alleged violator would be asked to respond by mail with a written statement of its position. If the state office did not receive a response after a reasonable amount of time, the letter and copy of the code would be sent again, this time by registered mail. If the firm owner admitted to the violation but could show evidence that he or she was now in compliance and that restitution had been paid (for example, back wages if the violation was paying less than the code minimum), the firm owner would be asked to sign a certificate of compliance, which was an agreement to continue comply in the future. At that point, the case would be considered "adjusted" and hence closed. If the firm owner denied any violation, then he or she would be invited to "appear at the office of the state director and state his case."[15] If the matter was still not resolved in the opinion of the state director's office, the director could assign a field adjuster to visit to the firm. If the field adjuster's visit was not successful in achieving compliance, the state office would send a threatening letter to the firm owner that stated: "Unless the respondent furnishes satisfactory evidence of compliance within a certain number of days, the case will be forwarded to the National Compliance Director in Washington for appropriate action."[16]

Ultimately, if no resolution was reached at the local level, the state director could choose to forward all materials related to the case to the NRA Compliance Division in Washington, DC. The national NRA authorities could undertake actions along the lines of those outlined above to try to bring adjustment. If such adjustment could not be attained, the case could be referred to the National Compliance Board, which then had four options: (1) Undertake further actions to try to attain adjustment, (2) call for a public hearing in the case, (3) remove the Blue Eagle and publicize this fact, and/or (4) recommend to the NRA administrator that the case be referred to the Department of Justice or the Federal Trade Commission, which could then bring criminal charges that could lead to the fines or jail time stipulated in the NIRA.[17] This system was hardly one of swift justice. Complaints could go on for weeks or months with nothing more than threatening letters arriving in the violator's mailbox.

Quantifying Complaints and Enforcement Actions

Between October 1933 and May 1935, the state offices of the NRA Compliance Division docketed 123,192 cases of alleged labor violations and 36,977 cases of alleged violations of code trade practice provisions. It also docketed another 5,933 cases of violations related to the President's Reemployment Agreement. These numbers exclude another 7,136 cases that the state offices referred to the national Compliance Division in Washington—cases that will be discussed separately. Additionally, these 166,000 docketed cases do not include complaints that were originally received and acted on by code authorities. Furthermore, it is important to note that these statistics reflect only reported violations—widespread violations could exist in absence of formal complaints if complaints were viewed as a waste of time due to a lack of any hope of enforcement.

The NRA classified each of these docketed cases into four categories: ad-

TABLE 6.1. Cases Accepted for Investigation by
NRA Compliance Division, 1933 to 1935

	Labor	Trade practice
Docketed	123,192	36,977
Adjusted	50,240	19,674
No violation found	47,312	8,094
Dropped	14,663	5,295
Pending	10,977	3,914

Notes: These numbers do not reflect the 7,136 cases
in which the state Compliance Division referred
a case that it was unsuccessful in adjusting to the
national NRA Compliance Division. Additionally,
they do not include the 5,933 cases of violation of
the President's Reemployment Agreement.

Source: Galvin, Reinstein, and Campbell (1936,
167).

justed, no violation found, dropped, or pending. Adjusted cases were those in
which the firm came into compliance after NRA action as outlined above (letters, visits from a field adjuster, etc.). Cases classified as dropped were those
where a violation was found and the case was not successfully adjusted; however, the case was considered unsuitable for litigation by the Federal Trade
Commission or Department of Justice—typically because of a lack of evidence of interstate commerce, the violation was minor, or the violator was
a very small firm and unimportant in its industry (Galvin, Reinstein, and
Campbell 1936, 165). Many of these cases were dropped after the state director ordered the removal of the Blue Eagle. Pending cases were those that had,
by the time of the May 1935 *Schechter* decision, been investigated sufficiently
to disclose the nature of the violation (i.e., they were not classified as "no violation") but were neither classified as dropped nor adjusted, nor were they
sent on to the national office for potential litigation. Thus, it is reasonable to
say that pending cases were those where a violation was likely still occurring.
Table 6.1 breaks down the complaints into these categories.

The NRA was often able to successfully adjust cases of violations through
education or threats of further action if the violations continued. Around
67 percent of the cases that were both docketed and found to be in violation
were successfully adjusted (this number is around 62 percent if we consider
the 7,136 cases that are uncounted here but that state offices referred to the
national office because they were unable to attain a successful adjustment).
Still, these numbers suggest that there were around 37,000 cases where vio-

lations were indeed found to have occurred and the offending firm was not brought into compliance.

The NRA state offices tried to respond to complaints in a timely manner. Of the 118,675 labor violation cases that were investigated (i.e., dropping 4,515 pending cases that the NRA classified as not having been fully investigated), in 14.5 percent of cases, the NRA took its first action (most likely a letter to the violator) on the day of receipt. In nearly 40 percent of cases, action was taken within two days of receipt of the complaint. In only about 13 percent of the cases did it take more than two weeks before the first action was taken.[18] In terms of the length of time between the date of first action and the closing of the case (these numbers do not account for any of the cases that were pending in May 1935), around 23 percent of the cases were closed within six days of action. However, 40 percent of the cases took more than a month to close after the first action was taken, and over 12 percent of cases took three months or more to close.[19]

Table 6.2 reports the methods through which successful adjustments were attained in labor code cases. Clearly person to person visits were far more effective than just sending letters or telegrams. A visit by a field adjuster to the place of business was by far the most common way to bring about compliance, as this method was reported as bringing about the success in 58 percent of the adjusted cases. A conference between the violator and an NRA official in the local office was cited as the method of bringing about compliance in nearly 22 percent of adjusted cases. In fewer than 15 percent of the adjusted cases was postal correspondence with the accused the means that brought this adjustment.

TABLE 6.2. Method of Bringing About Successful Adjustment in Labor Code Violation Cases

Method of closing with adjustment	Number of cases	Percentage
Total of all methods	49,785	100
Field adjuster visit	28,959	58.2
Office conference	10,811	21.7
Correspondence	7,381	14.8
Code authority	1,489	3.0
State or local adjustment board	500	1.0
Unknown or other	645	1.3

Source: Galvin, Reinstein, and Campbell (1936, 208), Table 12, "NRA State Office Complaint Statistics Method of Closing, Labor Code Cases, Total All Offices, October 1933–May 1935."

The NRA broke down the complaints received in the state office by each of the 557 industry codes. The restaurant (14,644 complaints) and food and grocery industries (13,620 complaints) were the two that had the most complaints of labor violations. In fact, these two industries accounted for around 23 percent of all labor violation complaints (Galvin, Reinstein, and Campbell 1936, 195). Violations were most commonly reported for small firms with between two and five employees (22,083 complaints) and for firms with between six and ten employees (12,144 complaints), while only 497 complaints were made against firms with 200 employees or more (Galvin, Reinstein, and Campbell 1936, 197). Perhaps large corporations were less likely to violate the labor provisions of their codes because they feared the negative publicity and blowback from a violation more so than a small mom-and-pop restaurant that may have been in a better position to skate under the public radar while being investigated or censured.

The NRA Statistics Division also sorted complaints into categories of the alleged violation. For example, out of a total of 121,157 labor provisions complaints handled in state offices, 57,684 (47.6 percent) were related to violations of maximum hours, and 58,039 (47.9 percent) were wage violations. Of the remaining 4.5 percent of violations, by far the most common involved the failure of a firm to post its code's labor provisions in the place of business. It is interesting to note that there were only 316 complaints against the use of child labor—indeed, it appears that most firms strictly abided by the NIRA's outlawing of the use of child labor. The NRA additionally reported numbers in each category of cases that were successfully adjusted. For complaints about wage violations, 70.2 percent of cases were successfully adjusted. For complaints about hours, 68.9 percent of cases were successfully adjusted. Thus, the success rates in adjusting these two types of provisions were largely the same.

With respect to 36,977 cases related to trade practice provisions, some of the docketed cases were classified as containing multiple distinct violations so that the NRA recorded a total of 41,197 total violations. The most common alleged violation was related to failure to comply with price filing provisions, which accounted for 9,313 of the total. The second most common alleged violation was the failure to file statistics with the code authority—these accounted for 7,298 cases. Violations of sales below costs were reported 5,454 times. There were 1,538 reported cases related to misuse of NRA labels or insignia, such as the failure to adhere Blue Eagle emblems to products or packaging. There were 99 reported violations of exceeding machine and plant hour limitations as well as 84 reported violations of production control provisions such as quotas.[20]

Geographically, the number of labor complaints docketed is broken down by each of the fifty-four state offices (recall that some populous states were broken into multiple offices).[21] New York City appears to have been a hotbed of labor violations (or at least complaints), as it had 13,718 cases docketed. This accounted for 11.6 percent of all docketed labor violation cases in the United States, while the city's population accounted for only around 5.6 percent of the nation's total population according to the 1930 census. Furthermore, New York City had a relatively poor record of successfully adjusting these labor provision cases. Only 57 percent of the docketed cases were either adjusted or reported no violation. In the rest of the country, 85.5 percent of all docketed cases were either adjusted or reported no violation. The state office with the second most docketed labor cases was Massachusetts, with 7,429. But 45.1 percent of these cases found no violation, and another 48.6 percent were successfully adjusted. Only 6.3 percent of docketed Massachusetts cases continued in violation or were pending at the time of the *Schechter* decision. Vermont had by far the fewest docketed labor complaints, with 132 — and 77 percent of these were either adjusted or there was no violation found.

Summary of Cases Related to the President's Reemployment Agreement. The state offices of the NRA Compliance Division also handled complaints dealing with the President's Reemployment Agreement. Most of this work occurred during the fall of 1933, but some industries were never covered by a code of fair competition, so these complaints were arriving up until the *Schechter* decision of May 27, 1935. There were a total of 5,933 docketed cases of violations of the PRA.[22] In many cases, the firm that was the subject of the complaint was allegedly violating both the wage and hour provisions of the PRA, so these cases contained a total of 9,921 violations — 4,765 violations of hours and 5,012 violations of wage provisions (plus an additional 144 "general" violations). The NRA had a fairly strong record of adjusting these cases: 79.6 percent of the hours violations and 72.7 percent of the wage violations were adjusted; the rest were dropped or pending, suggesting that violations likely continued. The NRA was able to secure $204,184 of restitution pay from violations of the PRA to 7,497 employees.[23]

Summary of Cases Referred to the NRA Compliance Division in Washington. I turn now to the 7,136 cases that were referred by the state offices to the NRA Compliance Division in Washington; this was a necessary step if litigation would be pursued to impose fines and jail time. Prior to the spring of 1934, the NRA showed little interest in pursuing judicial action. In the fall of 1933, some individuals brought (and won) cases against violators to courts seeking injunctions against actions in violation of codes and/or restitution. However, in December 1933, federal district judge Alexander Akerman ruled that the competitors of an alleged violator of the cleaning and dyeing industry code, Samuel Bazemore, lacked standing under the NIRA to bring a suit against Bazemore and that only the Justice Department could do so (Irons 1982, 36). In response, NRA general counsel Donald Richberg helped establish the NRA Litigation Division on March 26, 1934. Blackwell Smith, who had been serving as the NRA's top lawyer, was named director of enforcement for the division, and the division had over one hundred lawyers in its employment. The strategies of Smith and the NRA lawyers will be discussed shortly, but first a quantitative overview of these 7,136 docketed cases will be instructive.

According to the NRA statistical section, about half (3,634) of these cases were "closed by administrative action"—meaning that either a successful adjustment had been achieved or the NRA lawyers had simply decided that the case was not worth their time. In 1,795 of these cases, the Blue Eagle was ordered removed by the Compliance Division in Washington (Galvin, Reinstein, and Campbell 1936, 235). Since a total of 2,914 emblems were removed over the course of the NRA, we can infer that these additional 1,119 removals were ordered by state or local offices in the Compliance Division. Of the 7,136 cases, 2,064 were referred to the Litigation Division with recommendations for court action. Though I am unaware of any breakdown of the data in this manner, it is likely that most of the 1,795 cases of Blue Eagle removal were among these cases referred to the Litigation Division. In most of the files that I have seen in which a case was referred to the Litigation Division, the Blue Eagle was ordered removed at the time of this referral. Of the 2,064 cases referred to the Litigation Division, 564 reached court (Hursey et al. 1936, 54). According to a 1936 report from the NRA Division of Review, "These figures demonstrate clearly that there was a pronounced lack of litigation which should have been instituted in support of the compliance program [as this had] a very depressing effect on compliance and contributed in a material degree to the failure of code administration" (Hursey et al. 1936, 54).

The NRA Lawyers' "Machiavellian" Approach to Litigation

With hundreds of cases to choose from, Blackwell Smith's Litigation Division had to carefully select appropriate targets. Most of the violations that came to the attention of the Litigation Division involved small firms. After all, the NRA codes that covered large industries were generally drafted by big business and hence these concerns were largely content to abide by the codes that they had written. It was the small competitor that may have had a different cost structure and thus may have been more severely impacted that was, ceteris paribus, more likely to defect from its code's wage and hour or trade practice provisions (Alexander, 1997).

Smith outlined his litigation strategy in an April 9, 1934, memo to his staff titled "Objective: Results; Methods in General: Machiavellian—The End Justifies the Means (Almost)." [24] The end objective was, of course, to make firms and consumers believe that the NRA enforcement mechanism was a powerful one and that defections would spell trouble for firms. The means were to be a combination of "threats" and "tricks" that would "bring swift justice to locally known chiselers." Essentially Smith's approach was what Peter Klein and I (Taylor and Klein 2008) call a "pick your battles wisely" strategy of pursuing litigation in only those cases where there was clear evidence of egregious violations *and* where these firms resided in districts with judges who were more likely to rule in favor of the NRA—such a combination would lead to the highest likelihood of successful court verdicts.[25] The NRA would then provide maximum publicity to these selectively chosen litigation actions to give the illusion that punishment of violators was widespread and swift.

By June 1934, the Litigation Division had filed 201 cases in thirty-five states, and it would file around 600 cases in total. The Department of Justice or Federal Trade Commission was the official prosecutor, but NRA lawyers were often allowed to handle aspects of the preparation and courtroom arguments.[26] The majority of these cases were not yet resolved at the time of the *Schechter* decision in May 1935; however, in the cases that had concluded before *Schechter*, the NRA prevailed in 90 percent of them, most through pretrial settlements. In the sixty cases decided in district courts, forty-two resulted in a ruling in favor of the NRA (Irons 1982, 55). In percentage terms, the NRA's record looks strong, but when we consider the raw numbers, these victories represented well less than one-tenth of one percent of the 160,000 alleged violations of the program.

Some Examples from the NRA Litigation Case Files

This section provides a small sample of cases that were referred to the NRA Litigation Division. Each case details the attempts that were made to secure compliance both before and after the case was referred to Washington. These summaries are assembled from digests that were compiled in late 1935, after the *Schechter* decision. In addition to documenting the details of each case, the government digester also reflected on what problems plagued the case and how the situation could have been improved.

The Belcher Case, Alabama. The code authority for the lumber and tim-

ber products code (passed August 19, 1933) was the Southern Pine Association (SPA). The SPA filed a complaint on September 7, 1933, against William
Belcher, of Centreville, Alabama, owner of nine small lumber mills with about
fifty employees in total, stating that Belcher was not abiding by the wage and
hours provisions of the lumber code, nor was he abiding by the production
and pricing stipulations of the code.[27] A preliminary conference was held by
the SPA—as noted earlier, in cases where an industry had an approved code
in place, the first layer in the compliance and enforcement armor was the code
authority. Belcher said his reason for noncompliance was that he could not
stay in business if he paid code wages and that he was unable to sell his lumber at the high code prices. Since the SPA was unable to get Belcher to comply
with the code, it forwarded the case to the NRA national compliance director.
On December 11, the NRA stripped Belcher of the right to display the Blue
Eagle and referred the case to the Department of Justice. The *New York Times*
reported that Belcher was accused of working his men "unlimited hours and
paying 15 cents an hour."[28] This was the third case that the NRA had referred
to the Department of Justice for prosecution; the first and second cases had
related to firms in the coal industry.

On December 26, 1933, the NRA's chief lawyer, Blackwell Smith, asked
that the Department of Justice postpone action on the Belcher case for several
months since he did not want to risk a negative court decision, which could
harm or kill the NIRA. On April 14, 1933, the Justice Department asked the
US district attorney to proceed with the case, and on April 23, a grand jury
issued an indictment against the Belcher. On August 24, supplemental indict-
ments were issued related not only to wage and hours violations but to violations of production control, cost protection, and failure to file reports with the
code authority. On October 31, 1934, a demurrer was filed and was sustained.
On December 12, 1934, Alexander McKnight of the NRA Litigation Division
urged the Department of Justice to proceed with the case, and on January 15,
1935, Smith also said he wanted the case pushed along. Despite these pleas,
the Department of Justice did not pursue the case any further before the May
1935 *Schechter* decision, which ruled the NIRA unconstitutional. The government official who digested this case in August 1935, A. W. DeBirny, noted that
there were "too many cooks—Department of Justice and N.R.A.; also District
Attorneys." DeBirny suggested that the process could have been improved by
"Elimination of divided responsibility for enforcement."

Supreme Instruments Case, Mississippi. The Supreme Instruments Company was a relatively small corporation with 150 employees located in Greenwood, Mississippi. On December 13, 1933, the Greenwood postmaster filed
a complaint saying that he felt it his duty to report that the firm "had never

signed up on the NRA."[29] On December 16, the district compliance director requested that the postmaster provide specific instances of violations. The postmaster noted the company's defiant attitude toward the NIRA, but again he did not provide any specific evidence of violations. Thus, the NRA took no further action. However, on April 12, 1934, six employees of Supreme Instruments filed complaints about specific violations of wage and hour provisions. Nine days later, the NIRA sent Supreme a letter outlining the complaints and asking the company to come into compliance with the electrical manufacturing code. Having received no response, the NRA sent a follow-up letter on May 4 reminding the firm of its duty to comply with the code, including the filing of prices as specified by the code.

The firm replied that to file prices with the electrical manufacturing code authority would be "suicidal" since an officer of the authority was the firm's principle competitor and the company believed that it was this competitor's intention to use the code to put Supreme out of business. Furthermore, the company said that it could not comply with the code wage scale because doing so would force it out of business. (It had filed a petition for an exemption to the NRA wages and hours in August 1933 but had been denied.) Finally, the firm believed that it actually fell under the scientific apparatus industry code, which had been approved on November 14, 1933, rather than the electrical manufacturing code of August 4, 1933. The scientific apparatus code allowed a forty-hour week at fifteen dollars, while the electrical manufacturing code required a thirty-six-hour week for fifteen dollars. On July 16, 1934, the NRA sent a letter insisting that Supreme was indeed subject to the electrical manufacturing code.

A field adjuster was sent to the firm on August 14, 1934. Because this still did not result in compliance in wages and hours, a hearing before the Mississippi Adjustment Board was held on August 20. Representatives of the firm were present, and they admitted that the firm was in violation of the electrical manufacturing code. The board ordered that restitution of back wages be paid from July 31, 1934—which was fairly generous to the firm given that it had been in violation of the wage provisions for over a year—and that the firm immediately come into compliance with the electrical manufacturing code provisions. On August 23, sixty-one employees of Supreme Instruments filed a petition on behalf of their employer asking that the company be allowed to continue under the current wage scale. Apparently, they were worried that if the company had to pay higher hourly wage, it would go out of business and they would lose their jobs.

Because the firm still did not come into compliance, the NRA's national office held a hearing on December 3, 1934. Supreme did not send a representative to the hearing, and the entire file was reviewed by the NRA Compliance Division. At the conclusion of the hearing, the NRA stripped Supreme Instruments of the right to display the Blue Eagle emblem and referred the case to the Litigation Division. On February 4, 1935, an attorney from the Litigation Division advised the Mississippi state director that the case would receive attention soon. However, on February 11, the NRA was asked to withhold action due to the death of the company's president. In March, NRA Litigation Division lawyers expressed doubt that Supreme Instruments truly did fall under the electrical manufacturing code and that the firm was probably correct that it belonged under the scientific apparatus code after all. On April 6, 1935, the NRA Litigation Division said that it would not pursue the case further.

The government official who prepared the digested summary of this case, William L. Pencke, claimed that "a more generous view of the entire situation and handled by a higher administrative officer would have avoided a great deal of unpleasantness." Pencke noted that Supreme's employees seemed satisfied with their working conditions and that a member of the local NRA compliance board, a member of Congress, and a member of the chamber of commerce had all spoken in favor of the company and that this should have been given more weight. He also noted, "There is no doubt that this concern, employing 150 people . . . would have closed its doors had a suit been filed in Federal Court."

Goodman Case, Pennsylvania. On December 14, 1933, one of Michael Goodman's twenty-four employees filed a complaint that Goodman's Souderton, Pennsylvania, firm was violating the minimum wage provisions of the silk textile industry code. The government's digest of the case notes that the state director appeared to have done little or nothing to secure adjustment before sending the case along to the NRA Compliance Division in Washington.[30] The case was finally considered by the Compliance Division in a hearing on October 4, 1934. Goodman was held in violation of the code, "and after protracted correspondence by the state director and Compliance Division, [the firm] refused to make any restitution." Goodman claimed that he had a financial inability to pay back wages, but he said he would come into compliance with wages and hours going forward. After three months of attempts to get Goodman to pay back wages, the NRA ordered Goodman to cease displaying the Blue Eagle and said it would refer the case to the NRA Litigation Division for potential prosecution. This was done on January 18, 1935. On February 2, an attorney of the NRA requested the state director investigate whether Goodman was still violating the wage and hours provisions. On February 23, the state office replied that Goodman was in a "precarious financial condition" but that he had been complying since the October hearing. On

March 1, 1935, the case was closed by the NRA. The government official who digested the case, L. M. Barkin, wrote that the "Delay in obtaining restitution for approximately 3 months after the case was heard by the Compliance Council was not excusable . . . when the case was forwarded to the Enforcement Division, violations were almost a year old." Barkin suggested the process could have been improved by the "Elimination of delays in adjustment efforts" by the NRA at all levels.

High Ice Cream Company Case, Virginia. On April 17, 1934, an employee of the L. W. High Ice Cream Company of Richmond, Virginia, filed a complaint against this company saying that it was not abiding by the restaurant industry code's hours and wage provisions.[31] High responded that its competitors in the area were also violating the code, and it claimed that the employees in question were misclassified by the NRA. The code said that non-service workers would receive a minimum of $14 for a fifty-four-hour week, while the minimum for service workers, who would presumably receive tips, was $10.25.[32] Since the local compliance authorities could not successfully adjust the case, it was sent to the national Compliance Division in Washington on July 20, 1934. A hearing was held on September 26, 1934, and a representative for High was present. The NRA found the company to be in violation and ordered restitution be paid to its underpaid workers. High and its lawyers continued to dispute the interpretation of the classification, and the company did not paid restitution. Therefore, on November 16, 1934, the NRA ordered the Blue Eagle removed and referred the High case to the Litigation Division. A lawyer at the Litigation Division suggested that the case should be prosecuted under the Virginia State Recovery Act—Virginia was one of twelve states that passed legislation complementary to the NRA that could impose fines of up to $500 per violation on firms engaged in intrastate commerce (Heinemman 1981, 92). However, no further action was taken. The digester of the case wrote, "It seems this file was misplaced, and that no action thereon was ever taken." In the section asking for suggestions for improvement, the digester suggested a better "check up on files assigned to attorneys."

The Danger to Employees Who Filed Complaints

A major problem that the NRA faced was hesitancy among employees to file complaints against their employers for fear of retaliation. Many letter writers outlining complaints were careful to ask that their name be withheld for fear of being discharged. As an example, in a letter from November 20, 1933, addressed to the NRA's Hugh Johnson, Samuel Hoffman of the Bronx, New York, wrote that because of his public complaint against his employer of violating the NRA's wage standards, "all New York employers boycott me and thus I am faced with absolute starvation. Having to feed and clothe a family of eight . . . I humbly plead with you to kindly do something on my behalf."[33] The NRA responded with a letter dated December 1 that stated: "It is most unfortunate that retaliatory action on the part of the employer should be directed against you." The letter went onto say that the "Administration is doing everything in its power to prevent conditions such as you describe."

Five and a half months later, on May 15, 1934, Roosevelt issued Executive Order 6711, which forbade the dismissal or demotion of an employee in response to his or her report of an NRA violation. Shortly after this order was instituted, a complaint was filed in the Louisiana state office.[34] When the employer was notified of the complaint, he addressed all of his employees and said that unless the person who filed the complaint confessed to it, the entire shop would suffer. The employee who filed the complaint identified himself and was discharged. In response to this violation of the executive order, the Louisiana NRA adjustment board voted unanimously to recommend that unless the employer rehired the worker and paid back wages within five days, the case would be referred to Washington for possible prosecution. The employer refused to comply. After several conferences, the case was sent along to the NRA Litigation Division, where it sat for several weeks without action. During this time, the Louisiana state office sent several letters and telegrams urging the Litigation Division to take action. The case was finally referred to the district attorney. Several more weeks lapsed with no action—in fact, there is no record that any action was ever taken by that office. The frustrated state office decided to at least pursue the removal of the Blue Eagle emblem. Over seven months after the employee was discharged, the case was referred to the regional office in Atlanta and a hearing was held. The Regional Compliance Council voted to remove the Blue Eagle from the firm and refer the case back to the Litigation Division. No action was taken on the file, however, prior to the *Schechter* decision; the file had a notation that "no interstate commerce was shown" and, hence, the case was not eligible for prosecution. Needless to say, the worker was never reinstated.

Summary and Discussion

This chapter has outlined the NRA's complex system of enforcement. The chief weapon that the NRA had at its disposal was the threat of removing the Blue Eagle emblem. But this step was only taken after weeks—or, more likely, months—of pressure applied by letters, telegrams, visits from field adjusters, or hearings at local NRA offices. The NRA could recommend government prosecution, and the text of the NIRA noted that fines of up to $500 and imprisonment for up to six months could be imposed against violators. However, it was not until the spring of 1934 that the NRA even considered the path of litigation; mainly, it relied on local offices to cajole compliance from violators.

In total, around 166,000 cases of alleged violations were docketed by the NRA. Although the majority of these were successfully adjusted—that is, the violator was brought back into compliance—in about 37,000 cases, alleged violations were not successfully adjusted prior to the May 1935 *Schechter* decision. Of these cases, only about 3,000 resulted in removal of the Blue Eagle emblem, and only about 550 cases were actually brought to court. Thus, most violators of the NRA escaped any form of punishment. NRA lawyers were clearly worried about the effects that negative court decisions could have, so they employed a Machiavellian strategy of cherry-picking a few cases that they thought they could certainly win and then publicized those actions to make it appear that the emperor was wearing far more clothes than he, in fact, was.

While this chapter has focused much of its attention on quantifying the extent of violations and the NRA's success, or lack thereof, in bringing about adjustments, it has also provided some case studies of the NRA's attempts to punish firms that continued in violation long after the initial attempts to bring about adjustment had failed. These cases help illustrate, much more clearly than the raw numbers can, the important issues the NRA faced in trying to punish violators. The next chapter discusses the ramifications that the lack of enforcement had on compliance with the NRA. In fact, the program underwent a systematic "compliance crisis" in the winter and spring of 1934 after it became increasingly clear to firms that the NRA's bark was much worse than its bite.

The Economics of Compliance and Enforcement and the NRA Compliance Crisis

The previous chapter detailed the NRA compliance mechanism and showed that, despite its presence, tens of thousands of violations occurred. This chapter discusses the economic forces that drove firms' lack of compliance. In fact, the effectiveness of the NRA enforcement mechanism hinged largely on the economic power of the Blue Eagle emblem. As long as the emblem affected consumers' decisions on where to shop and firms believed that a defection from the NRA provisions would result in the loss of the emblem, compliance could generally be sustained. However, this chapter documents a systemic breakdown in compliance in early 1934—a breakdown that coincided with a decline in enthusiasm for the Blue Eagle. The chapter also explores the NRA's various attempts in the months following the compliance crisis to recapture the high level of respect that the government enforcement mechanism had enjoyed in the summer and fall of 1933.

A Microeconomic Model of Enforcement

The NIRA enforcement mechanism can be illustrated with a simple oligopoly model, and from this model we can glean insights into its workings and failings. Since the NIRA codes attempted to facilitate collusion, a cartel model is a suitable place to begin. When a cartel is successfully maintained, firms receive higher profits than they would under either perfect or Cournot competition. However, economic theory suggests that cartels often fail because, although collusion leads to a collectively better outcome for the firms, it is not individually rational—that is, any one firm does better by defecting from rather than complying with the cartel. This is always true in a one-shot or finitely repeated game, although collusion could potentially be sustained as a Nash equilibrium outcome in an infinitely repeated game so long as players do not discount future payoffs too much.

The stylized facts of the NIRA enforcement mechanism, however, add some important new components to the standard cartel model. First, complying firms had to increase wage rates. Second, firms that violated the NIRA risked possible fines and/or imprisonment. Third, violations could result in the loss of the Blue Eagle emblem, leading to a potential consumer boycott. Finally, firms that remained in compliance with the NIRA may have felt that they would gain additional "good patriot" payoffs from consumers who rewarded displays of the Blue Eagle.[1]

Consider first the simplest case of a one-period, n-firm symmetric Cournot game in which π^m is the industry's monopoly profit, $\pi_i^* = \pi^m/n$ represents firm i's payoff from successfully colluding, π_i^c is firm i's profit under Cournot competition, π_i^d is firm i's profit from defecting while the remaining $n - 1$ firms cooperate, and π_i^z is firm i's profit from cooperating while another firm defects. Under the standard assumptions that $\pi_i^d > \pi_i^*$ and $\pi_i^c > \pi_i^z$, firms have a dominant strategy to defect from the cartel. To make this easier to see, I will assume a market with two firms, a demand curve $P = 100 - Q$, and a constant marginal cost of 10 for each firm. In this case, the payoffs (rounded to the nearest 10) are reported in the two-player payoff matrix shown in figure 7.1. The Nash equilibrium is that each firm will defect, and the Cournot outcome of $900 of profit for each firm will be achieved.

The NIRA changes the payoffs in the following ways. First, let γ be the cost of complying with the NIRA codes—this primarily includes the cost of paying higher wages, but it could also include other compliance costs such as data reporting, the costs of using a less-than-optimal technology, and the additional cost of buying from NIRA-compliant supplier cartels. Let F be the expected value of the disutility from the government fine and prison sentence imposed on firms defecting from the cartel, and BE equal the expected cost of lost business from not being allowed to display the Blue Eagle when a firm has the right to display it taken away. Assume that defectors lose BE with expected probability θ_1 and F with expected probability θ_2 but avoid having to pay γ. Furthermore, when some firms comply with the NRA but others defect and lose the Blue Eagle, the firms in compliance gain additional business represented by GP (good patriot profits).[2] The payoff matrix now appears as shown in figure 7.2.

The firms will have a dominant strategy to abide by the NIRA codes so long as firm B

	Cooperate	Defect
Cooperate	1010 1010	1140 760
firm A	760	900
Defect	1140	900

FIGURE 7.1. Payoff Matrix under Cournot Competition

firm B

	cooperate	defect
cooperate	$1010-\gamma$ $1010-\gamma$	$1140- \theta_1 BE - \theta_2 F$ $760 +\theta_1 GP- \gamma$
firm A	$760 +\theta_1 GP- \gamma$	$900 - \theta_1 BE - \theta_2 F$
defect	$1140 - \theta_1 BE - \theta_2 F$	$900 - \theta_1 BE - \theta_2 F$

FIGURE 7.2. Payoff Matrix under the NIRA Codes

(1) $1010 - \gamma > 1140 - \theta_1 BE - \theta_2 F$

and

(2) $760 + \theta_1 GP - \gamma > 900 - \theta_1 BE - \theta_2 F.$

After rearrangement of terms, these expressions can be rewritten as

(3) $\theta_1 BE + \theta_2 F > 130 + \gamma$

and

(4) $\theta_1 BE + \theta_2 F + \theta_1 GP > 140 + \gamma.$

The left-hand side of inequality (3) represents the expected losses from defecting, and the right-hand side represents the expected gains from defecting when the other firm is maintaining compliance with the NRA codes. In inequality (4), the left-hand side represents the expected losses from defecting from the codes, and the right-hand side represents the expected gains from defecting when the other firm is also defecting.

Clearly, the decision to cooperate with the NRA codes in this model hinges on the perceived probabilities of enforcement with either removing the Blue Eagle or imposing fines or imprisonment (θ_1 and θ_2) as well as the perceived size of the BE and F penalties and the GP reward. Of course, F is essentially constant at a punishment of six months in prison and \$500, but it is important to note that θ_1, θ_2, BE, and GP are all variables that *change with beliefs*. Thus, we can see that if social pressure to abide by the codes of fair competition is high—giving the Blue Eagle compliance mechanism bite—the criminal punishment (F) from defecting, or its probability of being imposed (θ_2), need not be substantial. Ceteris paribus, a change from cooperation to defection could thus be caused by a change in firms' beliefs about of the cost of losing the Blue Eagle. Additionally, cooperation could change to defection if the firms' perceptions of the probabilities of losing the Blue Eagle when they violated the codes fell.

The NIRA was originally set to expire after two years, suggesting the program should be analyzed as a finitely repeated game. However, many business owners and policy makers expected the NIRA's cartel-enabling provisions to be renewed and maintained indefinitely. Given the uncertainty regarding the legislation's duration, it may be instructive to also view competition under the NIRA as an infinitely repeated game. Consider an n-firm infinitely repeated game in which firm i plays a grim trigger strategy (Friedman 1971): In period t, cooperate if all firms $j \neq i$ cooperated in period $t - 1$; otherwise, revert to Cournot output in period t and all subsequent periods. Furthermore, each firm faces a per-period discount rate of δ. Finally, assume that defection in period 1 yields π_i^d and that the punishments of fines, jail, and loss of the Blue Eagle occur beginning in period 2. Cooperation will be sustainable so long as the discounted payoff over time from cooperating when the other player is cooperating is higher than the discounted payoff from defecting when the other firm is cooperating, as shown in equation (5).

(5) $(1010 - \gamma)/(1 - \delta) > 1140 + (900 - \theta 1 BE - \theta 2 F)\delta/(1 - \delta),$

which can be rearranged to

(6) $\delta > [(130) + \gamma]/[(240) + \theta 1 BE + \theta 2 F].$

As in the one-shot or finitely repeated game, the NIRA enforcement mechanism's effectiveness depends on the relative magnitudes of θ_1, θ_2, BE, F, and γ. In both the one-shot and the infinitely repeated games, the likelihood of successful cartelization is increasing in θ_1, θ_2, BE, F and decreasing in γ. Of course, interest rates, to which the discount factor (δ) is directly related, also affect the ability to sustain collusion in a repeated game since the short-term gain from defecting increases as interest rates rise (and the long-term loss from being punished falls), ceteris paribus, making collusion more difficult to sustain. In fact, nominal interest rates remained relatively stable throughout the NIRA period, but the price level rose sharply and thus real interest rates fell. This should have made collusion easier to sustain as the NIRA went on, which is quite the opposite of what happened; in fact, collusion became less likely as the NIRA went on.

Public Attitude toward the NRA and the Blue Eagle over Time

The NRA seems to have been acutely aware that compliance hinged on the public's attitude toward the NRA (and the Blue Eagle emblem in particular), because it took great pains to not only promote the Blue Eagle but keep tabs on its standing in public opinion. Each NRA district (and beginning in January 1934, state) office sent standardized biweekly reports to Washington, which answered thirteen brief questions. One of these questions, and the one that often received the most attention in the answers, asked districts to provide a summary of the "Public attitude towards the President's plan." From these reports, it is clear that the public was behind the NRA and that the Blue Eagle emblem was a powerful economic symbol in the late summer and early fall of 1933. However, this enthusiasm waned significantly in the late fall and winter of 1933/1934. Furthermore, these reports directly point to the change in firms' and consumers' views of the probability of enforcement—which occurred after many defections went unpunished—as a major cause for the decline in the power of the Blue Eagle.

To illustrate, Detroit district compliance director A. J. Barnaud's reports to the NRA in August and September 1933 noted a highly favorable attitude toward the program and the Blue Eagle. Interestingly, his October 14 report stated that "Publicity given [to] cases where Blue Eagles have been ordered taken down has had [an] excellent effect."[3] As described in chapter 6, the first wave of the emblem's removals began on October 11. Along the same lines, Barnaud's report of November 18 noted that "support of lower courts . . . rendering judgements to underpaid employees to the balance due on their wages under the NRA has helped immensely in rendering better public attitude." This statement was in response to two cases decided in Detroit Common Pleas Court. On November 14, Judge Gerald W. Groat ruled in favor of Alex Rush against the owner of Bert's Bar-B-Q. Rush was awarded $70.80 in back wages because he had worked at the restaurant for a total of 384 hours after Bert's had signed the PRA, but he was paid only between 9.5 and 11 cents per hour. Judge Groat wrote, "Where codes have been signed and the Blue Eagle is displayed in a sign of compliance, there is a guarantee of minimum wage and that obligation must be respected."[4] In the second case, Judge Ralph W. Liddy ruled in favor of May Bethel, who had likewise sued her employer for violations of a signed NRA code.[5]

On December 30, Barnaud's public attitude report noted that the successful adjustments of many complaints in Detroit—particularly those involving the payment of back wages—had been carried out in the last week. Barnaud wrote, "When a man parts with his money he is convinced of one of two things: either the law has teeth or it is the right thing to do." In his January 13, 1934, report, Barnaud wrote that the Detroit office had found complaints "are more easily dealt with and this is undoubtedly the result of local and national publicity to the effect that the government means business when it comes to code compliance."

As the winter progressed and turned to spring, however, Barnaud's reports from the Detroit office became far less rosy. On March 17, Barnaud wrote, "The public had spotty reactions to the NRA [and] the situation is aggravated by [beliefs] that manufacturers are violating the code." In his April 14 report, Barnaud noted, "During the last three weeks the number of complaints arriving in this office has increased materially. . . . This tends to indicate that more firms . . . are not complying with the codes." On April 21, Barnaud highlighted the concerns of employees of small business, who have lost "faith in the NRA as a beneficial factor." Barnaud's May 19 report outlined the deleterious effects on public attitude of a scathing article in the *Detroit Free Press* titled "NRA in Retreat." On July 28, 1934, Barnaud noted that his office had received "considerable criticism in the press," and he reported "a decided increase in complaints filed, which indicates that firms are not continuing to live up to the provisions of the codes governing their industry." In his August 11 report, Barnaud wrote, "The criticism of the NRA is getting more severe as each day goes by." His August 25 report likewise noted, "The publicity in the press on the NRA continues to be severe and bitter. . . . We are of the opinion that it is materially affecting compliance." Interestingly, the memo included a handwritten note, clearly written by an administrator in the Washington office, stating, "Similar reactions reported from other offices."

In his November 17, 1934, report, Barnaud highlighted some good news: a decision in the NRA's favor by federal judge Raymond "has had, we feel, a beneficial effect on our compliance work [as it is] a warning to recalcitrants that the NRA does mean something in Michigan." The case Barnaud referred to involved Reginald S. French, a coat dealer from Caledonia, Michigan. French had been ruled in contempt of court for continuing to violate the

NRA's wage and hours provisions, but he objected on the grounds that the injunction was invalid. Judge Raymond upheld the contempt of court charge.[6]

In Louisville, Kentucky, NRA district manager Prentiss Terry's weekly reports to the NRA also indicated a waning of public attitude toward the program over time—although in this case, the decline began far earlier than it had in Detroit.[7] Throughout August and September, Terry reported high favorability, but on October 7, he wrote of "misapprehension and upsetting of mind" toward the NRA. Among other things, Terry noted, "There are those who are irritated because only Washington has authority with regard to enforcement of compliance." In his October 14 report, Terry wrote, "The general attitude towards the President's plan is becoming apathetic . . . the spirit of the Blue Eagle drive is waning." A week later, Terry wrote that some large concerns were considering "giving up their Eagles in order to meet competition of their competitors who are not flying the Eagle." Terry's November 4 report indicated that "people want teeth vested in compliance groups." He suggested that the NRA's current methods of "conciliation, mediation, and persuasion" should be replaced with "firmness" and that the codes "should be enforced." On November 18, Terry's report regarding public attitude was extremely blunt and brief: "The public wants to know whether those few who are inclined to ignore the provisions of permanent and temporary codes will be forced to comply with them." On November 25, Terry wrote, "What the NRA needs now more than anything else is an authority to enforce compliance with codes."

Throughout the next two months, Terry continued to hammer home the same point about the need for strict enforcement from the NRA. Beginning in late January, the reports from the Louisville office came from the newly organized state director's office, headed by J. R. Layman. Layman's reports also expressed hope of stronger enforcement to give the Blue Eagle more bite. For example, in his March 24, 1934, report Layman wrote, "There is an earnest desire for . . . speedy enforcement against those offenders who show no spirit of compliance." Layman's May 19 report noted the increase in "business to openly violate the provisions of the Codes governing their industries." In his July 28 report, Layman wrote, "The lack of power to enforce by court action compliance on the part of those who recognize no moral obligation toward their employees or toward the Government is retarding the problem of compliance considerably." In his August 11 report, Layman noted a sharp increase in complaints of violations and noted that employers were far less willing to work with NRA field adjusters than they previously had been.

In the Chicago office, district manager F. L. Roberts likewise expressed concerns about compliance. As early as his September 23, 1933, report, Roberts noted that the public's attitude was "Not as favorable lately due to failure to punish violators of the PRA."[8] Roberts's November 11 report noted that compliance boards in Illinois and Wisconsin were frustrated by the delay experienced with regard to their recommendations to Washington to remove Blue Eagles from area firms. In his December 2 report, Roberts wrote of "Increasing signs of dissatisfaction . . . in this district due to violators of the PRA not being penalized." He also reiterated that local compliance boards were extremely frustrated by Washington's unwillingness to act on their recommendations for removals of the Blue Eagle. Finally, on December 9, Roberts noted that the removal of several Blue Eagles in the area helped stem the rising tide of violations. Still, by March 10, the Chicago report noted that things had gotten so bad that even the removal of Blue Eagles had no appreciable effect on the business of those firms. On March 24, the attitude report put it bluntly: "The general public is not displaying any considerable interest in patronizing businesses . . . so far as the Blue Eagle is concerned." In a May 28, 1934, response to a questionnaire from Washington, the Chicago district answered the question, "Does the public give preference to Blue Eagle businesses?" with a direct, one-word answer: "No."

Similar to other districts, the reports from the San Francisco office generally showed high approval for the NRA and the Blue Eagle in the summer and early fall of 1933.[9] On September 30, the report by district manager E. Tildon Mattox revealed the first small chink in the armor when he wrote that lack of local authority "to settle cases of noncompliance [is] believed, in some quarters, to be conducive to laxity on the part of employers to live up to the PRA." While conditions were reported as largely favorable over the rest of the fall, on December 16, Mattox noted a "considerable feeling that the effectiveness of the NRA [is being] retarded because no drastic action [is taken] against violators." On January 20, state director George Creel filed the report from the San Francisco office, noting that the general "complaint is that the NRA has not prosecuted chiselers in California up to this time. To make an example of one or two will change the attitude of the small employer, and especially when convictions are secured." Creel speculated that firms would "fall in line when [they saw that] the NRA actually has some backing by the courts."

In fact, the February 17, 1934, report noted that the district attorneys of San Francisco and Santa Clara Counties were successful in attaining injunctions against two prominent dry cleaners and that these "actions have cleared the atmosphere in Northern California. . . . Compliance as a whole is much better since these actions were taken." Still, as it turns out, this optimism was misplaced. The March 10 report noted that the removal of the Blue Eagle from the dry cleaner in Santa Clara County actually had a *positive* effect on its business. "He cut his price to 29 cents for cleaning and pressing suits immediately upon removal of the Blue Eagle and his business has increased since that time tremendously."

The conclusion from these reports and others from all over the country is clear: An important driver of compliance with the NRA was the public's (both consumers and firms) belief in the probabilities of punishment for violations, which are represented by θ_1 and θ_2 in the model above. Furthermore, consumers' collective response to the Blue Eagle emblem, represented in the model by *BE* and *GP*, was driven by their belief that the emblem was indeed doing what it was designed to do—that is, signal to consumers which firms were, or were not, in compliance with the NIRA. When violations did not result in the Blue Eagle's removal, the emblem was viewed as increasingly ineffective in accomplishing the task for which it was created. This is consistent with the findings of the government's final review of the NIRA, conducted in 1937, which wrote, "The loss of the right to display the Blue Eagle, to the extent that the public interest in patronizing only enterprises which displayed it waned, gradually becoming a penalty of little consequence" (US Committee of Industrial Analysis 1937, 70). The model presented here suggests that the loss of respect for the Blue Eagle emblem could have created a cascade effect of further noncompliance since noncompliance itself fed into a lack of respect for the emblem.

Analysis of Blue Eagle Emblems in Newspaper Advertisements

Since the above analysis from NRA public attitude reports is anecdotal, it would be useful to obtain systematic quantitative data on the effectiveness of the Blue Eagle as an enforcement mechanism. One potential proxy for a firm's attitude toward the importance of the emblem is its willingness to pay to display it. Firms complying with the NRA were allowed to include it in their advertisements. An example of such an ad from Quaker Oats is shown in figure 7.3.

To quantify the prominence of the Blue Eagle, I examined a diverse sample of eight daily newspapers: *Atlanta Journal-Constitution, Chicago Tribune, Christian Science Monitor, Lansing State Journal, New Orleans Times-Picayune, New York Times, San Francisco Examiner,* and *Washington Post.*[10] To make this task manageable, the first twenty-five advertisements in each paper were examined every Thursday between August 3, 1933, and June 6, 1935. This method provides two hundred weekly observations from which to

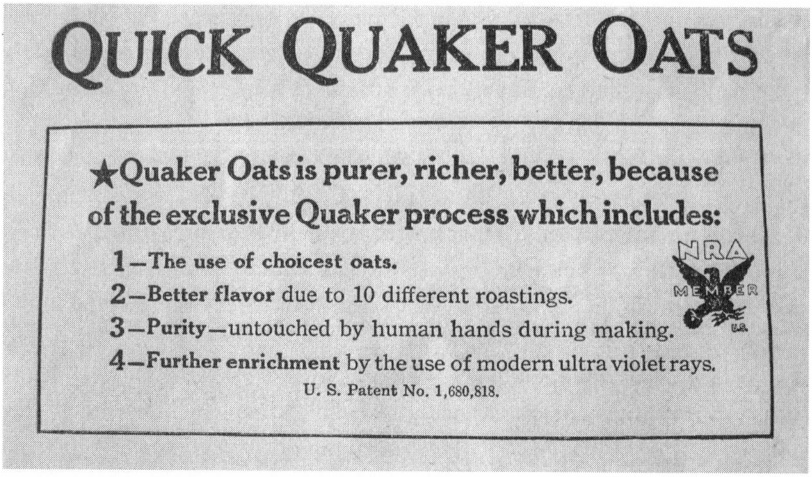

QUICK QUAKER OATS

★Quaker Oats is purer, richer, better, because
of the exclusive Quaker process which includes:

1—The use of choicest oats.
2—Better flavor due to 10 different roastings.
3—Purity—untouched by human hands during making.
4—Further enrichment by the use of modern ultra violet rays.
U. S. Patent No. 1,680,818.

FIGURE 7.3. Example of Ad with Blue Eagle
Source: *Christian Herald* magazine, November 1933, 32.

calculate the percent of advertisements that displayed the Blue Eagle emblem.
Figure 7.4 shows the percentage of ads carrying the patriotic emblem between
August 1933 and May 1935.

Consistent with the analysis of the attitude reports, the advertisement data
suggest that firms' beliefs in consumer enthusiasm for the Blue Eagle emblem were strongest in September and October of 1933, when between 40 and
45 percent of all ads contained the emblem. But in addition to the level, the
movement in this percentage over time is important. A sharp drop-off in the
percentage of ads displaying the emblem began in November and December
1933. As noted in the previous section, these months coincided with a sharp
rise in dissatisfaction over enforcement of the PRA/NRA. Compliance boards
in many cities and states expressed deep frustration over their lack of ability
to do more than employ words to try to convince recalcitrant firms to comply. Even when they recommended removal of the Blue Eagle, action from
Washington was generally very slow. In fact, on December 2, 1933, the entire
Lincoln, Nebraska, compliance board resigned in protest of a lack of enforcement resources from Washington.[11] Ten days later, the seven-member compliance board of Lowell, Massachusetts, stepped down for the same reason.[12]
These resignations were national news that could only have reduced firms'
expectations that violations would result in punishment (i.e., θ_1 and θ_2 in the
enforcement model above). Furthermore, they could only have further re-
duced consumers' belief that the Blue Eagle was in fact distinguishing patriotic compliers from violators—without this belief, consumers would be un-

likely to consider the Blue Eagle in their shopping decisions (thus affecting *BE* and *GP* in the model).

Another wave of the emblem's disappearance in newspapers occurred in early June of 1934, when the percentage dropped from around 25 percent to around 15 percent of ads. This period fell directly after the release of a report by the National Recovery Review Board, headed by Clarence Darrow, which suggested that the NRA had helped create monopolies at the expense of small businesses. The percentage held steady at around 15 percent through October, and then fell again in November to around 10 percent; it continued to slide so that by the time of the *Schechter* decision in May 1935, only 4 percent of advertisements displayed the Blue Eagle.

If the economic significance of the Blue Eagle was indeed a major factor in the decision to comply with or defect from the NRA, we would expect to see a relationship between this proxy—the percent of ads displaying the Blue Eagle—and other measures related to compliance or a lack thereof. I begin by looking at the relationship between the percentage of advertisements displaying the Blue Eagle and the number of complaints about violations of the NRA received in state offices. Chapter 6 discussed the aggregate number of

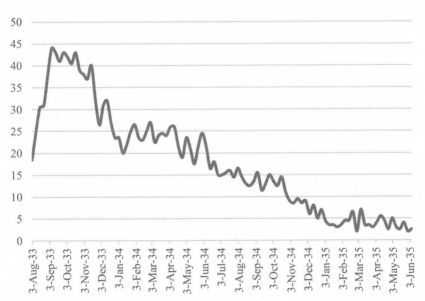

FIGURE 7.4. Percentage of Advertisements Displaying Blue Eagle Emblem in Eight Newspapers
Notes: Data are based on a sample of the first twenty-five advertisements in eight newspapers (200 ads per observation) from every Thursday between August 3, 1933, and June 6, 1935. Newspapers: *Atlanta Journal-Constitution, Chicago Tribune, Christian Science Monitor, Lansing State Journal, New Orleans Times-Picayune, New York Times, San Francisco Examiner,* and *Washington Post.*

complaints and whether they were successfully adjusted. Not discussed, however, was how these varied over time. Figures 7.5 and 7.6 show the number of complaints received every two weeks in state offices. Unfortunately, these data are not available prior to November 25, 1933, and hence we are missing valuable information about the variation in complaints between August and early November.

The theoretical model above suggests that firms would be less likely to violate the NRA if the Blue Eagle was viewed as a powerful enforcement tool, which would suggest a negative correlation between complaints and percentage of ads with the Blue Eagle. In fact, the correlation coefficient between trade practice complaints received and percentage of ads with the Blue Eagle is −0.68, and it is statistically significant at the 1 percent confidence level. This strongly suggests that the Blue Eagle played an important role in compliance with trade practice aspects of the codes. The relationship is not nearly as strong, however, with complaints of violations of the NRA's labor provisions. The correlation coefficient is negative, but it is relatively small (−0.09), and it is not statistically significant.

It would also be interesting to investigate whether economic measures such as wage rates, hours, output, and prices (which were impacted by the NRA codes, according to the analysis in chapter 5) were affected by the degree of importance economic actors placed on the Blue Eagle emblem (as proxied by its placement in advertisements). To undertake this, I converted the weekly Blue Eagle advertisement data reported in figure 7.4 to monthly data by averaging the weekly percentage data. This monthly data series can be used in fixed-effect panel regressions, such as those reported in chapter 5. Table 7.1 reports the results of four regressions with four different dependent variables. Each regression includes the same control variables employed in table 5.5, but the coefficients are not reported in the interest of space. I also include a dummy variable for August and September 1933 because these were the months in which the PRA was implemented in most industries and hence were the two months when the growth rate in wages and hours was strongly affected—controlling for these months should make it much more difficult to find statistically significant results in table 7.1.

Specification (1) in table 7.1 essentially duplicates of the same specification in table 5.5, except that it also contains the percentage of advertisements displaying the Blue Eagle emblem as well as the monthly change in this variable. The result suggests that output fell when enthusiasm for the Blue Eagle was higher and that it also fell when the change in percentage of ads with Blue Eagles rose, other factors held constant—although the second of these measures is only marginally significant. Since falling output is what we would

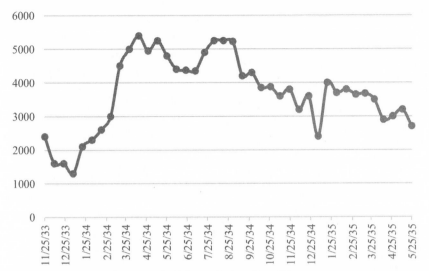

FIGURE 7.5. Biweekly Labor Complaints Received in NRA State Offices
Source: Galvin, Reinstein, and Campbell (1936, p. 174), Chart 1, "NRA State Office Labor Complaints."

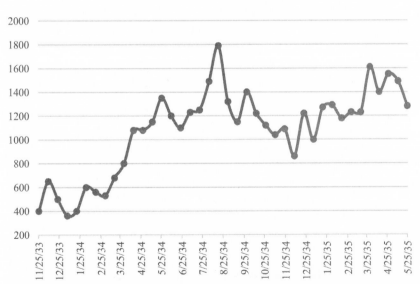

FIGURE 7.6. Biweekly Trade Practice Complaints Received in NRA State Offices
Source: Galvin, Reinstein, and Campbell (1936, p. 213), Chart 2, "NRA State Office Trade Practice Complaints."

TABLE 7.1. The Impact of the Blue Eagle Emblem's Prominence on Key Economic Variables

Dependent variable	(1) Output	p	(2) Prices	p	(3) Wage rates	p	(4) Hours worked	p
Percentage of ads with Blue Eagle	-0.00087	.00	0.00001	.42	0.00020	.05	-0.00070	.00
Change in percentage of ads with Blue Eagle	-0.00059	.13	0.00014	.31	0.00236	.00	-0.00213	.00
Unreported controls	Yes		Yes		Yes		Yes	
Number of industries	38		24		18		15	
Number of observations	4,720		2,932		2,260		1,876	

Notes: Dependent variables are expressed in growth rates (log differences). All regressions employ industry fixed effects, cross-section weights, and White standard errors, in duplication of tables 5.5 and 5.7. The unreported controls include those used in chapter 5: capacity utilization lagged one period, the dependent variable lagged one period, the growth rate in the money supply, the growth rate in government spending, the growth rate in government revenue, the growth rate of the S&P 500 stock index, the growth rate in the spread between AAA and BAA bonds, and a dummy variable for June and July 1933. Additionally, they all include a dummy variable for August and September 1933—the two months when the PRA wage and hours provisions were primarily implemented.

expect under successful collusion, this finding is consistent with the notion that the Blue Eagle played a role in bringing about compliance with the trade practice provisions of the NIRA. Specification (2) shows no evidence that the Blue Eagle affected the growth rate of industry prices. However, specifications (3) and (4) suggest that wage rates grew significantly faster and hours worked fell significantly more when the Blue Eagle was most prominent and when its appearance in ads rose, ceteris paribus. Again, these findings are consistent with the story that firms were more likely to abide by the NRA's labor provisions when they believed that Blue Eagle emblem had economic weight so that losing the ability to display it would result in lost business.

The Compliance Crisis of 1934

Contemporaries of the NIRA have long highlighted that the NIRA had a "compliance problem." New Deal historians in the latter half of the twentieth century such as Hawley (1966), Bellush (1975), and Brand (1988), among others, agreed that the breakdown in compliance resulted from a lack of enforcement and a decline in enthusiasm for the program. But what these studies generally neglect to emphasize is that the NIRA did strongly affect firm behavior in the months prior to the breakdown in compliance. The major theme of this book is that the NIRA's impact was much more heterogeneous than past studies have suggested. Thus far, this heterogeneity has primarily been demonstrated in the NIRA's differential impact on various industries. In this section, I highlight the NIRA's heterogeneous impact over time. It is an oversimplification to say the NRA failed due to compliance problems. After all, these problems did not plague it uniformly over the twenty-three months of its existence.

My contention, which is supported by the analysis presented thus far in this chapter, is that the NRA provisions as they related to wages, hours, and trade practice provisions were successfully implemented in the late summer and early fall of 1933 and were broadly effective through the winter of 1934. Beginning in the spring of 1934, however, compliance broke down in many industries with respect to many trade practice provisions. This is not to say that all collusion was lost, but an increasing number of firms that had been previously complying with the codes began to violate them. Figures 7.5 and 7.6, which display the number of labor and trade practice complaints received by the NRA, suggest that March 1934 was a key turning point in compliance—at least if one views complaints as a reasonable proxy for defections. In the two weeks prior to March 3, around 3,000 labor complaints were reported. This number surged to 4,500 complaints received over the next two weeks and then to 5,400 complaints received in the first two weeks of April. Likewise, in the two weeks prior to March 3, there were 530 complaints of violations of trade practice provisions, and this more than doubled to 1,080 complaints during the first two weeks of April.

Empirically, if we look closely at wage rates and workweeks around the time of the crisis in compliance in the late winter and early spring of 1934, we would expect to see wage rates fall and hours worked rise as firms violated the codes in line with the jump in complaints about violations. In fact, such movements do not appear in the aggregate wage and hour data, which show hourly wage rates in manufacturing actually rose from 56 to 58 cents in April 1934 while the average workweek fell slightly from 36.4 to 35.8 hours. In the industry-level data, again there is no strong evidence that wage rates fell or hours rose systematically in the spring of 1934. This suggests that, while there may have been more firms paying wages below code minimums or working employees beyond code maximum hours, these defections were not significant enough to affect the aggregate or industry-level data.

Still, it can be shown that, ceteris paribus, economic variables did change far more in the direction the NRA codes were designed to push them during code months prior to April 1934 than they did afterward. Table 7.2 shows the results of four fixed-effects panel regressions that are again in line with those from chapter 5—except that the NRA code dummy variable is broken into two periods. The NRA code *precompliance crisis* dummy variable turns on the month of code passage and stays on through March 1934. The NRA code *postcompliance crisis* dummy variable turns on only during the months the industry was covered by a code after March 1934. As with table 7.1 above, I do not report the control variables in the interest of space, but instead only report the coefficients of interest. Specification (1) in table 7.2 suggests that output fell slightly more on average in the months prior to the compliance crisis than it did in the months after, but the difference is negligible. However, specification (2) shows that prices rose twice as quickly during code months prior to spring 1934 than they did in code months after this time. Finally, specifications (3) and (4) suggest that the average increase in wage rates and the average decline in hours worked were greater by a factor of three in the months prior to the compliance crisis compared to those after.

I ran some unreported regressions (unreported in the interest of space) that duplicated those shown in table 7.2, but I split the sample into industries with long (twenty pages or more) and short codes (fewer than twenty pages) as was done in chapter 5. The purpose was to determine whether the compliance crisis differentially affected these two industry subgroups. There is no evidence to suggest that industry code length impacted the severity of the compliance crisis with movements in output, prices, wage rates, or hours.

TABLE 7.2. The Impact of the NRA Codes before and after the Compliance Crisis

Dependent variable	(1) Output	p	(2) Prices	p	(3) Wage rates	p	(4) Hours worked	p
President's Reemployment Agreement dummy variable	−0.0143	.00	0.0079	.00	0.0361	.00	−0.0396.	.00
NRA code dummy variable: code passage through March 1934	−0.0091	.06	0.0031	.03	0.0178	.00	−0.0214	.00
NRA code dummy variable: April 1934 through May 1935	−0.0081	.00	0.0016	.07	0.0061	.00	−0.0076	.00
Unreported controls	Yes		Yes		Yes		Yes	
Number of industries	38		24		18		15	
Number of observations	4,792		2,976		2,294		1,904	

Notes: Dependent variables are expressed in growth rates (log differences). All regressions employ industry fixed effects, cross-section weights, and White standard errors, in duplication of tables 5.5 and 5.7. The unreported controls include those used in chapter 5: capacity utilization lagged one period, the dependent variable lagged one period, the growth rate in the money supply, the growth rate in government spending, the growth rate in government revenue, the growth rate in growth rates of the S&P 500 stock index, and the growth rate in the spread between AAA and BAA bonds.

Although these findings are consistent with the notion that compliance declined after the spring of 1934, it is important to note that in all four cases, output, prices, wages, and hours continued to move in the direction (and by a statistically significant amount) that would be predicted by the NIRA provisions. This suggests that compliance was not completely lost, even if it did wane significantly. The fact that the NRA provisions continued to affect the industrial economy between April 1934 and the Supreme Court's *Schechter* decision in May 1935 is a testament to the NRA's work to regain adherence with the codes in the months after the compliance crisis.

The NRA's Fight to Bring Back Compliance with the Codes

It was clear that the NRA was on the ropes with compliance in the spring of 1933. Rather than throw in the towel, however, the government employed new strategies. Chapter 6 highlighted the creation of the NRA's Litigation Division on March 26, 1934, and its strategies to publicize the carefully selected cases that it pursued in courts. This was the first step in the NRA's attempt to regain credibility with respect to its enforcement (i.e., to raise the perceived values of θ_1 and θ_2). Another important step followed from the NRA's recognition that Washington had become a bottleneck where complaints from state offices sat in a long queue. The narrative evidence reported earlier suggested that the lack of quick action sowed dissatisfaction from state and local compliance offices and fed into the belief that the NRA enforcement mechanism had no bite. Thus, to further speed up the process of enforcement, on April 6, 1934, the NRA amended its policy whereby state directors, if they were convinced that the facts conclusively established a violation and the respondent showed no intention to amend, could refer the record of the case directly to the US district attorney for action rather than sending the case to the national Compliance Division in Washington. While this eased the Washington bottleneck, it created new ones with the district attorneys. Additionally, many cases were still sent along to Washington for further attempts at adjustment or for removal of the Blue Eagle emblem.

To further ease the Washington bottleneck, in January 1935, regional compliance offices were set up in Boston, New York, Washington, Atlanta, Cleveland, Chicago, Omaha, Dallas, and San Francisco (Galvin, Reinstein, and Campbell 1936, 128). These offices were given the power to remove the Blue Eagle and to select cases to be referred to the Department of Justice for prosecution. After the regional offices were up and running, the ability of state directors to directly submit cases to the attorney general was removed—cases would instead be referred to the relevant regional office. An ex-post NRA report noted that "the decentralization of the compliance administration and enforcement was a marked improvement over the old method of handling unadjusted complaints. The average length of time necessary in order to bring about adjustment of complaints or to initiate action against unadjusted cases was substantially reduced" (Galvin, Reinstein, and Campbell 1936, 138).

Blue Eagle Makeover: The NRA Code Eagle

The Blue Eagle was originally created as a symbol of compliance with the PRA, but by the spring of 1934, most firms were covered by a specific code of fair competition rather than the PRA. With enthusiasm for the Blue Eagle emblem fading quickly, the NRA decided to renovate the emblem via the creation of the new "Code Eagle," which would serve as a symbol of compliance with the NRA codes of fair competition. Similar to what had been done in the summer of 1933, postmasters distributed applications for Code Eagles to all firms prior to May 1, 1934. Firms were asked to apply for the emblem through the NRA state offices by indicating under which code they were operating. The Code Eagle was essentially a duplicate of the old Blue Eagle except that it dropped the "We Do Our Part" text and instead specified what industry code the firm was operating under. The Code Eagle would also include a firm-specific registration number created by its code authority. Two examples of NRA Code Eagles are shown in figure 7.7.

The NRA publicity machine ramped up to introduce the new emblem. On Sunday, April 30, the Code Eagle was formally unveiled in New York City with a ceremony that featured the Marine and New York City police bands. The NRA highlighted the Code Eagles as an improved method of enforcement, and the New York State director of the National Emergency Council, Nathan Straus, noted that the new emblem marked the beginning of "a militant drive" toward compliance. "The educational part of the campaign is now over and we will no longer be as kind and considerate toward violators as we have been in the past. . . . From [May 1] on any who fails to adhere to a code will be punished first by widespread publicity and, second, if unfavorable publicity does not make him toe the mark, by prosecution on the part of the District Attorney."[13]

To the disappointment of the NRA, few firms applied for the new emblems prior to their initial distribution date of May 1. Two weeks later, in the hopes that a different layer of the bureaucracy would be more effective, the NRA ceded the responsibility to distribute Code Eagles to the code authorities associated with each industry. The code authorities viewed the new emblems as a potential way to get more firms to formally join and pay dues to

FIGURE 7.7. Code Eagles for the Distilled Spirits Rectifying and Retail Food and Grocery Trade Industries

Source: National Archives, Record Group 9, ARC Identifier 16703546, "Pictorial Materials" Entry Number PI 44–43, Box 3.

FIGURE 7.8. Blue Eagle Week Window Display in Washington, DC
Source: National Archives, Record Group 9, ARC Identifier 16703546, "Pictorial Materials" Entry Number PI 44–43, Box 3.

the authorities, as sometimes required in the codes. The NRA pushed for June 16, 1934, the one-year anniversary of the NRA, to be the date by which firms should all have their Code Eagles in place. Despite the administration's best efforts, enthusiasm for the new Code Eagle continued to be extremely disappointing. According to the final report of the insignia section, of the three million firms that were entitled to display the Code Eagle, only 1,856,000 even received one (Duvall 1936, 15).

Blue Eagle Week

In an attempt to boost the public's opinion of the fledgling Blue Eagle, Washington, DC, announced that the week of September 24, 1934, would be "Blue Eagle Week." Residents of the city were strongly encouraged to shop at businesses that displayed Blue Eagles, and businesses were likewise encouraged to highlight the emblem in their advertisements and window displays. Figure 7.8 shows a window display of a Washington firm during Blue Eagle Week. The Blue Eagle Week promotion was subsequently copied by at least one other city:

FIGURE 7.9. *Dayton Herald*, October 22, 1934
Source: National Archives, Record Group 9, ARC Identifier 16703546, "Pictorial Materials" Entry Number PI 44–43, Box 3.

Dayton, Ohio, declared the week of October 22, 1934, to be Blue Eagle Week in the city. Figure 7.9 shows the front page of the city's newspaper, the *Dayton Herald*, announcing the week's beginning with a banner headline and a full-page display of the Blue Eagle. Many of the advertisements in the paper were created for this special edition and announced their firm's pride in displaying the Blue Eagle in an appeal for the business of patriotic consumers. These attempts to resuscitate the Blue Eagle suggest that the NRA felt the symbol to be of high economic importance for firms' compliance with the codes.

The Mass Compliance Drive

Perhaps the most noteworthy attempt of the NRA to increase compliance with the codes was the mass compliance drive that began in the late summer and early fall of 1934. The need for the new approach was outlined in an October 8, 1934, memo from L. J. Martin, the head of the NRA Compliance Division, to the NRA administrative officer, George Lynch, who had replaced Hugh Johnson in that position two weeks earlier.[14] Martin noted that the Compliance Division wanted to see "a fundamental change in its method of obtaining compliance," because the current method had many flaws. Among them was that the NRA did nothing to *discover* violations, but instead only acted on those that were reported to it. This system not only brought risk to employees who, as noted in the previous chapter, were sometimes discharged after making complaints but also was unfair to the employer who was asked to comply with a code that his competitors were not abiding by. Martin's proposal was for "a systematic universal inspection of all business establishments under codes." Specifically, Martin suggested that NRA field adjusters go door to door in a sweep of an entire geographic area, or of an entire industry, and check whether each employer was in compliance. The field adjuster could also furnish copies of labor provisions that were to be posted, furnish Code Eagles to those in compliance who did not have them, and determine on the spot any restitution that was owed for violations that were found. Martin pointed to a successful experiment of this sort that was carried out in Mansfield, Ohio, in August 1934, and he recommended that the NRA immediately undertake complete canvasses of smaller locations in each state and give them high national and local publicity. This action "would greatly increase compliance even in advance of the inspection," because it would suggest to firms that an inspection may be forthcoming.

The Mansfield experiment to which Martin referred had been conducted over ten days beginning on August 20, 1934. Four NRA field adjusters from the Ohio office visited all 483 firms in Mansfield. A September 10, 1934, memo from Benedict Crowell, the Ohio state compliance director, to Stanley Posner, the NRA Compliance Division's chief economist, outlined the findings of the survey.[15] "Our men soon found that the NRA was a dead issue in Mansfield; the Blue Eagle was either in the back part of the store or had been thrown out." Crowell noted that many employers "had never seen a copy of the code under which they were operating; they had read in the paper about the NRA and that was the extent of their knowledge. They had not received, or had ignored, application cards for [the] Code Eagle." During their visits, the field adjusters discussed the provisions of the codes with firm owners and managers and checked their payroll books. They found that less than one-third of firms even kept wage and hours records, but Crowell noted that most employers agreed to start keeping such records immediately.

When cases of noncompliance were found, adjustments and agreements of restitution were made on the spot, and Code Eagles were given to complying firms along with copies of the labor provisions, which were to be posted. "In most instances, employers were very cooperative. They assured our adjusters that they would gladly comply with their code, but insisted that their competitors should also be made to conform." Only 5 employers out of the 483 were reported as antagonistic toward the drive. During the second week of the campaign, the Blue Eagle was removed from the Southern Hotel, because the firm was flagrantly violating the hotel code and refused to come into compliance. "Word of this action soon spread around Mansfield, and business firms seemed greatly impressed." Crowell closed his memo saying that a week after the campaign had ended, one of the adjusters returned to the city. "He found clean new Code Eagles in practically every store window. . . . We believe that as a result of our campaign, compliance in Mansfield has improved at least 90% and the business community has a better and more sympathetic understanding of the NRA than ever before."

The Ohio NRA office followed up the Mansfield experiment with another one in Zanesville, Ohio, a city of similar size. Between September 9 and September 30, 1934, five NRA field adjusters visited 498 Zanesville firms and found that "compliance with the codes was at a low ebb."[16] It was estimated that only one store in five was displaying the Blue Eagle or Code Eagle. By the time the campaign had ended, this number had reversed so that four out of five stores were displaying an emblem. Still, the field adjusters noted, "We did not find the same spirit of cooperation among employers that we found in Mansfield," and while "we cannot believe that there is effective compliance with the codes in Zanesville at the present time, we do believe that conditions are considerably better than they were before the campaign."

Similar campaigns of mass compliance were carried out in several other cities in northeast Ohio and across the country between October 1934 and May 1935. Although the NRA did not collect explicit data or give a final evaluation of this program, anecdotal data suggest that these programs were relatively effective. A report from August 1935 by the Ohio state office showed the amount of restitution payments collected in three cities—Akron, Canton, and Youngstown—in 1934 prior to the mass compliance drive and in the five months between January and May 1935 that followed the drive. In Youngstown, restitution rose from $962 in 1934 to $13,648 in the first half of 1935. In Canton, the amount rose from $882 to $6,156. Finally, in Akron, it rose from $1,180 to $4,551 (Galvin, Reinstein, and Campbell 1936, 157).

Encouraged by these city-level experiments, the NRA decided to try a similar tactic on an entire industry: boot and shoe manufacturing. This industry was suspected of widespread noncompliance, and the NRA touted its national survey of firms as an "aggressive action" against "chiselers."[17] Beginning in the last week of March 1935, and lasting for around four weeks, NRA field adjusters attempted to visit every boot and shoe manufacturing firm in the nation. For example, on April 10, NRA field adjuster J. E. Campion visited the Berkshire Shoe Co. of Reading, Pennsylvania. Campion interviewed the company's president, C. B. Kuntz, as well as several employees, and he was allowed access to the company's records. He noted that the Blue Eagle was being displayed but that "a number of the girls in the packing room are being underpaid to the extent of $2.50 per week [and other] employees have been working more than an eight hour day and received no extra pay."[18] An auditor was brought in the next day to determine the exact amount of restitution that Berkshire would have to pay to be considered in compliance. In another case, field adjusters W. C. Young and J. R. Brunozzi visited Sam Biron & Co. of Philadelphia on March 27, 1935. Interviews with employees as well as an examination of the plant's payroll records revealed "consistent violations of the Hour and Wage Provisions of the Code." As a result, Biron was instructed to bring his payroll records to the local NRA compliance office for a full audit so that restitution amounts could be determined.[19] When violations such as these were found, the standard procedures applied: Attempts would be made to adjust the case through these initial meetings, and if that did not work, a formal hearing could result in removal of the Blue Eagle and the case could be referred to the Litigation Division for further action.

In Ohio, all thirty-four boot and shoe manufacturing plants were visited. Field adjusters reported that none of them were in violation of the hours provisions of the industry's code, but three were in violation of the wage provisions. These violations affected only 31 employees out of a total of 14,285 — thus, the adjusters reported a 99.8 percent rate of compliance.[20] The findings were far less positive in New England, where some degree of violation was found in 43.8 percent of the 491 boot and shoe manufacturing plants visited by field adjusters. Still, the final report from New England noted that adjustments were successfully achieved in almost every instance.[21] The Chicago district's final report of April 12 noted that, of the thirty-seven factories visited, ten were in full compliance, seventeen were deemed minor violators, and ten were considered major violators. The report noted that nearly $9,000 worth of necessary restitution payments had been found and that this number would certainly rise into five figures when all was said and done.[22] The New York office completed its mass compliance survey of boot and shoe manufacturers prior to the *Schechter* decision but did not file its report until August 1935. New York reported that ninety-seven of the two hundred firms visited were in violation of the NRA wage and hour provisions. Thirty-three of these cases were reported as being "immediately adjusted," bringing $3,029 of restitution payments. Other attempts at obtaining restitution were abandoned after *Schechter* held the NIRA unconstitutional.[23]

Because not all the reports from state and regional offices had come in prior to the NIRA's demise, I am not aware of any final national tally of compliance in the boot and shoe industry. But the reports described above — with Ohio being a strong outlier — suggest a compliance rate of only a little more

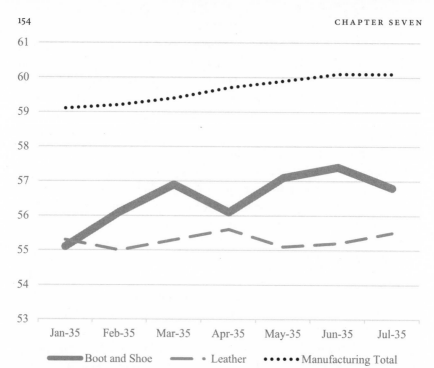

FIGURE 7.10. Average Hourly Earnings in the Boot and Shoe, Leather, and Overall Manufacturing Industries, January–July 1935

Source: Data from National Bureau of Economic Research, *NBER Macrohistory Database*, chap. 8, http://www.nber.org/databases/macrohistory/contents/.

than half. Given this high level of noncompliance and the fact that the field adjusters claimed they were often able to attain successful adjustments, did the mass compliance survey of the boot and shoe industry cause wage rates to rise and workweeks to fall in this industry after the visitations occurred, but prior to *Schechter*? Figures 7.10 and 7.11 show wage rates and workweeks in the boot and shoe industry as well as the overall averages in the manufacturing industry. Also included in the figures are the wages and hours in the leather industry, which generally moved closely with the shoe industry.

Average hourly earnings in the boot and shoe industry were 56.9 cents in March 1935. Since these data represent the average for the middle of the month, this data point should not be affected by the mass compliance surveys, which began in the last week of March. The hourly wage rate fell a bit in April to 56.1 and then rose nearly 2 percent in May to 57.1. Still, these movements are not substantially different from the overall trend in manufacturing industries, where average hourly earnings rose from 59.4 in March to 59.9 in May. For workweeks, however, figure 7.11 reveals evidence consistent with an effect from mass compliance. The average workweek in the boot and shoe industry

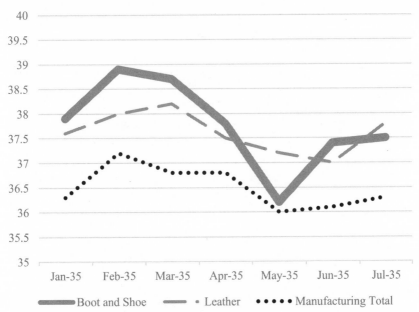

FIGURE 7.11. Average Number of Hours Worked per Week in the Boot and Shoe, Leather, and Overall Manufacturing Industries, January–July 1935
Source: Data from National Bureau of Economic Research, *NBER Macrohistory Database*, chap. 8, http://www.nber.org/databases/macrohistory/contents/.

fell by 7.2 percent between March and May 1935, while the average workweek in total manufacturing fell by only 2.1 percent (and declined in the leather manufacturing industry by only 2.6 percent).

Although the industry results suggest only modest progress from the mass compliance drive, there is little doubt that the NRA was in the process of moving away from its original method of compliance and enforcement and toward this more systematic method. A 1936 report on the history of the NRA Compliance Division noted that it was "unfortunate that the rapid strides being made in the development of mass compliance methods were abruptly terminated by the invalidation of codes" with *Schechter* as the experiments had convinced many in the Compliance Division "that the use of mass compliance methods presented a more practical means of administration . . . than the reliance originally placed on complaints as the sole basis of activity."

Conclusion and Discussion

Appearances were supremely important for the success of the NRA enforcement mechanism. The government did everything it could to give the impression that any violation of NRA rules would be, in Hugh Johnson's words, "a sentence of economic death." If consumers showed a strong preference for Blue Eagle firms and violating firms were quickly stripped of the right to display the emblem, then violators would indeed have been punished severely with a sharp loss of business—and, as a result, further violations would have been few and far between.

The model of compliance and enforcement developed in this chapter highlights the importance of perceptions. It was less important that the actual likelihood of a firm owner being fined or imprisoned for a violation (θ_2 in the model) was close to zero than whether the government could create the illusion that defections brought significant risk. Similarly, it did not matter that no Blue Eagle was removed until ten weeks after the compliance emblem began to cover the nation. As long as the perception that violators would lose the emblem (θ_1 in the model) was strong and that this loss would create a damaging consumer boycott (*BE* in the model), the rate of compliance with the program would be high. In the late summer and early fall of 1933, the NRA did its part to ensure that Blue Eagle mania swept the nation; as a result, compliance with NRA labor and code provisions was very strong.

But while violations were relatively few in those early days, they were not zero. When the initial violations were met not with swift punishment but only with further threats and long delays, perceptions of enforcement among firms and consumers ratcheted downward. More firms fell out of compliance and defections were not punished, creating a vicious cycle that led to a full-blown compliance crisis engulfing the program by spring 1934. Complaints of violations flooded NRA offices in March and April 1934 at about double the rate of February. These complaints and defections from the NRA were closely correlated with the perceived strength of the Blue Eagle: When the emblem's prominence (as proxied by its appearance in newspaper ads) fell, violations of the NRA rose. Furthermore, output, wage rates, and hours moved significantly more in the directions prodded by the NRA codes during months prior to April 1934 than they did in the months between then and the *Schechter* decision in May 1935, which overturned the program. That the NRA had any economic effects after the spring of 1934 is a testament to its renewed efforts at enforcement—the introduction of the Code Eagle, new promotions such as Blue Eagle Week, and the mass compliance drives—as it tried to convince the nation that now it really meant business.

The *Schechter* Decision and the Lingering Effects of the NIRA

The NIRA was passed as a two-year program and thus was set to expire on June 16, 1935. Still, congressional debate in the spring of 1935 was focused not on whether the NIRA would be extended but on the length of such an extension. Roosevelt had pushed for a two-year extension while the Senate Finance Committee had approved in early May a resolution extending the NIRA only through March 1936. On May 26, 1935, the *Chicago Tribune* noted that a compromise bill mandating a 21.5-month extension through March 1937 was gaining broad support.[1] But three weeks earlier, the Supreme Court had heard a case, *A.L.A. Schechter Poultry Corp. v. United States*, in which the NIRA's constitutionality would be determined. The Circuit Court of Appeals had ruled against Schechter Poultry with respect to the NIRA's ability to regulate trade practices in industry. At the same time, the Court had ruled against the NIRA's ability to control the wages and hours of Schechter, which slaughtered chickens in New York that were sold in New York, and hence was not engaged in interstate commerce. The government had hoped the Supreme Court would settle this question of interstate commerce versus intrastate commerce, which had long vexed NIRA enforcement efforts. Both sides appealed the aspects of the rulings that they had lost so that the constitutionality of the entire law was to be determined by the Supreme Court. With the decision expected by the end of the month, many in Congress preferred to wait for the outcome of this case before approving an extension of the law.

On May 27, 1935, the Supreme Court ruled unanimously that the NIRA was unconstitutional. First, the Court ruled that the NIRA had given the office of the president what Justice Cardozo called "a roving commission" to make laws through industry codes of fair competition and that this was a constitutional breach—the legislative branch is to make laws, and the executive branch is to enforce them. Second, even if Congress, rather than the president, had enacted the codes, the Court ruled that the NIRA was illegally regulating intrastate commerce. With the *Schechter* ruling, the NIRA was completely invalidated. The wage and hour provisions, the cartel provisions, and the requirement of firms to recognize labor's right to collective bargaining were all terminated.

Within hours of the ruling some members of Congress began to formulate a potential piecemeal approach to bringing back key aspects of the NIRA by quickly entertaining some existing bills that involved NIRA-type regulations. For example, Senator Hugo Black's thirty-hour bill, which was introduced prior to the passage of the NIRA in 1933, could implement the work-sharing aspects of the NIRA. A bill submitted in January 1935 by Pennsylvania senator Robert Guffey would impose enhanced NIRA-style regulations in the bituminous coal industry. In February 1935, Senator Robert Wagner proposed a bill that would permanently institute the right of collective bargaining along the lines of the NIRA's Section 7(a).

In fact, Wagner's bill would become the National Labor Relations Act, which was signed into law in June 1935. Black's thirty-hour bill eventually morphed into the Fair Labor Standards Act of 1938, which set a 40-cent per hour federal minimum wage and a forty-hour workweek (with time and a half paid for hours above forty) and said that children under age sixteen could not be employed during school hours. The Guffey Coal Act was passed in August 1935; however, the Supreme Court found the legislation unconstitutional in 1937, saying that the Tenth Amendment prohibited the federal government from assuming regulatory powers not explicitly granted to it in the Constitution. While the National Labor Relations Act and Fair Labor Standards Act had succeeded in making the NIRA's guarantee of collective bargaining, minimum wages, and maximum hours permanent parts of the economic landscape, the regulation of industry through anything resembling government-enforceable codes of fair competition would not continue beyond 1937.

These formal efforts to reinstate aspects of the NIRA were not the government's only course of action. The Roosevelt administration also asked industries to voluntarily continue to abide by their codes of fair competition in the wake of the *Schechter* decision. Because the history of the demise of the NIRA has been well documented (see Hawley 1966 and Bellush 1975 among others), this chapter will not rehash it. I will, however, examine the effectiveness of these attempts to keep the NIRA in force after the *Schechter* decision. Specifically, I will examine data on wage rates, hours, employment, and output to examine the effects of the *Schechter* decision in the months that followed.

The Media's Reaction to the *Schechter* Decision[2]

The *New York Times* asked newspapers across the nation to telegraph summaries of their editorial viewpoints regarding the *Schechter* decision so that it could publish a roundup of opinions. The *Times* headline summarized that "Newspapers throughout the country express editorial satisfaction" with the *Schechter* ruling.[3] For example, the *Phoenix Republican* wrote that "The sweeping decision will have a clarifying effect . . . and will tend to relieve the uncertainty which has held business and recovery in check." The *Denver Post* called the *Schechter* ruling "the most reassuring development this country has experienced in many a year" as it will "loosen the bureaucratic brakes which have been clamped on business and individual initiative." The *Dallas News* editors wrote, "The codes have not ended labor troubles or brought the expected golden age into industrial life. Fiat has demonstrated its incompetency to legislate a payroll out of proportion to industry's receipts." The *Boston Herald* hoped that the ruling would "mean the end of slovenly legislative procedure. Congress has stupidly enacted measure after measure without explicitly providing just what is to be accomplished." The *Los Angeles Times* declared, "The days of a virtually uncontrolled one man dictatorship in the United States are at an end."

While a strong majority of opinions in the *New York Times* article expressed support for the ruling, some expressed hope that at least certain aspects of the NIRA could be maintained. The *Kansas City Star* wrote that, while "on the whole [the NIRA] retarded recovery . . . there were certain features of the codes that ought to be lived up to. Business would make a fatal mistake if it [were] to bring back sweat-shop conditions, throw men out of work and return to child labor." The *Birmingham Age-Herald* wrote, "Many of the standards set by NRA are now so well established that a continued widespread observance of them on a voluntary basis may be expected."

The *Wall Street Journal* provided a sample of reactions to the *Schechter* ruling from members of the business community. The *Journal* reported that, although many were not willing to put their comments on the record, "industry leaders were generally agreed that the Supreme Court's decision . . . will have many stimulating and few adverse effects on the immediate future of business."[4] The *New York Times* likewise reported that "Leading bankers and industrialists characterized the decision on the NRA as 'the best thing in years.'"[5] The *Wall Street Journal*'s editors seconded the sentiments of Congressman Hamilton Fish Jr. of New York when he had heard about the ruling: "Thank God for the Supreme Court of the United States."[6] An examination of the nation's leading newspapers suggests a strong consensus that the removal of the NIRA provisions was more likely to help the struggling economy than hurt it.

Business leaders had generally been in favor of the NIRA bill when it was debated in the spring of 1933—so why were they so overwhelmingly pleased with the news of its demise via the *Schechter* decision? Businesses generally embraced the NIRA early on because they viewed it as a "quid pro quo."[7] Business would grant concessions to labor, and in return it would have the right to coordinate activity at the industry level—something it had pushed for throughout the 1920s. Furthermore, the government would provide an enforcement mechanism to punish violators of these industry-level agreements. By the spring of 1934, however, compliance with the codes' trade practice provisions—such as those forbidding sales below costs, imposing production quotas, and requiring firms to notify the industry in advance of prices changes—was largely lost. Despite the loss of the "quo," firms were still expected to supply the "quid" by complying with the labor aspects of the law, and thus many (though certainly not all) in the business community welcomed the program's end.

Voluntary Compliance with the Codes Post-*Schechter* and the Findings of the Robert Committee

Just hours after the *Schechter* ruling, Donald Richberg, chairman of the National Industrial Recovery Board, announced that NRA enforcement of the codes of fair competition would cease.[8] However, Richberg asked firms to voluntarily continue to abide by code provisions: "I hope that all employers . . . will cooperate in maintaining those standards of fair competition in commercial and labor relations which have been written into codes."[9] NRA officials' hopes of success in this endeavor were buoyed by the number of telegrams they received from firms across the country saying that they would continue to comply with their industry codes despite the Supreme Court's ruling. The directors of the National Boot and Shoe Manufacturers Association released a statement urging its members to continue to conform to its industry code's wage, hour, and child labor provisions.

In the weeks after the *Schechter* decision, the NRA directed its regional offices to conduct surveys of major businesses to gauge the extent to which the NRA codes were still being followed. To illustrate, the South Carolina NRA office kept daily tabs on news of violations—both those by specific companies and more broadly of overall compliance in different industries—and reported these observations to the NRA national office.[10] For example, on June 1, it was reported that the Piedmont Shirt Co. reduced its hourly wage rates 25 percent and increased its hours to forty-four per week. On June 4, the office reported "that various industries have extended hours with decreased wages" and that "price cutting in general [was] evidenced among industries." On June 8, the office reported that Smith Coal Co. had truck drivers working eleven hours per day, six days a week, with no provision for overtime. On June 10, it reported that the O. L. Williams Furniture Co. (which had 575 employees) decreased its hourly wage rates below code levels. On June 12, it reported that the Reamer Ice and Fuel Co. had reduced its wages for black workers to 20 cents per hour. On June 14, it reported that the Tuxbury Lumber Co. increased its workweek from forty to forty-eight hours with no change in weekly pay.

The South Carolina office also noted that the degree of noncompliance varied dramatically by industry. For example, the textile industry experienced a "comparatively small departure from code standards," while the manufacturing of forest products, motor vehicle retailing, and construction industries all saw "a sharp departure from code standards." Retail establishments, the office noted, were mostly in continued compliance. Of the 142 retailers surveyed, which together employed 2,569 workers, 134 (94 percent) were adhering to the wage standards of the retail trade code, and 128 (90 percent) were adhering to the hours provisions.

On June 17, 1935, Roosevelt asked Richberg to form a committee charged with obtaining and reporting systematic and nationwide information on the extent to which industries were deviating from the standards that were set up under the NRA codes of fair competition. This committee, headed by W. P. Robert, was directed to report its findings by the end of the year. The committee gathered reports from the regional offices and ultimately aggregated the data for forty-four industries. The survey was completed in November 1935, but its results were not made public until spring of 1936.

To provide a bit of flavor regarding the execution of this survey, consider an August 17, 1935, report filed by Edward P. Halline, an NRA field adjuster from the Milwaukee office, pertaining to the graphic arts industry in Wisconsin. Halline noted that the commercial printing and lithographing industry "maintains its allegiance, with minor deviations, to the 40-hour week and the graphic arts code wage rates."[11] Furthermore, what deviations that did exist were generally minor—for example, some companies had raised the workweek from forty to forty-four hours. With respect to trade practices, Halline reported that firms felt "price cutting was just as bad as ever—codes or no codes," indicating that even prior to *Schechter*, many of the trade practice provisions of the graphic arts code were ignored. In fact, the survey revealed that only seventeen employers with 279 employees were in favor of maintaining the *trade practice* provisions of the code, while twenty employers with

356 employees were against this notion, and another nine employers with 171 employees were indifferent. On the other hand, thirty-two of the employers agreed with the principles behind the *wage and hour* provisions of the code, while only seven employers were against (and seven more were indifferent).

The Milwaukee office surveyed conditions in the department store industry in the city since May 27.[12] E. M. Berliner, the field officer who filed the report, wrote that he had conducted an initial survey of eight department stores about two weeks after the *Schechter* ruling and found that no changes in wages or hours had been made. As of mid-August, he wrote that the stores continued in complete compliance. Furthermore, the report noted that trade practice difficulties had never been a major problem in this industry thanks to the work of the Milwaukee Better Business Bureau, which had been administering the trade practice provisions of the retail trade code prior to *Schechter*, and it was still acting in this manner.

A September 19, 1935, report to the NRA from the Los Angeles district office by executive assistant Chas Cunningham reported the results of a survey of around seven hundred firms in thirteen industries.[13] Nine of the thirteen industries reported that over half of their firms were in violation of labor provisions of their relevant code. However, only one of the thirteen industries had over 50 percent of firms in violation of trade practice provisions of the codes. Furthermore, in all but one industry (paint, varnish, and lacquer) at least 64 percent of firms reported a favorable attitude toward the NRA and the notion of continuing to follow the codes after *Schechter*—most firms were, in fact, reported to be desirous of the NIRA being restored. Still, in the text of the report, Cunningham wrote, "We believe there are more violations than this [report] shows . . . in view of the fact that we were required to take the word of the employer or management of the firms." For instance, Cunningham noted that only 10 percent of firms in the "Crushed Rock, Sand & Gravel, Etc." industry were reported to be in violation of the code's trade practice provisions; however, "the entire industry today is selling at a price 50% lower than the price filed under the Code." Cunningham's statement suggests that the Robert Committee survey results should be taken with a grain of salt—respondents may have simply told the government surveyors what they thought they wanted to hear.

The New York NRA state office reported to the Robert Committee that in the state's retail drug industry, 67 percent of the 432 firms surveyed admitted noncompliance with the trade practice provisions of its industry code.[14] However, over 70 percent indicated compliance with the wage and hours provisions of the retail drug code. None of the surveyed firms said it was in violation of the code's provision against hiring child labor under the age of sixteen.

In the motor vehicle retailing industry, 326 New York firms were surveyed by NRA canvassers. Of these, 86 percent had reported noncompliance with the trade practice provisions of the industry's code, 51 percent reported non-compliance with the wage provisions, and 52 percent were not in compliance with the hours provisions.[15] As was the case in the retail drug industry, all 326 retail vehicle firms indicated continued compliance with the restriction on the employment of child labor. In the shipbuilding and ship repair industry, all thirty-nine firms surveyed said they were still in compliance with the industry code's trade practice provisions, although 21 percent of them said that they were in violation of the code's wage provisions and 74 percent admitted violation of the code's hour provisions.[16]

The Robert Committee's final analysis suggested that in nearly three-quarters of industries surveyed, over half of the firms reported full compliance with the wage and hours provisions of codes of fair competition. This suggests that the NIRA codes were still impacting economic behavior—at least to some degree—in the months after the *Schechter* decision. The final report stated, "In no industry has there been complete abandonment by all establishments surveyed of both the labor and trade practice provisions of a code. Code standards have broken down in particular respects rather than in all respects."[17] The report noted that perhaps the most disregarded aspect of the codes was the payment of overtime rates for hours in excess of the maximums specified in the codes. Another common deviation from code rules was that many firms had increased hours worked without boosting weekly pay, thus resulting in a decrease in hourly earnings. The committee's survey suggested almost universal adherence to the code's rules against child labor; however, the committee noted that "various sources [have] indicated a larger employment of child labor than has been shown in our returns."[18]

Interestingly, the Robert Committee's findings show tremendous industry-level heterogeneity in the degree of compliance. For example, 136 of the 143 (95 percent) iron and steel industry firms reported full compliance with the labor provisions of the industry's code. However, at the other extreme, only 215 of the 1,936 (11 percent) firms in the cotton garment industry reported no departures from that industry code's wage and hours provisions.[19] Given the analysis presented earlier in this book, such heterogeneity is not surprising—after all, hourly wage rates in the iron and steel industry were already relatively high (averaging around 48 cents in May 1933) and hourly work-weeks relatively low (averaging around 35 hours) prior to the imposition of the NIRA. Thus, the NIRA wage and hour rules had relatively little impact on labor in this industry, so its demise would likewise be expected to have minimal impact. On the other hand, the cotton garment industry was historically

TABLE 8.1. Average Hourly Earnings (Cents per Hour) and Average Workweek in May 1935 and May 1936

Industry	Hourly earnings May 1935	Hourly earnings May 1936	Workweek May 1935	Workweek May 1936
Chemical manufacturing	60.6	62.4	38.3	39.7
Cotton goods manufacturing	45.0	44.9		
Electrical manufacturing	66.3	66.9	35.5	39.2
Furniture	54.2	54.8	35.4	39.4
Leather	55.1	56.7	37.2	38.4
Machinery	63.3	63.8	39.4	43.6
Meatpacking	57.2	56.1	41.8	42.5
Paper production	53.0	53.8	38.6	42.3
Passenger cars	74.8	78.5	34.7	40.7
Rayon	54.3	52.0	29.3	30.4
Rubber products	80.5	76.8	32.9	37.2
Iron and steel	65.5	65.9	33.9	40.5
Boot and shoe	57.1	56.6	36.2	32.3
Wool	51.1	52.7	36.1	34.6

Source: National Bureau of Economic Research, *NBER Macrohistory Database*, chap. 8, http://www .nber.org/databases/macrohistory/contents/.

a low-wage (under 30 cents per hour prior to the NIRA) and long-hour one. The NIRA had far more dramatic effects on labor in this industry, and hence we would expect the withdrawal of the legislation to result in relatively shaper declines in wages and increases in hours.

Table 8.1 shows the average hourly earnings and average hourly workweeks in fourteen industries in May 1935, just before the *Schechter* decision, and in May 1936, a year after *Schechter* (compare with table 4.2, which displays the wage and hour data for these industries for May 1933 and May 1934). It is interesting to note that hourly wage rates were largely unchanged in the year after the demise of the NIRA—in fact, on average, they *rose by 0.5 percent*. Three factors could have played a role in preventing a fall in average hourly earnings after the NRA codes were ruled unconstitutional: (1) The economy grew fairly sharply during these twelve months, and hence market forces may have kept earnings from falling despite the removal of the industry minimum wage rates. (2) Firms could have continued to abide by the minimum wage provisions of their codes voluntarily. (3) Falk, Fehr, and Zehnder (2006) report the results of laboratory experiments suggesting that wage rates did not fall substantially after the removal of a minimum wage policy. They attribute this behavior to the imposition of a minimum wage permanently raising the reservation wage of workers. Such an effect could have played out after the effective removal of the minimum wages in 1935.

With average workweeks, the *Schechter* decision appears to have had much stronger effects. The workweek rose in all but two industries, and the average increase was around 7 percent. This is consistent with the results of the Robert Committee study, which generally (though not always) found that firms were more likely to voluntarily abide by the wage provisions than to implement the restrictions on hours. Still, the growing economy could have contributed to the growth in average hours worked per week if firms were expanding the hours of full-time workers or hiring fewer part-time workers as they ramped up production. Furthermore, perhaps economic growth accelerated in the months after *Schechter* because, as the *Denver Post* hypothesized after the ruling, the end of the NIRA loosened "the bureaucratic brakes which have been clamped on business"—this growth could have kept equilibrium wage rates from falling while also causing firms to expand workweeks.

Figure 8.1 provides a more aggregate (rather than industry-level) approach by looking at the manufacturing sector as a whole. The chart shows movements of wage rates (average hourly earnings), workweeks, employment, and

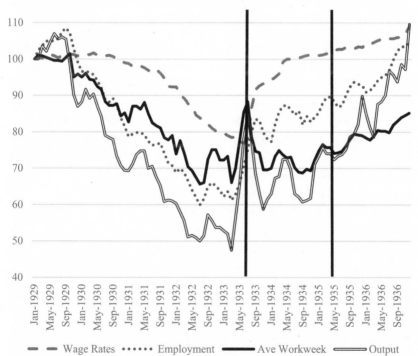

FIGURE 8.1. Movement of Manufacturing Indexes (January 1929 = 100); NIRA Start and End Dates Marked

Source: Data from National Bureau of Economic Research, *NBER Macrohistory Database*, http://www .nber.org/databases/macrohistory/contents/.

production in the manufacturing sector during the 1930s. July 1933 and May 1935 are marked with vertical lines representing the first and last months of the NIRA. This graph makes it quite clear that the NIRA's beginning had far more of an effect on wage rates and workweeks than did its official end after the *Schechter* decision. Average wage rates jumped sharply and average workweeks fell sharply in August 1933, the month the President's Reemployment Agreement was instituted so as to quickly implement the NIRA's labor provisions. However, no such mirror jump in these variables occurred after May 1935; both wage rates and workweeks were largely unchanged in June and July 1935 from their May levels, although workweeks did begin to rise after August. The other item that stands out is the relatively strong increase in manufacturing production in the eighteen months that followed the *Schechter* decision. Much of this strong growth can be attributed to fiscal and monetary expansion, but my empirical work with Todd Neumann and Jerry Taylor suggests that the repeal of the NIRA likely contributed to this recovery (see Neumann, Taylor, and Taylor 2012; Taylor and Neumann 2013).

Did the NIRA Have Long-Lasting Impacts?

While the NIRA lasted for just under two years, the findings of the Robert Committee suggest that the effects of the law may have persisted. By the end of the 1930s—via other legislative acts—child labor was regulated, the standard workweek was forty hours (generally eight hours per day, five days a week), and labor was guaranteed the right to collective bargaining. With respect to hourly earnings, earlier chapters show that the NIRA caused a large shock to wage rates in the summer of 1933—and I have demonstrated in this chapter that a decline in wage rates did not follow the NIRA's demise. This raises some important questions. *Did the NIRA cause a permanent boost to real hourly earnings? And if so, were low-wage industries affected by the NIRA more than high-wage industries in the long run?*

Table 8.2 reports the average inflation-adjusted (1982–84 dollars) wage rates in the five lowest- and the five highest-wage industries (as of July 1929) in our sample. In all ten industries, real wage rates rose between July 1929, just before the Great Depression began, and July 1938, shortly before the Fair Labor Standards Act took effect. Surprisingly, however, the largest percentage gain occurred in the automobile industry—an industry that also had the highest hourly wage rate in July 1929. Furthermore, the smallest gain came in the rayon yarn industry—an industry that had among the lowest hourly wage in 1929.

On average the five lowest-wage industries saw real hourly earnings rise

TABLE 8.2. Real Hourly Wage Rates (1982–84 Dollars) during the Great Depression

	Real hourly wage July 1929	Real hourly wage July 1933	Real hourly wage July 1938	Percentage change 1929 to 1938
Cotton goods manufacturing	$2.40	$2.41	$3.45	43.6
Wool manufacturing	$2.73	$2.71	$4.25	55.6
Rayon yarn	$2.82	$2.65	$3.68	30.5
Meatpacking	$2.95	$2.96	$4.91	66.5
Furniture manufacturing	$3.13	$2.72	$4.63	47.7
Machine manufacturing	$3.57	$4.02	$5.09	42.4
Electrical manufacturing	$3.61	$4.08	$5.63	55.9
Iron and steel	$3.71	$3.79	$5.97	60.9
Rubber products	$3.79	$4.45	$5.92	56.1
Automobiles	$4.03	$4.36	$6.73	66.9

Notes: Nominal wage data are converted to real via the consumer price index (1982–84 = 100) from the Bureau of Labor Statistics.

Source: National Bureau of Economic Research, *NBER Macrohistory Database*, chap. 8, http://www.nber .org/databases/macrohistory/contents/.

by an impressive 49 percent between July 1929 and July 1938. However, the five highest-wage industries experienced an even more impressive 56 percent average wage rate increase during this time. Thus, while the results presented earlier in this book suggest that the NIRA had a greater impact on the wage rates of low-wage industries than on high-wage industries in the summer of 1933, we cannot say the same thing regarding the longer-term impact of the NIRA.[20] Of course hourly earnings (when determined by markets) are largely a function of labor productivity, which is largely driven by technology. Whereas the short-term increase in wage rates that accompanied the NIRA was clearly driven by government fiat, the longer-term increase in wage rates during the Great Depression of the 1930s was likely driven by rapid productivity gains. Indeed, Field (2011) calls this decade "the most technologically progressive" in history. Looking at the list of industries in table 8.2, it seems feasible, if not likely, that technological gains were sharper in the five high-wage industries than in the five low-wage industries. Of course, we cannot discount the high-wage policies embedded in New Deal programs such as the NIRA, which encouraged firms to adopt capital- and technology-intensive forms of production rather than more expensive labor-intensive ones. For example, Seltzer (1997) shows that firms in the seamless hosiery industry shifted toward capital-intensive production in response to the institution of the minimum wage that accompanied the Fair Labor Standards Act of 1938. Still, it seems safe to say that the NIRA did not have a significantly greater long-term effect on low-wage industries than it did on high-wage industries.

Industry Output Growth after *Schechter*

Figure 8.1 reveals that production in the manufacturing sector rose very rapidly in the eighteen months after the *Schechter* decision, but this swift rise did not begin in the immediate wake of the ruling; July 1935 output was only 2 percent higher than it was in May 1935. By December 1935, however, it was up 24 percent from its May level, and by May 1937, it was over 40 percent above its level at the time of *Schechter*. In this section I examine how output changed in different industries in the months after the NIRA's demise. As discussed in chapter 5, there was tremendous heterogeneity within the codes in their trade practice provisions—some codes were many pages long and contained a plethora of provisions regulating output, pricing, and other economic decisions. Other codes did nothing but offer wage and hour regulations. One may hypothesize that the *Schechter* decision would have had a much larger impact on industries with complex codes than on industries with simple codes since they would be the ones in which, to quote from the *Denver Post*, the "bureaucratic brakes" were most loosened. For example, the lumber code was fifty-two pages long and contained, among other regulations on economic activity, explicit production quotas. In fact, the seasonally adjusted output of the lumber industry jumped 8.4 percent in June 1935 and then jumped another 20.2 percent in July 1935 in the immediate wake of the *Schechter* decision. By December 1935, lumber production was up a whopping 66 percent from its May level. Furthermore, these output movements were much higher than those of the manufacturing sector as a whole.

To test whether industries with codes that contained more detailed trade practice provisions were differentially impacted by the *Schechter* decision, I ran regressions similar to those shown in table 5.4, where my sample of thirty-eight industries is split into two sets: those with codes twenty or more pages and those whose codes were shorter than twenty pages. In this case I include a simple dummy variable for the five months following the *Schechter* decision—June through October 1935. The results, reported in table 8.3, suggest that industries with more complex codes saw a larger post-*Schechter* output bounce as output rose 1.77 percent per month during these five months, ceteris paribus, compared to an increase of only 0.86 percent per month in industries with shorter codes.

Specifications (3) and (4) in table 8.3 hold constant movements in hourly wage rates and workweeks.[21] In industries with long codes, output rises by 1.1 percent per month in the five-month post-*Schechter* era, even holding changes in labor variables constant. Thus, the regressions suggest that over 60 percent (1.1/1.77) of the post-*Schechter* boost in output can be attributed to

TABLE 8.3. Growth in Output in Industries with Short and Long Industry Codes

	(1) Eighteen longest codes		(2) Twenty shortest codes		(3) Eighteen longest codes		(4) Twenty shortest codes	
	Coefficient	p	Coefficient	p	Coefficient	p	Coefficient	p
Intercept	0.0333	.00	0.0318	.00	0.0330	.00	0.0212	.11
President's Reemployment Agreement (August 1933 to code passage)	-0.0146	.02	-0.0100	.18	-0.0124	.26	0.0045	.62
Industry-specific NIRA code (code passage to June 1935)	-0.0091	.02	-0.0011	.68	-0.0117	.00	0.0019	.50
Schechter dummy variable (June 1935–October 1935)	0.0177	.02	0.086	.01	0.0107	.00	0.0060	.17
Growth rate in workweek					0.6395	.00	0.3608	.00
Growth in wage rates					0.2596	.11	0.1160	.48
Controls	Yes		Yes		Yes		Yes	
Cross-sections	18		20		5		10	
Number of observations	2,510		2,282		638		1,264	

Notes: Dependent variable is growth rate in industry output minus growth rate in index of general business activity. Regressions employ industry fixed effects, cross-section weights, and White robust standard errors. Unreported control variables include a lagged dependent variable, pre-NIRA dummy variable, capacity utilization lagged one period, growth rate in government spending, growth rate in government revenues, growth rate in the M–1 money supply, growth rate in the S&P stock index, and growth in the AAA-BAA bond spread.

relaxation in the cartel-oriented aspects of the codes rather than simply the relaxation of the labor provisions. Interestingly, however, in industries with short codes, the *Schechter* dummy variable is not statistically different than zero once wages and hours are held constant. This suggests that any bump that these industries experienced was due to industries diverting from the wage and hours provisions of the NIRA after *Schechter*—there was no output bump from relaxation of trade practice rules since these industries generally had few, if any, rules regulating output.

Discussion

The demise and aftermath of the NIRA are well trodden paths in the historical literature. Because this book's focus is the heterogeneity of the impact of the NIRA, this chapter's discussion has largely centered on how industries were differentially impacted by the *Schechter* decision. Figure 8.1 shows that, while the implementation of the NIRA wage and hour provisions in August 1933 (under the President's Reemployment Agreement) had dramatic effects on workweeks and average hourly earnings, the *Schechter* decision brought little or no discernable change in either measure. One possibility is that firms followed the request of Roosevelt and the NRA and continued to voluntarily abide by their industries' codes of fair competition. The Robert Committee found substantial violations of the NRA codes—which is not surprising considering that there was no enforcement mechanism in place and compliance was purely voluntary. Still, the report noted that the code provisions were far from abandoned completely. In around three-quarters of industries, over half of the firms reported full compliance with the wage and hours provisions of the codes of fair competition.

Interestingly, however, the Robert Committee reported a great deal of industry-level heterogeneity with respect to continued compliance with the codes after *Schechter*. In the iron and steel industry, 95 percent of firms reported full compliance with the industry code's labor provisions. On the other hand, in the cotton garment industry, only 11 percent of firms reported no departures from that industry code's wage and hours provisions. This is consistent with the overall picture painted in this book. As hourly wages in the iron and steel industry were relatively high and hourly workweeks relatively low prior to the imposition of the NIRA, the law had relatively less impact on labor in this industry—both coming and going—than it did on, say, the cotton garment industry, which traditionally had low wages and long hours.

On the whole, the two years after the *Schechter* decision were positive ones for the US economy. Output, wage rates, employment, and average workweeks all rose—and the increase in output and employment was particularly sharp. According to Vedder and Gallaway's (1993, 77) monthly estimates, the unemployment rate fell from 20.1 percent when the *Schechter* ruling was handed down in May 1935 to 12.3 percent two years later. Expansionary monetary and fiscal policy certainly contributed to this sharp recovery. Still, to the extent that firms now freed from the NRA codes engaged in behavior that would have led to more hiring, such as wage rate cuts and expansions in productive capacity or output, the *Schechter* decision likely contributed to this two-year boom. My empirical findings suggest that industries with more complex codes of fair competition saw a larger post-*Schechter* output boom than did industries with shorter codes. These findings offer further evidence of the heterogeneous impact that the NIRA—and its demise—had on various industries.

9

Conclusion

This book argues that the general view of the NIRA as a monolithic two-year negative supply shock has been exaggerated. Yes, the program broadly raised wage rates and cut hours worked across the nonfarm economy. Furthermore, the NIRA promoted collusive outcomes whereby output was reduced and prices were raised. And it is true that the law was in effect for just under two years. Despite the veracity of these broad statements, however, *the effects of the NIRA varied dramatically by both industry and time period.* This concluding chapter summarizes the main argument of the book—the vast heterogeneity of effects and outcomes within the NIRA—and I will attempt to employ the microeconomic insights gleaned here to provide some macroeconomic insights into the overall impact of the program.

Heterogeneity of the Codes of Fair Competition

The degree of success that industries had in creating codes that promoted monopolistic behavior varied dramatically by industry. Many industry codes were just a few pages long and contained nothing more than statements creating minimum wage rates and maximum workweeks and recognizing the right of workers to bargain collectively. The photographic manufacturing code, for example, was a short code that set the maximum workweek at forty hours and the minimum wage at 35 cents per hour; it did not contain any trade practice provisions dealing with fair competition, prices, or output. Similarly, the rayon and synthetic yarn production code specified a forty-hour maximum workweek and a 32.5-cent minimum wage for the industry, but again it contained no trade practice provisions whatsoever. These two codes, and scores of others like them, are nothing like the familiar cartel-enabling caricature of the NRA codes.

On the other hand, many industries passed codes that were dozens of pages long and contained highly detailed provisions regulating prices, output, productive capacity, and other important aspects of economic behavior. For example, the copper code was 29 pages long and it contained an industry "sales plan" with monthly production quotas for each firm in the industry. The 24-page cement industry code likewise set up an "equitable allocation of available business" among its firms. The 20-page pickle-packing code allowed for the imposition of minimum (fixed) prices. The lumber code was 52 pages and contained provisions for both production quotas and fixed prices. The longest code, for the graphic arts industry, was 68 pages long. In total, the 557 codes took up 8,046 pages of text, yielding an average length of 14.4 pages. However, the standard deviation of code length was about eight pages. As with snowflakes, no two codes were the same.

In short, when one dives into the codes of fair competition, it is apparent that, while some of the codes closely fit the caricature of the NIRA monolith, many others do not. Thus, it should not be surprising to find that, while ample evidence indicates that cartel outcomes were achieved under the NIRA, this evidence is generally restricted to those industries that had complex codes that intensely regulated behavior. Little or no evidence exists that industries with basic codes saw output fall or prices rise because of collusion. While we can indeed "cement" the case that collusion occurred in some industries—such as cement—if we randomly drop our hooks in the code water, we may just as easily catch an industry like fishing tackle, which had one of the shortest and simplest of the 557 codes. The NIRA's effect on this industry looks nothing like that of a cartel-enabling program.

The Heterogeneous Effects of the NIRA's Labor Provisions

The NIRA instituted minimum wage rates across the manufacturing sector. However, as continues to be true today, these minimums generally affected low-wage industries such as yarn and cotton garment manufacturing far more than they did high-wage industries such as automobile and electrical manufacturing. Likewise, the NIRA reduced workweeks—usually to between thirty-five and forty hours per week, which was far less than the standard full-time week of forty-eight hours at the time. But again, many industries, such as iron and steel and machinery manufacturing, had already instituted thirty-five- to forty-hour workweeks by 1933. Hence, the NIRA affected hours worked in these industries far less than it did in, say, the meatpacking industry, where the average workweek a month before the NIRA's passage was nearly fifty hours.

Furthermore, it is an oversimplification to say that the NIRA imposed a binding 40-cent minimum wage across the economy. The President's Re-employment Agreement, which was instituted in August 1933, was indeed a relatively monolithic program in that it affected every industry identically. The PRA simultaneously mandated a 40-cent minimum wage and thirty-five-hour workweek for manufacturing workers in all industries (though firms could appeal for exemptions once their industry code of fair competition had been submitted for approval). Indeed, the data show a 17.5 percent jump in wage rates as well as a 15.6 percent decline in average workweeks between July and September of 1933 across the manufacturing sector as a whole. However, once an industry's code of fair competition was enacted, the wage and hour rules outlined in those codes superseded the PRA—and labor provisions varied dramatically by industry code. In some industries the minimum wage was as low as 20 cents an hour. Minimum wage rates below 30 cents were particularly common in codes that allowed for regional wage differentials—these generally stipulated lower minimum wage rates for firms located in the American South or in low-population cities. In some industries, such as petroleum, the minimum rates stipulated by the code were higher than 40 cents an hour. Workweeks also varied within the codes, although forty hours was relatively common. Still, the NIRA was not like the one-size-fits-all law that followed it (and that still exists today): the Fair Labor Standards Act, which set a common set of wage and hour guidelines for all firms.

Heterogeneity of the Timing of Code Passage

While the NIRA began on June 16, 1933, and continued until the Supreme Court ruled it unconstitutional on May 27, 1935, the effects of the program did not switch on like a light on the former date and then go black on the latter. Until an industry's code of fair competition was approved by the government, the NIRA had little or no effect on the trade practices in that industry. By August 1, 1933, only three industries had approved codes. Fourteen industry codes were passed in August, and thirteen more were approved in September. Code approvals finally began to speed up in the fall of 1933, with forty-five codes approved in October and sixty-eight in November. By year's end, around two hundred industries had codes in place. Still, this represents less than 40 percent of the total of 557 industry codes that were approved at the time of the NIRA's demise. The steam heating equipment industry accounted for the 279th code, the median in terms of the number passed. This code was approved on February 12, 1934. To say that the NRA was a cartel-enabling program from June 1933 to May 1935 clearly misses the mark, because no industries had their codes in effect in June 1933, and most did not have them in place until early 1934.

Compliance Issues and the Heterogeneous
Intertemporal Effects of the NIRA

Compliance issues were a major constraint on firms' abilities to achieve collusive outcomes under the NRA codes. Chapters 6 and 7 provide a detailed evaluation of the NRA enforcement mechanism and model the factors that determined its effectiveness. In the summer and fall of 1933, firms were generally convinced that defection from the NIRA would result in stiff penalties— specifically, a combination of lost business from a consumer boycott caused by the loss of the patriot Blue Eagle compliance emblem, government fines, and even imprisonment. However, during the winter of 1933/1934, it became clear that the NRA enforcement had far more bark than bite. Relatively few Blue Eagle emblems were removed, even in the face of clear violations, and the NRA's attempts to prosecute defectors in the courts were extremely rare. Instead, the 166,000 reported violations were generally met with a series of letters and visits from various NRA offices asking the firm to come into compliance. As it became clear that violations were unlikely to be met with punishment, many firms' calculus regarding their profit-maximizing behavior changed such that defection had a higher expected payoff than compliance.

By March and April of 1934, the NIRA was in a full-fledged "compliance crisis." Certainly not every firm broke the rules imposed by the codes, but complaints of violations of both labor and trade practice code provisions flooded NRA Compliance Division offices—the number of complaints received in March and April was more than double the number received in January and February. Thus, while those industries that were able to implement detailed and cartel-oriented codes of fair competition may indeed have achieved the collusive outcome of lower output and higher prices in late 1933 and early 1934, their ability to maintain collusive results was greatly hindered after this time. As firms defected, the NIRA's potential to act as a negative supply shock lessened. In fact, my regressions suggest that the effects of the NIRA on output, wage rates, and hours worked were stronger between the month an industry's code was passed and March 1934 than they were between April 1934 and the end of the program—a result consistent with a compliance crisis having wounded the program less than halfway through its two-year run.

From Micro to Macro

This book has focused on the microeconomics of the NIRA. My examination of economic decisions made under the program has concentrated on either the individual (firms and consumers) or the industry level. From the government's perspective, I have focused a great deal on the behavior of the individual city or state NRA offices as well as the actions of individual NRA field adjustors in their quest to enforce the program. Empirically, I have employed industry-level panel data to examine the effects of the NIRA over time. This microeconomic approach paints a far more complex picture of the program than that painted by scholars who employ the macroeconomic approach that is common in the NIRA literature (e.g., Cole and Ohanian 2004; and Eggertsson 2008, 2012, which employ macro-oriented general equilibrium models). From a bird's-eye view, the NIRA may indeed look like a monolithic program that created a two-year negative supply shock by artificially raising wage rates and reducing hours worked while also mandating that firms behave collusively. But the view on the ground shows that its economic effects were far more nuanced.

What can we say now that the NIRA monolith has been deconstructed—can these microeconomic pieces be employed to glean new insights into the macroeconomic implications of the program? I will use my concluding thoughts to try. Figure 9.1, which shows movements in industrial production during the 1930s, is produced to supplement this discussion.

The NIRA was announced with great fanfare in the summer of 1933. As Eggertsson (2008, 2012) correctly points out, the program raised inflation expectations and seemed to greatly boost general optimism. The government's Blue Eagle campaign, complete with parades and brass bands, was enormously successful in raising public morale—and macroeconomic models predict that economic confidence begets prosperity. Indeed, the US economy experienced its largest four-month growth spurt in history from April 1933, when the NIRA was being formulated, to July 1933, just before its labor provisions were to be put into effect through the PRA. Todd Neumann and I have called this remarkable episode in which industrial production rose 57 percent "Recovery Spring" (Taylor and Neumann 2016). During these four months, the economy climbed nearly halfway back from its trough in March 1933 to its prior peak in August 1929. Eggertsson's (2008, 2012) arguments are highly relevant to this time period.

The euphoria continued into the early fall—the Blue Eagle emblem covered the nation, and most economic actors expressed optimism that the recovery generated during President Roosevelt's first few months in office

FIGURE 9.1. Index of Industrial Production, July 1929–May 1937
Notes: The two lines at July 1933 and June 1935 mark the start and end of the NIRA.
Source: Federal Reserve Industrial Production and Capacity Utilization (G.17), Major Industry Groups, series B50001.S (seasonally adjusted).

would continue unabated. However, the imposition of the sharp hourly wage increases of the PRA in August and September 1933 coincided with a severe economic slowdown as industrial production fell nearly 20 percent between August and November 1933. Economic theory suggests that an artificial wage shock—this one was on the scale of a nearly 20 percent one-time rise—would cause firms to reduce employment and production and raise their prices. In other words, it would create the negative supply shock that Cole and Ohanian (2004) point toward. Indeed, the empirical analysis in Taylor and Neumann (2016) supports the notion that much of the slowdown in the fall can be attributed to the NIRA wage shock.

Furthermore, by October and November, many large industries such as iron and steel, lumber, petroleum, cotton textiles, bituminous coal, and automobile manufacturing were covered by their specific codes of fair competition. And by the end of 1933, the majority of all nonagricultural workers were in an industry that was covered by a code. Some, although certainly not all—and probably not even close to half—of these industry codes promoted collusive outcomes. To the extent that some industries were able to act monopolistically by raising prices and curtailing output (overproduction was said to be a major problem in many industries leading up to the NIRA, so indeed some codes focus heavily on means of reducing output), this would have fed further into the negative supply shock of the fall of 1933, consistent with Cole and Ohanian.

Still, some of the NRA code provisions such as those forbidding false advertising or lying about a competitor, were, from an economic welfare perspective, harmless at worst and perhaps even procompetitive. More-over, the work-sharing aspects of the NRA codes — that is, the reduction in workweeks — promoted the employment of more workers. Aggregate hours worked in the economy fell after the PRA wage hikes, but the number of Americans with jobs rose since scarce work was effectively shared (Taylor 2011). One could argue that this aspect of the NIRA was highly successful. Likewise, enthusiasm for the Blue Eagle emblem — and the NIRA in general — while waning in the fall of 1933, was still relatively high, and this boost of con-fidence certainly offset some of the negative effects that the labor provisions had on recovery.

The economy began to recover again in the winter and spring of 1934 (see figure 9.1). The timing coincides with a surge in noncompliance with the NRA — in terms of firms' obedience with labor provisions guiding wages and hours as well as trade practice provisions implementing production quotas, price filing provisions, and forbidding sales below costs. At this point, I have not attempted to establish causality between the defections from the NRA codes and the macroeconomic upswing in the winter and spring of 1934. Still, the regression results reported in chapter 7 — which link the enthusiasm for the Blue Eagle emblem (proxied by its presence in newspaper ads), violations of the NRA (proxied by complaints received in NRA offices), and changes in output, prices, wages, and hours — are at least suggestive of such a possibility. This is an avenue that appears worthy of future research. Indeed, to the extent that compliance with the NRA's labor and trade practice provisions waned, the negative supply shock that these policies brought would have waned as well.

Chapter 7 also describes the NIRA's renewed efforts to bring industries back into compliance with the NRA codes. Among these was the introduc-tion of the Code Eagle in the late spring and early summer of 1934 as well as mass compliance drives beginning in the late summer of 1934. Although these actions did not bring compliance back to the fall 1933 levels (at least not in the economy as a whole, although in some cities, such as Mansfield, Ohio, where mass compliance experiments were attempted, they appear to have been highly successful), they at least appear to have halted the trend of rising defections that the economy experienced in the spring of 1934. The

NRA provisions, while certainly not having as much of an impact as they did in the fall of 1933, continued to affect the economy in the last half of 1934 and the first half of 1935.

Figure 9.1 also shows that industrial production began a sustained increase in the months immediately following the Supreme Court's *Schechter* decision, which invalidated the NIRA. The regression findings reported in table 8.3 suggest that output grew twice as fast in the six months after *Schechter* in industries that had complex codes—that is, those where collusive outcomes were most likely to have occurred—than it did in industries with simple codes. From a macroeconomic perspective, this is suggestive of the removal of a cartel-oriented supply shock having occurred in these industries after the *Schechter* decision. Indeed, it is notable that the result of faster output growth post-*Schechter* in the complex-code industries holds even when changes in wages and hours are held constant—that is, the boost in output in these industries is not simply attributable to the relaxation of NIRA labor standards.

The discussion here suggests that I largely concur with the broad macroeconomic conclusions of Cole and Ohanian, who point to the NIRA's labor and collusive provisions as a general obstacle to recovery. However, I also concur with Eggertsson in regard to the NIRA's positive impact via the expectations channel in the initial months of the program, when enthusiasm was high. By deconstructing the time line of the NIRA, we can essentially synthesize the findings of these two sides of the debate and show that, rather than being mutually exclusive, they both provide important truths about the NIRA's macroeconomic impact.

Still, while I generally value the overall conclusions conveyed by macroeconomics studies of the NIRA, the models employed in these studies are inaccurate caricatures of the NIRA. They are missing the heterogeneous impact of the NIRA both by industry and by time period. To the extent that the results of macroeconomic general equilibrium studies are a function of the underlying models they employ, their results likely overstate the NIRA's effects on the macroeconomy as well as the timing of these effects. The negative supply shock that the NIRA created was strongest between August 1933 and March 1934, and then it waned significantly after that. Likewise, the "great expectations" that Eggertsson notes the NIRA created—with respect to raising both inflation expectations and consumer and business confidence more generally—was strongest between the late spring and early winter of 1933. Enthusiasm for the program as a tonic for recovery (or inflation) waned rapidly as 1933 ended and 1934 began. The positive demand shock (enhanced expectations) and the negative supply shock (high wages and collusion) overlapped in the late summer and early fall of 1933. The deflationary spiral had ended, but this did not bring swift recovery—at least not until after the NIRA ended in 1935. Output rose sharply in the two years after the *Schechter* decision invalidated the NIRA.

In closing, I strongly encourage further exploration into the microeconomics of the NIRA. Carefully designed studies of the program can help economists glean important insights into economic theory—specifically related to labor, industrial organization, and public choice theory. But scholars must account for the fact that the NIRA is not the monolith it is often characterized as. Recent case studies that focus on the contents of codes in a specific industry, such as Vickers and Ziebarth (2014), are a large step in the right direction. At the same time, given the compliance issues under the NIRA, scholars must take better care to consider the precise timing of when the effects under consideration actually occurred. A careful unpacking of the NIRA into industry-level code attributes, as well as into appropriate temporal periods, can yield fruitful insights into contemporary economic issues. It can also paint a more accurate picture of the NIRA's impact on the depressed economy of the 1930s.

Acknowledgments

I am grateful to many people who have contributed in some way to this book. First, Price Fishback, thank you for kind encouragement of my NIRA-related research over the past decade. Thanks also to all my various coauthors of NIRA-related articles upon which this book builds, especially Todd Neumann, Peter Klein, Bernard Beaudreau, and Robert Schuldt. I also want to acknowledge the critical role played by three former professors who mentored and inspired me toward economic research on the Great Depression: Richard Vedder, Fred Bateman, and George Selgin. Over the past twenty years I have had a veritable army of student research assistants who have been extremely helpful gathering the materials and data used in this research. Four in particular—Robert J. Lee, Vlad Radoias, Jason Turkiela, and Wyatt Bush—stand out for their contributions. Finally, I want to thank Holly Smith and Jane Macdonald of the University of Chicago Press for their valuable assistance in the final stages of completing this book.

Notes

Chapter 1

1. The details of the Liberty Baking case were reported in various memos in National Archives, Record Group 9, ARC Identifier 1107059, "Records of the Compliance Division, Closed Case Files," PI 44-102 [hereafter cited as Compliance Division, Closed Case Files], box 1.

2. Details of the case against Bernard Levine are from Compliance Division, Closed Case Files, box 83.

3. Details of the case against the A. N. Smith Lumber Company are from Compliance Division, Closed Case Files, box 133.

4. Such information generally is supplied in the preface to each industry's specific code of fair competition.

5. The 40/40 wage and hour standards were to be phased in beginning with less restrictive levels in 1938.

Chapter 2

1. This chapter draws from my work in Beaudreau and Taylor (2018), which also addresses this question.

2. Eggertsson (2012), which will be discussed in more detail later in the book, builds a model of emergency economic conditions whereby the NIRA is expansionary because it promotes rising prices. In his model, anything that raises inflation expectations is expansionary.

3. O'Brien (1989), Vedder and Gallaway (1993), and Taylor and Selgin (1999) discuss the importance of this doctrine in 1930s policy.

4. "Presidential Statement on the National Industrial Recovery Act," in *The Public Papers and Addresses of Franklin D. Roosevelt*, vol. 2, *The Year of Crisis, 1933* (New York: Random House, 1938), 251.

5. United States v. American Linseed Oil Co., 262 U.S. 371 (1923) at 262.

6. Maple Flooring Manufacturers Association v. United States, 268 U.S. 563 (1925) at 268.

7. Herbert Hoover, speech to the American Federation of Labor, October 6, 1930, "The Depression Papers of Herbert Hoover," http://www.geocities.ws/mb_williams/hooverpapers/1930/paper19301006.html.

8. "Text of the President's Speech," *New York Times*, May 5, 1933.

9. "Franklin Roosevelt's Statement on the National Industrial Recovery Act," June 16, 1933, http://docs.fdrlibrary.marist.edu/odnirast.html.

10. A large body of literature discusses the efficacy of modern work-sharing policies and their impact. For example, see Calmfors and Hoel (1988), Brunello (1989), Marimon and Zilibotti (2000), Rocheteau (2002), and Pencaval (2014).

11. *Historical Statistics of the United States Millennial Edition Online*, Table Ba470-477, "Labor Force, Employment, and Unemployment: 1890–1990."

12. National Bureau of Economic Research, "US Average Hours of Work per Week, Manufacturing Industries, Total Wage Earners, NICB," NBER Macrohistory Database, series m8029a.

13. "The Merchant's View," *New York Times*, April 30, 1933.

14. "30 Hour Work Bill Will Be Deferred: Works Plan in Jam," *New York Times*, May 2, 1933.

15. "Business Control: To Plan or Not to Plan No Longer Seems to be the Question," *Wall Street Journal*, May 5, 1933.

16. "Industry Control Modified in Bill," *New York Times*, May 7, 1933.

17. "The Merchant's Point of View," *New York Times*, May 7, 1933.

18. "The President's Message," *New York Times*, May 18, 1933.

19. "Recovery Measure Called a Trade Boon," *New York Times*, May 16, 1933.

20. "Trade Groups Here Hail Industry Bill," *New York Times*, May 19, 1933.

21. "Baruch Endorses Industry Measure," *New York Times*, May 20, 1933.

22. "Predicts Pay Rise in 10,000,000 Jobs," *New York Times*, May 21, 1933.

23. "Electrical Group for Industry Act," *New York Times*, May 24, 1933.

24. "Manufacturers Attack Bill," *New York Times*, May 27, 1933.

25. "Higher Pay Urged as Recovery Step," *New York Times*, June 3, 1933.

26. "Licensing Power Killed," *New York Times*, June 3, 1933.

27. "Senators Bar Sales Tax," *New York Times*, June 4, 1933.

28. All quotes in this paragraph are from "Members Grow Restive," *New York Times*, June 8, 1933.

29. "Lund and Harriman Back Recovery Act," *New York Times*, June 15, 1933.

Chapter 3

1. This discussion is largely based on Dearing et al. (1934, 79–90).

2. US National Recovery Administration, *Codes of Fair Competition* (1933), vol. 1, 22.

3. "Dress Group Works on Trade Compact," *New York Times*, May 5, 1933.

4. "Recovery Measure Called Trade Boon," *New York Times*, May 16, 1933.

5. "Business World," *New York Times*, May 20, 1933.

6. "Trade Groups Hail Industry Bill," *New York Times*, May 19, 1933.

7. "Control Bill Puts Industry on Trial," *New York Times*, May 21, 1933.

8. "Two Trades in Line with Federal Plan," *New York Times*, May 23, 1933.

9. "Business World," *New York Times*, May 26, 1933.

10. "Cotton Group Named," *New York Times*, May 24, 1933.

11. "For Organization of Dress Industry," *New York Times*, May 27, 1933.

12. US National Recovery Administration, *Codes of Fair Competition*, vol. 2, 84.

13. "Electric Trade Drafts New Codes," *New York Times*, May 29, 1933.

14. "Retailers to Act on Industry Bill," *New York Times*, June 4, 1933.

15. "N. D. Baker to Form Rubber Trade Code," *New York Times*, June 8, 1933.

16. "Industries Act to Adopt US Control Plan," *Chicago Tribune*, June 16, 1933.

17. "Coal Men Draft Code," *Chicago Tribune*, June 16, 1933.

18. "Warn Industries to Simplify Codes," *New York Times*, June 18, 1933.

19. "Recovery Act Aimed at Rehabilitation," *New York Times*, June 8, 1933.

20. US National Recovery Administration, *Codes of Fair Competition*, vol. 1, 4.

21. Because it was the first of its kind, some details of this hearing were outlined in "Code of Fair Competition for the Cotton Textile Industry," *Monthly Labor Review* 37, no. 2 (August 1933): 265–72.

22. "Cotton Men Raise Minimum Wage $2," *New York Times*, July 1, 1933.

23. "Textile Mills First to Meet Control by US," *Chicago Tribune*, June 27, 1933.

24. "Cotton Men Raise Minimum Wage $2," *New York Times*, July 1, 1933.

25. "New Codes Rushed; Work Rate Is 4% in Recovery Loans," *New York Times*, July 2, 1933.

26. "Warn Industries to Simplify Codes," *New York Times*, June 18, 1933.

27. "Labor Board Asks Firm Trade Codes," *New York Times*, July 23, 1933.

28. Franklin D. Roosevelt, "Statement on N.I.R.A," June 16, 1933, http://www.presidency.ucsb.edu/ws/?pid=14673.

29. "Wide Work Spread Asked by Johnson," *New York Times*, June 17, 1933.

30. "Committee Named to Draft Oil Code," *New York Times*, June 23, 1933.

31. "Oil Code Adopted; Asks Price Fixing," *New York Times*, June 25, 1933.

32. "President Orders Curb on Illegal Oil," *New York Times*, July 13, 1933.

33. "Oil Men Warned to Agree on Code," *New York Times*, July 25, 1933.

34. "Federal Oil Curb Proposed by NRA," *New York Times*, August 1, 1933.

35. "Sinclair Assails Oil Code," *New York Times*, August 6, 1933.

36. "Code Drawn by Shipbuilding Industry," *New York Times*, July 13, 1933.

37. "Wool Code Terms Opposed By Labor," *New York Times*, July 25, 1933.

38. Ibid.

39. "Two Textile Groups End Code Hearings," *New York Times*, July 26, 1933.

40. Memorandum, Leslie Smith to The Ice Industry, May 22, 1933, National Archives, Record Group 9, ARC Identifier 1102650, "Records Relating to Code Drafting and Approval, 1933–1935," PI 44-20, box 23 [hereafter cited as Code Drafting and Approval].

41. Memorandum, Smith to The Board of Directors, May 24, 1933, Code Drafting and Approval.

42. Memorandum, Smith to The Ice Industry, June 19, 1933, Code Drafting and Approval.

43. Smith, "Present Status of Ice Industry Code under Industrial Recovery Act," July 17, 1933, Code Drafting and Approval.

44. Memorandum, Lucy Mason to R. A. Paddock, September 6, 1933, Code Drafting and Approval.

45. Memorandum, Jos. Moreschi to Hugh Johnson, September 8, 1933, Code Drafting and Approval.

46. "Warn Industries to Simplify Codes," *New York Times*, June 18, 1933.

Chapter 4

1. "Johnson to Offer Blanket Schedule to Speed Up Codes," *New York Times*, July 11, 1933.

2. "Blanket Code Next Step," *New York Times*, July 18, 1933.

3. The PRA stated that fourteen- and fifteen-year-olds could be employed for up to three hours per day as long as it was not during school hours and the hours were between 7:00 a.m. and 7:00 p.m.

4. Arthur Krock, "Blue Hawk Spreads Its Wings This Week in Colossal Experiment," *New York Times*, July 25, 1933.

5. Franklin D. Roosevelt, "Fireside Chat (Recovery Program)," July 24, 1933, American Presidency Project, http://www.presidency.ucsb.edu/ws/index.php?pid=14488.

6. Two weeks later, Roosevelt signed an executive order saying that all firms with federal contracts—which accounted for around $500 million—had to abide by the PRA or their contracts would be canceled.

7. "President Sees Higher Pay, Shorter Hours for All Workers," *New York Times*, July 26, 1933.

8. "450,000 NRA Blanks Distributed Here," *New York Times*, July 28, 1933.

9. All information in this paragraph is reported in "Response Is Nationwide," *New York Times*, July 28, 1933.

10. See Dearing et al. (1934, 64–65) for more detail about the organization of the Blue Eagle drive.

11. "Force Blue Eagle on Shop by Strike," *New York Times*, August 30, 1933.

12. "15,000 March under the NRA Banner While Thousands of Spectators Cheer Detroit's Response to Recovery Drive," *Detroit Free Press*, September 1, 1933.

13. "Fervor Sweeps Throngs," *New York Times*, September 14, 1933.

14. "750,000 Affected in Banks," *New York Times*, August 3, 1933.

15. "New Exemptions from NRA Code," *New York Times*, August 1, 1933.

16. "26,233 State Firms under NRA Banner," *Detroit Free Press*, August 6, 1933; "Tentative Auto Code Possible," *Detroit Free Press*, August 14, 1933.

17. "80,000 Consumers Sign NRA Pledge," *Detroit Free Press*, September 8, 1933.

18. "908 More Local Employers Sign Recovery Code," *Chicago Tribune*, August 15, 1933.

19. "Strike Threats Arise as 3,442 More Firms Sign NRA Codes," *Chicago Tribune*, August 19, 1933.

20. "Retail Code Rigid on Unfair Tactics," *New York Times*, August 6, 1933.

21. "City NRA Dive Asks Aid of Trade Groups," *New York Times*, August 9, 1933.

22. "Hodgson Assails Failure to Join NRA," *New York Times*, August 30, 1933.

23. Associated Press, "NRA Campaign to 'Buy Now' Is Under Way," *State Journal* (Lansing, MI), August 7, 1933.

24. "Johnson Gives New Warning," *Detroit Free Press*, August 12, 1933.

25. These figures from local newspapers are reported in Taylor (2011).

Chapter 5

1. Supplementary codes were those passed by subindustries within a broader industry code. For example, on April 4, 1934, a supplementary code for the wrench manufacturing industry was passed. This code was supplemental to the fabricated metal products manufacturing and metal finishing and metal coating industry code, which was passed on November 2, 1933. The subindustries within these codes often replaced certain provisions in the broader code with one that catered to their own needs or added new provisions that were relevant to their subindustry.

2. Michael Bernstein (1987) documents that heterogeneous impact that the Great Depression had between industries, with some dynamic industries doing well while others experienced dramatic declines.

3. Codes generally specified that they would take effect a few days after government approval—the second Monday after approval was commonly stipulated as the date the code would become binding.

4. I have compiled monthly data from about seventy industries that were covered by a specific code of fair competition, and the median date of code passage of these industries is November 17, 1933. Of course, the government tended to collect data from large industries, and this bias toward code approval in large industries can account for the difference in the date of median code passage for all codes (February 12, 1934) and the median date of code passage in these seventy industries (November 17, 1933). The actual date on which the median worker was covered by a code was probably between these dates but closer to the earlier one—thus, my estimate of December 1, 1933.

5. Alexander used growth rate in establishment size between 1929 and 1933 as a proxy for cost heterogeneity between firms in an industry.

6. This length includes the introductory material provided by the NRA—generally a letter of recommendation of approval from Hugh Johnson or another NRA administrator summarizing the key points from the code hearing as well as the state of the industry. Essentially this is the number of pages the industry's code discussion takes up in the NRA's printed volumes of approved codes. US National Recovery Administration, *Codes of Fair Competition* (1933–35), vols. 1–23. The codes have been digitized and are available here: https://babel.hathitrust.org/cgi/pt?id=mdp.35112101846592;view=1up;seq=332.

7. Temin and Wigmore (1990) build a similar case, which Eggertsson extends. Romer (1999) concludes that the NIRA wage and price provisions, along with a relatively high rate of economic growth, were the key factors in the inflation that occurred between 1933 and 1935 despite the economy being well below trend.

8. Monthly output data are from National Bureau of Economic Research, NBER Macrohistory Database. The index of business activity is from the same source—specifically, "Index of Physical Volume of Business Activity," series 1001. The business activity index is seasonally adjusted using the same procedure as with the output data.

9. If a code was passed on or before the fifteenth of the month, that month is counted as an NIRA month. If passed on the sixteenth or after, it was a PRA month. For example, the code covering the furniture production industry was passed on December 7, 1933, so August through November were counted as PRA months and the NIRA dummy variable turns on in December. The code covering tires was passed on December 21, 1933, so August through December were PRA months and the NIRA dummy variable turned on in January 1934.

10. Ideally, the sample would have been divided in half—nineteen in each subsample. However, the nineteenth and twentieth longest codes (construction and fertilizers) were both eighteen pages. The results are qualitatively the same regardless of whether these two are placed in the long or short code group.

11. When a trade association existed in an industry, it typically helped the industry formulate and administer the provisions of the code.

Chapter 6

1. Executive Order 6205-A, July 15, 1933.

2. "Restores Blue Eagle," *New York Times*, October 13, 1933, 26.

3. All information and quotes in this paragraph and the next are from Memorandum, Leighton H. Peebles to Alvin Bailey, National Recovery Administration, October 17, 1933, in

"Proceedings of Meeting No. 20 of the Special Industrial Recovery Board," Appendix B, Department of Commerce, October 23, 1933.

4. "First Blue Eagle Removal Ordered," *Detroit Free Press*, October 11, 1933, 1.

5. "Blue Eagles Taken from 2 Employers," *New York Times*, October 12, 1933, 1.

6. "Seeks Blue Eagle Return," *New York Times*, October 13, 1933, 26.

7. *State Journal* (Lansing, Michigan), October 11, 1933, 1.

8. "National Whirligig: News behind the News," *Detroit Free Press*, October 11, 1933, 6.

9. "Roosevelt Orders Fine, Jail Terms for NRA Violators," *New York Times*, October 18, 1933, 1.

10. US National Recovery Administration, *Codes of Fair Competition*, vol. 6, 198 (from the hat manufacturing code of fair competition).

11. The sworn affidavit of April 18, 1934, from Pollack titled "In the Matter of Complaint against the Adamstown Hat Company" is from Compliance Division, Closed Case Files, box 2. (See note 1 of chapter 1 for the full citation of Closed Case Files.)

12. Memorandum to Vincent Powers, NRA Compliance Adjuster, April 18, 1934, Compliance Division, Closed Case Files, box 2.

13. From National Archives, Record Group 9, ARC Identifier 1107065, "Complaints Regarding the President's Reemployment Agreement," PI 44-109.

14. Ibid.

15. National Recovery Administration, "Manual for the Adjustment of Complaints by State Directors and Code Authorities," bulletin no. 7 (January 22, 1934), 14.

16. Ibid., 16.

17. Ibid., 18.

18. Galvin, Reinstein, and Campbell (1936, 206), Table 10, "NRA State Office Complaint Statistics Time Elapsed between Docketing and First Action, Labor Code Cases, Total All Offices, October 1933–May 1935."

19. Ibid., 207, Table 11, "NRA State Office Complaint Statistics Time Elapsed between First Action and Closing, Labor Code Cases, Total All Offices, October 1933–May 1935."

20. Ibid., 214–19, "Table 20, NRA State Office Complaint Statistics, Violations of Trade Practice and Administrative Provisions."

21. Ibid., 168, "Table 1, NRA State Office Complaint Statistics, Number of Labor Code Cases Investigated, Offices by Region."

22. Ibid., 231, "Table 13, NRA State Office Complaint Statistics: Violations of the President's Reemployment Agreement."

23. Ibid., 232, "Table 10, NRA State Office Complaint Statistics: Amount of Restitution and Number of Employees Paid."

24. This memo is cited in Irons (1982, 39).

25. Irons (1982, 56) notes that in the subset of nineteen cases decided by district judges on constitutional grounds, 71 percent of Republican judges held the NIRA unconstitutional while 80 percent of Democratic judges upheld the NIRA—so it does appear that "partisanship clearly colored constitutionalism at the district court level."

26. Irons (1982, 40–53) discusses the uneasy relations between the Justice Department and the NRA regarding the handling of many of these cases.

27. Unless otherwise noted, the source of the material on the case against Belcher is National Archives, Record Group 9, ARC Identifier 1103131, "Records of Enforcement Division, Digests of Litigation Cases," PI 44-59 [hereafter cited as Records of Enforcement Division], box 1. The case was digested by A. W. DeBirny on August 12, 1935.

28. "100 Cleaners Face NRA Prosecution," *New York Times*, December 12, 1933, 6.

29. All information on the Supreme Instruments Company is from Records of Enforcement Division, box 1. The case was digested by William L. Pencke on September 27, 1935.

30. All information on the Michael Goodman case is from Records of Enforcement Division, box 1. The case was digested by L. M. Barkin on November 7, 1935.

31. All information on the High Ice Cream case is from Records of Enforcement Division, box 2. The case was digested by L. M. Barkin on October 11, 1935.

32. US National Recovery Administration, *Codes of Fair Competition*, vol. 6, 517 (from the restaurant industry code of fair competition).

33. This correspondence is from National Archives, Record Group 9, ARC Identifier 1107065, "Complaints Regarding the President's Reemployment Agreement," PI 44-109, box 26.

34. The information regarding this case is from Galvin, Reinstein, and Campbell (1936, 154).

Chapter 7

1. This model is based on my work with Peter Klein (Taylor and Klein 2008).

2. In Taylor and Klein (2008), we go into more detail regarding how the size of *GP* depends on the percentage of the *n* firms that are complying and defecting. For the analysis here, the focus is more on the intuition of the good patriot effect.

3. The records discussed from the Detroit office on public attitude are from National Archives, Record Group 9, ARC Identifier 1105784, "Records of the Compliance Division, Public Attitude Reports," PI 44-128 [hereafter cited as Compliance Division, Public Attitude Reports], box 1.

4. "Court Upholds NRA Pay Scale," *Detroit News*, November 14, 1933.

5. "NRA Wages Suit Won by Waitress," *Detroit Free Press*, November 15, 1933.

6. "Attempt to Test NRA Is Rejected," *Detroit Free Press*, November 15, 1934, 2.

7. The records discussed from the Louisville office on public attitude are from Compliance Division, Public Attitude Reports, box 2.

8. The records discussed from the Chicago office on public attitude are from Compliance Division, Public Attitude Reports, box 1.

9. The records discussed from the San Francisco office on public attitude are from Compliance Division, Public Attitude Reports, box 1.

10. These data were collected and employed in Taylor (2007a) and Taylor and Klein (2008).

11. "NRA Board Quits at Lincoln Nebr," *Washington Post*, December 2, 1933, 8.

12. "NRA Board of 7 Resigns in Bay State," *Washington Post*, December 12 1933, 1.

13. "New Blue Eagles to Appear Monday," *New York Times*, April 27, 1934, 22.

14. Memorandum, L.J. Martin, Chief, Compliance Division, NRA, to Col. G. A. Lynch, Administrative Officer, "Mass Compliance," October 8, 1934, from National Archives, Record Group 9, ACR Identifier 1105785, "Records Relating to Mass Compliance Surveys, 1934–45," PI 44-129 [hereafter cited as Records Relating to Mass Compliance Surveys], box 2.

15. Memorandum, Benedict Crowell, State NRA Compliance Director, to Stanley Posner, Chief Economist, NRA Compliance Division, "Compliance Campaign," September 10, 1934, from Records Relating to Mass Compliance Surveys, box 2.

16. Memorandum, M. E. Woods, Executive Assistant, Cleveland Field Office, to John Swope, Chief, Field Branch, Attention: Stanley Posner, "Zanesville Compliance Campaign," September 10, 1934, from Records Relating to Mass Compliance Surveys, box 2.

17. "Chiseling Inquiry Set on Shoe Code," *New York Times*, March 23, 1935.

18. Report from J. E. Campion of the Berkshire Shoe Company, April 10, 1935, from Records Relating to Mass Compliance Surveys, box 1.

19. Report from W. C. Young and J. R. Brunozzi of Sam Biron & Company, March 27, 1935, from Records Relating to Mass Compliance Surveys, box 1.

20. Report from M. E. Woods, Ohio State Compliance Director to John Swope, NRA Mass Compliance Officer, April 13, 1935, from Records Relating to Mass Compliance Surveys, box 1.

21. "Find Shoe Plants Broke Code Rules," *New York Times*, April 17, 1935.

22. Report from Chicago State Office to John Swope, "Boot and Shoe Industry Mass Compliance Survey," April 12, 1935, from Records Relating to Mass Compliance Surveys, box 1.

23. "Summary of Mass Compliance Activities," New York Office, August 5, 1935, from Records Relating to Mass Compliance Surveys, box 2.

Chapter 8

1. "New Deal to Use Steam Roller to Extend NRA," *Chicago Tribune*, May 26, 1935, 20.

2. This subsection largely follows a similar section from Neumann, Taylor, and Taylor (2012).

3. "Press Generally Sees Ruling as Victory for Fundamental Law," *New York Times*, May 28, 1935, 12. All quotes in the following two paragraphs are from this article.

4. "Industry Cheered by NIRA Ruling: Retail Trade and Automobile Manufacturers Especially Welcome Outcome: Cross Section of Views," *Wall Street Journal*, May 28, 1935, 1.

5. "Wall Street Hails New Deal Defeats," *New York Times*, May 28, 1935, 1.

6. "Review and Outlook: Realists on the Bench," *Wall Street Journal*, May 29, 1935, 4.

7. This was terminology used by Lyon et al. (1935) in their contemporary study of the NIRA.

8. After Hugh Johnson's resignation in late August 1934, the National Industrial Recovery Board, a five-member (and later seven-member) governing body was formed to steer the NRA. Richberg was named chairman of this board in March 1935.

9. "Richberg Issues Plea. He Calls on Employers to Maintain Labor, Fair Practice Standards," *New York Times*, May 28, 1935, 1.

10. "Reports from Field Offices Regarding Changes in Industrial Conditions Subsequent to the Supreme Court Decision of the Schechter Case," South Carolina, "Reports of Non-Compliance with Code Standards," National Archives, Record Group 9, ARC Identifier 1105783, "Records Relating to the Robert Committee Investigation, 1935," PI 44-127 [hereafter cited as Robert Committee Investigation], box 9.

11. Memorandum 2056, Milwaukee Office (E. T. Anderson, Executive Assistant) to National Recovery Administration, Major General Amos A. Fries, "Survey of Graphic Arts Industry in Wisconsin," August 17, 1935, Robert Committee Investigation, box 9.

12. Memorandum 2054, Milwaukee Office (E. T. Anderson, Executive Assistant) to National Recovery Administration, Major General Amos A. Fries, "Survey of Graphic Arts Industry in Wisconsin," August 16, 1935, Robert Committee Investigation, box 9.

13. Memorandum 2056, Charleston S.C. State Office to Chairman of the Committee on Business and Labor Standards, "Daily Report on Industries," July 30, 1935, Robert Committee Investigation, box 9.

14. "Extent of Departure from Code Standards . . . New York Figures Only," Retail Drug Industry, Robert Committee Investigation, box 2.

15. "Extent of Departure from Code Standards . . . New York Figures Only," Motor Vehicle Retailing Industry, Robert Committee Investigation, box 2.

16. "Extent of Departure from Code Standards . . . New York Figures Only," Shipbuilding and Ship Repair Industry, Robert Committee Investigation, box 2.

17. "NRA Code Rules Still Maintained in Most Industries," *New York Times*, March 17, 1936, 1.

18. Ibid.

19. The Robert Committee data were published in *Monthly Labor Review* (May 1936): 1237.

20. Hausman (2016) suggests that hourly wage rates in the automobile industry during the 1930s rose due to waves of labor strife, which became particularly acute in 1936 and 1937.

21. As mentioned in chapter 5, the rationale for treating wage rates and hours worked as exogenous is that the NIRA mandated exogenous changes to these variables, which could have indirectly affected output. Thus, when these factors are held constant, we can better isolate the impact of the NIRA's trade practice provisions on output.

References

Alexander, Barbara. 1994. "The Impact of the National Industrial Recovery Act on Cartel Formation and Maintenance Costs." *Review of Economics and Statistics* 76 (2): 245–54.

———. 1997. "Failed Cooperation in Heterogeneous Industries under National Recovery Administration." *Journal of Economic History* 57 (2): 322–44.

Alter, Jonathan. 2006. *FDR's Hundred Days and the Triumph of Hope.* New York: Simon & Schuster.

Badger, Anthony J. 2008. *FDR: The First Hundred Days.* New York: Hill and Wang.

Beard, Charles. 1933. Review of *Industrial Discipline and the Governmental Arts,* by Rexford G. Tugwell. *American Political Science Review* 27 (5): 833–35.

Beaudreau, Bernard, and Jason E. Taylor. 2018. "Why Did the Roosevelt Administration Think Cartels, Higher Wages, and Shorter Workweeks Would Promote Recovery from the Great Depression?" *The Independent Review: A Journal of Political Economy* 23 (1): 91–107.

Bellush, Bernard. 1975. *The Failure of the NRA.* New York: W. W. Norton.

Berle, A. A., Jr., John Dickinson, A. Heath Onthank, Leo Pasvolsky, Alexander Sachs, Herbert J. Tily, Willard L. Thorp, Rexford G. Tugwell, and Leo Wolman. 1934. *America's Recovery Program.* New York: Oxford University Press.

Bernstein, Irving. 2010. *The Lean Years: A History of the American Worker, 1920–1933.* Chicago: Haymarket Books. First published in 1969 by Houghton Mifflin.

Bernstein, Michael A. 1987. *The Great Depression: Delayed Recovery and Economic Change in America, 1929–1939.* New York: Cambridge University Press.

Best, Fred. 1981. "The History and Current Relevance of Work Sharing." In *Work Sharing: Issues, Policy Options, and Prospects,* 1–17. Kalamazoo, MI: W. E. Upjohn Institute for Employment Research.

Biles, Roger. 1991. *A New Deal for the American People.* DeKalb: Northern Illinois University Press.

Brand, Donald. 1988. *Corporatism and the Rule of Law: A Study of the National Recovery Administration.* Ithaca, NY: Cornell University Press.

Brookings, Robert. 1932. *The Way Forward.* New York: Macmillan.

Brunello, Giorgio. 1989. "The Employment Effects of Shorter Working Hours: An Application to Japanese Data." *Economica* 56: 473–86.

Calmfors, Lars, and Michael M. Hoel. 1988. "Work Sharing and Overtime." *Scandinavian Journal of Economics* 90: 45–62.

Chicu, Mark, Chris Vickers, and Nicolas L. Ziebarth. 2013. "Cementing the Case for Collusion under the NRA." *Explorations in Economic History* 50: 487–507.

Cohen, Adam. 2009. *Nothing to Fear: FDR's Inner Circle and the Hundred Days That Created Modern America*. New York: Penguin Press.

Cole, Harold L., and Lee E. Ohanian. 2004. "New Deal Policies and the Persistence of the Great Depression: A General Equilibrium Analysis." *Journal of Political Economy* 112 (4): 779–816.

Dearing, Charles L., Paul T. Holman, Lewis L. Lorwin, and Leverett S. Lyon. 1934. *The ABC of the NRA*. Washington, DC: Brookings Institution.

Duvall, Walker M. 1936. "NRA Insignia." Work Materials No. 22. Washington, DC: Office of National Recovery Administration, Division of Review.

Eggertsson, Gauti B. 2008. "Great Expectations and the End of Depression." *American Economic Review* 98, 1476–516.

———. 2012. "Was the New Deal Contractionary?" *American Economic Review* 102 (1): 524–55.

Falk, Armin, Ernst Fehr, and Christian Zehnder. 2006. "Fairness Perceptions and Reservation Wages—The Behavioral Effects of Minimum Wage Laws." *Quarterly Journal of Economics* 121: 1347–81.

Field, Alexander J. 2011. *A Great Leap Forward: 1930s Depression and U.S. Economic Growth*. New Haven, CT: Yale University Press.

Filene, Edward A. 1923. "The Minimum Wage and Efficiency." *American Economic Review* 13: 411–15.

Fisher, Irving. 1930. *The Stock Market Crash—And After*. New York: Macmillan.

Fisher, Waldo E., and Charles M. James. 1955. "Efforts to Regulate the Bituminous Coal Industry Prior to 1937." In *Minimum Price Fixing in the Bituminous Coal Industry*, 20–38. Princeton, NJ: Princeton University Press. http://papers.nber.org/books/fish55-1.

Ford, Henry. 1922. *My Life and Work*. Garden City, NY: Doubleday.

———. 1926. *Today and Tomorrow*. Cambridge, MA: Productivity Press.

Foster, William Trufant, and Waddill Catchings. 1928. *Business without a Buyer*. Boston: Houghton Mifflin.

Friedman, James W. 1971. "A Non-Cooperative Equilibrium for Supergames." *Review of Economic Studies* 38 (1): 1–12.

Galvin, W. M., J. J. Reinstein, and D. Y. Campbell. 1936. "History of the Compliance Division." Work Materials No. 85. Washington, DC: Office of National Recovery Administration, Division of Review.

Gelderman, Carol. 1981. *Henry Ford: The Wayward Capitalist*. New York: Dial Press.

Hartshorn, Peter. 2011. *I Have Seen the Future: A Life of Lincoln Steffens*. Berkeley, CA: Counterpoint.

Hausman, Joshua. 2016. "What Was Bad for General Motors Was Bad for America: The Auto Industry and the 1937–38 Recession." *Journal of Economic History* 76: 427–77.

Hawley, Ellis W. 1966. *The New Deal and the Problem of Monopoly*. Princeton, NJ: Princeton University Press.

Hay, George A., and Daniel Kelly. 1974. "An Empirical Survey of Price Fixing Conspiracies." *Journal of Law and Economics* 17, 13–38.

Heinemman, Ronald L. 1981. "Blue Eagle or Black Buzzard: The National Recovery in Virginia." *Virginia Magazine of History and Biography* 89: 90–100.

Himmelberg, Robert F. 1976. *The Origins of the National Recovery Administration: Business, Government, and the Trade Association Issue*. New York: Fordham University Press.

Hobson, John A. 1909. *The Industrial System: An Inquiry into Earned and Unearned Income*. London: Charles Scribner's Sons.

———. 1930. *Rationalisation and Unemployment*. London: Unwin Brothers.

Hoover, Herbert. 1921. *Report on the President's Conference on Unemployment* (Herbert Hoover, Chairman). Washington, DC: US Government Printing Office.

———. 1952. *The Memoirs of Herbert Hoover: The Great Depression 1929–41*. New York: Macmillan.

Hopkins, William. 1933. Review of *The Industrial Discipline and the Governmental Arts* by Rexford G. Tugwell. *Economic Journal* 43 (171); 500–2.

Hursey, Frank, John B. Jago, Mackenzie Shannon, Donald Frothingham, W. W. Swift, and Howard C. Dunn. 1936. "Code Compliance Activities of the National Recovery Administration." Work Materials No. 61. Washington, DC: Office of National Recovery Administration, Division of Review.

Irons, Peter. H. 1982. *The New Deal Lawyers*. Princeton, NJ: Princeton University Press.

Johnson, Hugh. S. 1968. *The Blue Eagle from Egg to Earth*. New York: Greenwood Press. Original Doubleday, 1935.

Kovacic, William E., and Carl Shapiro. 2000. "A Century of Economic and Legal Thinking." *Journal of Economic Perspectives* 14 (1): 43–60.

Krepps, Matthew B. 1997. "Another Look at the Impact of the National Industrial Recovery Act on Cartel Formation and Maintenance Costs." *Review of Economics and Statistics*, 79: 151–54.

Lauck, W. Jett. 1936. "Coal Labor Legislation: A Case." *Annuals of the American Academy of Political and Social Science* 184: 130–37.

Levenstein, Margaret C., and Valerie Y. Suslow. 2006. "What Determines Cartel Success?" *Journal of Economic Literature* 44 (1): 43–95.

Lewis, David. 1976. *The Public Image of Henry Ford: An American Folk Hero and His Company*. Detroit: Wayne State University Press.

Lyon, Leverett S., Paul T. Homan, Lewis L. Lorwin, George Terborgh, Charles L. Dearing, and Leon C. Marshall. 1972. *The National Recovery Administration: An Analysis and Appraisal*. New York: Da Capo Press. Reprint of 1935 first edition.

Malthus, Thomas. 1827. *Definitions in Political Economy*. London: John Murray-Albemarle Street.

———. 1836. *Principles in Political Economy*. London: William Pickering.

Marimon, Ramon, and Fabrizio Zilibotti. 2000. "Employment and Distributional Effects of Restricting Working Time." *European Economic Review* 44: 1291–326.

Marshall, Leon C. 1935. *Hours and Wages Provisions in NRA Codes*. Washington, DC: Brookings Institution.

Martin, Arthur T. 1935. "The President's Reemployment Agreement." *Ohio State Law Journal* 1 (3): 155–68.

Neumann, Todd C., Jason E. Taylor, and Jerry L. Taylor. 2012. "The Behavior of the Labor Market between *Schechter* (1935) and *Jones & Laughlin* (1937)." *Cato Journal* 32 (3): 605–27.

Neumann, Todd C., Jason E. Taylor, and Price Fishback. 2013. "Comparisons of Weekly Hours over the Past Century and the Importance of Work-Sharing Policies in the 1930s." *American Economic Review Papers and Proceedings* 103, 105–10.

O'Brien, Anthony Patrick. 1989. "A Behavioral Explanation for Nominal Wage Rigidity during the Great Depression." *Quarterly Journal of Economics* 104: 719–35.

Ohanian, Lee E. 2009. "What—or Who—Started the Great Depression?" *Journal of Economic Theory* 144: 2310–35.

Owen, Robert. (1820) 1970. *Report to the County of Lanark: A New View of Society.* Reprint, London: Penguin.

Pearce, Charles Albert. 1939. *NRA Trade Practice Programs.* New York: Columbia University Press.

Pencaval, John. 2014. "The Productivity of Working Hours." IZA Discussion Paper No. 8129. Bonn, Germany: Institute for the Study of Labor.

Posner, Richard A., 1970. "A Statistical Study of Antitrust Enforcement." *Journal of Law and Economics* 13: 365–419.

Raff, Daniel M. G., and Lawrence H. Summers. 1987. "Did Henry Ford Pay Efficiency Wages?" *Journal of Labor Economics* 5: S57–S86.

Rocheteau, Guillaume. 2002. "Working Time Regulation in a Search Economy with Worker Moral Hazard." *Journal of Public Economics* 84: 387–425.

Romer, Christina. 1999. "Why Did Prices Rise in the 1930s?" *Journal of Economic History* 59: 167–99.

Rose, Jonathan D. 2010. "Hoover's Truce: Wage Rigidity in the Onset of the Great Depression." *Journal of Economic History* 70 (4): 843–70.

Seltzer, Andrew. 1997. "The Effects of the Fair Labor Standards Act of 1938 on the Southern Seamless Hosiery and Lumber Industries." *Journal of Economic History* 57 (2): 396–415.

Schuldt, Robert, and Jason E. Taylor. 2017. "Cartel Attributes and Cartel Performance: The Impact of Trade Associations." *Journal of Industrial Economics.* doi:10.1111/joie.12155.

Taylor, Jason E. 2002. The Output Effects of Government Sponsored Cartels during the New Deal." *Journal of Industrial Economics* 50, 1–10.

———. 2007a. "Buy Now! Buy Here! The Rise and Fall of the Patriotic Blue Eagle Emblem, 1933–1935." *Essays in Economic and Business History* 25, 117–30.

———. 2007b. "Cartel Code Attributes and Cartel Performance: An Industry-Level Analysis of the National Industrial Recovery Act." *Journal of Law and Economics* 50, 597–624.

———. 2011. "Work-Sharing during the Great Depression: Did the 'President's Reemployment Agreement' Promote Reemployment?" *Economica* 78, 133–58.

Taylor, Jason E., and Peter G. Klein. 2008. "Anatomy of a Cartel: The National Industrial Recovery Act of 1933 and the Compliance Crisis of 1934." *Research in Economic History* 26: 235–71.

Taylor, Jason E., and Todd C. Neumann. 2013. "The Effect of Institutional Regime Change within the New Deal on Industrial Output and Labor Markets." *Explorations in Economic History* 50: 582–98.

———. 2016. "Recovery Spring, Faltering Fall: March to November 1933." *Explorations in Economic History* 61: 54–67.

Taylor, Jason, and George Selgin. 1999. "By Our Bootstraps: Origins and Effects of the High-Wage Doctrine and the Minimum Wage." *Journal of Labor Research* 20: 447–62.

Temin, Peter, and Barrie A. Wigmore. 1990. "The End of One Big Deflation." *Explorations in Economic History* 27: 483–502.

Tugwell, Rexford G. 1933. *The Industrial Discipline and the Governmental Arts.* New York: Columbia University Press.

US Committee of Industrial Analysis. 1937. *The National Recovery Administration: Report of the President's Committee of Industrial Analysis.* Washington, DC: Department of Commerce.

US National Recovery Administration. 1933–1935. *Codes of Fair Competition*. 23 vols. Washington, DC: US Government Printing Office.

Vedder, R. K., and L. E. Gallaway 1993. *Out of Work: Unemployment and Government in Twentieth-Century America*. New York: Holmes and Meier.

Vickers, Chris, and Nicolas L. Ziebarth. 2014. "Did the NRA Facilitate Collusion? Evidence from the Macaroni Industry." *Journal of Economic History* 74: 831–62.

Weinstein, Michael M. 1980. *Recovery and Redistribution under the NIRA*. Amsterdam: North-Holland.

Wolvin, Andrew D. 1968. "The 1933 Blue Eagle Campaign: A Study in Persuasion and Coercion.

Index